To Arthur
with much love
From Celia for 40

500

G000270965

Traditional Food
in Yorkshire

Traditional Food in Yorkshire

PETER BREARS

JOHN DONALD PUBLISHERS LTD
EDINBURGH

© Peter Brears 1987

All rights reserved. No part of this publication may be
reproduced in any form or by any means without the
prior permission of the publishers, John Donald
Publishers Ltd., 138 St Stephen Street, Edinburgh, EH3
5AA.

ISBN 0 85976 169 X

Exclusive distribution in the United States and Canada
by Humanities Press Inc., Atlantic Highlands, NJ07716,
USA.

Typesetting by Print Origination, Formby, Liverpool.
Printed in Great Britain by Bell & Bain Ltd., Glasgow.

Acknowledgements

My grateful thanks are due to the many people, too numerous to mention individually, who have generously provided material for this book. Particular acknowledgment must go to the following however: Mr David Bostwick, Ms Caroline Davidson, Mr Jeffrey Dent, Mr & Mrs John Gall, Mr John Goodchild, Mr Stephen Harrison, Mr Clarence Hellewell, Mrs Kate Mason and Mrs Jennifer Stead. Substantial help has also been received from the members of a wide variety of local groups and societies, the discussions held at the close of their lecture sessions giving a particularly fruitful insight into the domestic life of Yorkshire.

My colleagues in the museum profession have readily granted access to the reserve collections and related information in their care, those at Beamish, at Shibden Hall, Halifax, the Tolson Memorial Museum, Huddersfield, the Ryedale Folk Museum, Cliffe Castle, Keighley, the Nidderdale Museum, Pateley Bridge, the Whitby Museum and Castle Museum, York, giving the greatest assistance. Similarly, the staff in the Bradford, Calderdale, Rotherham, Scarborough and Sheffield reference libraries have all provided an excellent service, frequently drawing my attention to material which I would never have found but for their help and interest. My especial thanks must also go to Mrs Ann Heap and her staff in the Leeds Local History Library for access to the city's magnificent Yorkshire collections. Without these the present volume would have been almost impossible to prepare.

I am most grateful to the Yorkshire Archaeological Society for enabling me to study its extensive manuscript collections, to Bradford Libraries for permission to reproduce their illustrations of the Faxfleet Street development, and also to the Brotherton Library, University of Leeds, for permission to publish extracts from the notebooks of the late Dr H. Bedford.

Peter Brears

Contents

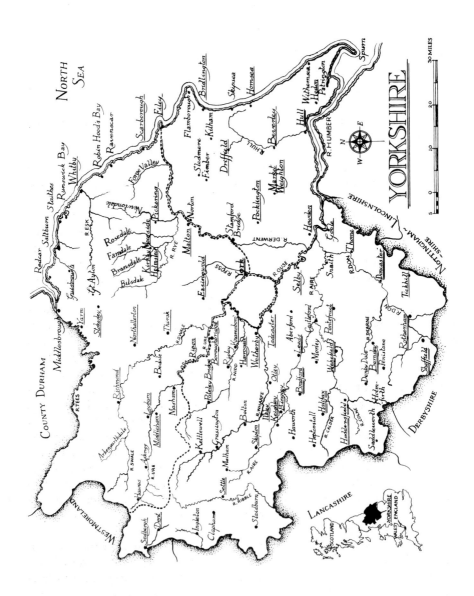

Introduction

Along with politics and religion, food used to be one of those prohibited topics which were rarely, if ever, allowed to enter polite conversation. Perhaps it is for this reason that this most fascinating and revealing aspect of human life has never been given much serious study. Over the past few years, however, there has been a great revival of interest in food, with overseas travel and the influx of shops and restaurants offering rich and flavoursome new dishes completely breaking down the old taboos and apathy. In fact, the success of French, Italian, Greek, Chinese and American foods has been so complete that it can now be quite difficult to obtain a purely English meal. As a reaction to this state of affairs, interest is now turning to the traditional regional foods of this country, numerous collections of local recipes being issued by a whole series of national publishers, local groups, and private individuals. Recipes in themselves form only a small part of culinary history, however, for they need to be considered within the much larger context of domestic life.

This book sets out to study the food and drink prepared and eaten in ordinary Yorkshire homes during the nineteenth century. This massive county, its 6,000 square miles occupying about a tenth of the area of England, or some three-quarters of Wales, provides an ideal area for study. In landscape terms, it slopes down from the high Pennines, across to the North Sea, including large areas of bleak hill country, with moors and fells intersected by long dales. Then there are the rolling Wolds, the fertile plains and vales, and the flat peat wastes to the east of Doncaster. In economic terms, its rich mineral deposits made the central and southern parts of the West Riding into one of the world's great industrial centres for engineering and wool textiles, while lead mining in the Dales provided a useful dual economy when combined with farming. These elements, along with many others, have left the county with an extremely diverse series of human environments, ranging from isolated hill-farms set in the most beautiful countryside to crowded rows of back-to-backs buried deep within massive urban conurbations, each area having its own distinctive way of life.

Throughout the towns and villages of early nineteenth-century Yorkshire most working families maintained a pattern of living which had gradually evolved over many hundreds of years. Each generation had successively responded to local environmental and economic circumstances to obtain the best possible lifestyle, one which came closest to satisfying its physical and emotional needs at both a personal and a communal level. On the whole, the population had remained largely static for centuries, so that visitors to the county were still able to recognise 'the three principal varieties of Yorkshiremen. There was the tall, broad-shouldered rustic,

1

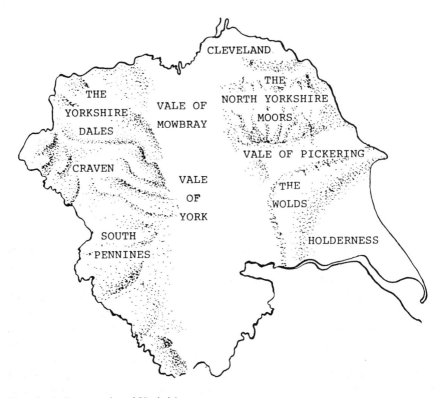

The physical geography of Yorkshire.

whose stalwart limbs, light grey or blue eyes, yellowish hair and open features indicate the Saxon; there was the Scandinavian, less tall and big, with eyes, hair and complexion dark, and an intention in the expression not perceptible in the Saxon face; and last, the Celt, short, swarthy, and Irish-looking. The first two appeared most numerous in the East and North Ridings, the last in the West'.[1] Had surveys of blood-grouping been available at this period, they would probably have confirmed this distribution, suggesting that there had been little major movement in the population here over the past millennium. In fact, there is a considerable body of evidence which suggests that most communities took active steps to discourage any form of social mobility. People seldom left their own immediate localities, thus fostering narrow prejudices. If, for example, a man went from one part of his village to another to look for a girl to marry he was looked on as an interloper by the young men there, and could receive very rough treatment. Many had to give up in despair after being covered in mud and suffering considerable bodily harm. If the man ventured to a nearby village, meanwhile, his neighbours, especially the women, turned against him, telling him he could have got as good a girl, and a good deal better, around his own home. Just to enter a Yorkshire village either as a casual visitor or as a new resident could be an extremely unpleasant and dangerous experience, leading to constant insult and assault until either initiation or naturali-

Yorkshire boundaries up to 1974.

sation occurred. Even then, the most certain way of gaining acceptance was to courageously fight in self-defence, since a quiet, inoffensive and submissive manner brought absolutely no respect.[2]

As long as these attitudes prevailed, the rural communities of Yorkshire, isolated from major trade routes and the spread of new ideas, retained numerous beliefs and domestic traditions from past centuries. Witches and wise-men were still active, 'celtic' heads were still carved on spring-sites, doorways and gables, for example, and rowan-tree crosses and holed stones still protected both houses and domesticated animals. Within many homes, life in the early nineteenth century can have been little different from that of the medieval period four or five hundred years earlier, but then the entire population began to be affected by a whole series of dynamic changes as a direct result of the industrial revolution. The rise of industry and the need for large labour forces brought people from the Yorkshire countryside and from most other parts of Britain flooding into the great iron, steel and textile towns of the West Riding. Agricultural improvements involving the enclosure of hundreds of thousands of acres of common land tended to remove the cottagers' grazing-rights, and made their traditional way of life quite untenable. New forms of transportation – the canals, turnpikes and railways – made travel much more accessible, and promoted the movement of people, produce, and ideas. At the same time the Church of England awoke from its comfortable eighteenth-century slumber, the absentee clergy, pluralists and hunting squarsons being replaced by a new breed of earnest young men intent on reforming the spiritual, moral and social life of their parishioners. Along with their non-conformist competitors, they built new churches and chapels, established new schools, and introduced new standards of behaviour. The harvest home, one of the great joyful celebrations of the agricultural year, had to be discouraged, its dancing, drinking and feasting being replaced by staid harvest festivals held in church. The lively customs associated with weddings and the traditional forms of funeral had to be deprived of their communal drinking and feasting, and brought into line with standard church practice, while families who had lived together in single rooms from the time when man built his first permanent shelters thousands of years ago had to be taught that such shameful

Yorkshire boundaries since 1974, when parts of the county were transferred to County Durham, Cumbria, and even Lancashire, while most of the East Riding was combined with North Lincolnshire to form Humberside.

habits were no longer acceptable. These influences when combined had a revolutionary effect on the diet and lifestyle of every section of the community, the nature of the various changes being traceable in a wide range of documentary sources.

To date, most serious work on English food history has been carried out on a national level, fine pioneering work being published in volumes such as Drummond and Wilbraham's *The Englishman's Food* of 1939, John Burnett's *Plenty and Want* of 1966 and Anne Wilson's *Food and Drink in Britain* of 1973. In contrast, this book deals with the food eaten by the ordinary people of a single region during the nineteenth century, emphasising the differences between the national and the local scenes.

Some information has been drawn from national surveys, including government reports etc. The majority has come from essentially local sources. Many of these are rarely used by the academic historian, but a surprising amount of detail can be gathered from dialect glossaries, dialect poetry, antiquarian local histories, memoirs and novels. The nature of these sources depends largely on regional occupations and traditions. Workers in physically demanding and potentially dangerous occupations, including fishermen, miners and steelworkers, seldom generate much literature of their own, for example, while workers in more routine or even contemplative occupations, such as woolsorters or handloom weavers, readily produce a mass of poems, memoirs and other writing expressing the thoughts of their communities. In the more rural areas, the task of recording the changing pattern of everyday life was taken up either by the squirearchy, with men such as Richard Blakeborough or Arthur Pease, or by the clergy. Major contributions were made by the Rev. J.C. Atkinson of Danby, the Rev. Sabine Baring-Gould of Horbury Bridge, the Rev. Thomas Browne of Hull, the Rev. A.N. Cooper of Filey, the Rev. M.C.F. Morris of Newton-on-Ouse, and the Rev. George Young of Whitby, to name but some.

Further information has been drawn from the mass of reminiscences and memories recorded by a miscellaneous group of writers towards the end of the nineteenth century. Having lived through one of the greatest periods of industrial expansion and social upheaval, they felt that it was important that every detail of the old ways of life should be recorded in permanent form before they were lost for ever. The greatest interest in local studies has always taken place in the periods of greatest social change, for then the community feels a real need to establish its roots and to confirm its identity in the face of economic and political forces far beyond its control. This has been clearly illustrated by the spate of local histories produced by civic and amenity groups over the years since local government reorganisation in 1974 destroyed the independence of numerous towns and villages, at the same time that their traditional industries were being destroyed by external economic pressures.

In addition to documentary sources, the most valuable body of information has been gathered by speaking to groups of people who can remember the period before the First World War. Over the past few years I have given some hundreds of talks to local history societies, church groups and old-age pensioners, always encouraging questions, and debate. Memories of former times have frequently come flooding back, bringing with them a wealth of detail, humour and stories which could never have been obtained in any other way. Lively descriptions of bloody pig-killings, delicious stews, and great baking-days poured out with great enthusiasm, then being noted down in longhand for use in the following pages.

Having gathered together a considerable mass of detail regarding traditional foods in Yorkshire, it was then necessary to arrange it in some logical order. It soon became apparent that food habits can only be effectively studied in relation to occupational groups. Although the diet, lifestyle and culture of the aristocracy or gentry were relatively uniform throughout the country, so that they could be considered as single 'classes', the term 'working class' as used by many social historians included such a wide range of differing circumstances as to be virtually worthless. This will be seen in the following chapters, where groups of wool textile workers, coal miners, farm workers and the urban poor are considered in detail, such factors as their economic state, their working lives, their housing, their furnishings and their social life all being taken into account. It would have been possible to have considered other groups, such as the fishermen of the East Coast, the lead miners, or the farmers in the Dales or Moors, but most of these have already been studied in some detail, especially in the fine works of Marie Hartley and Joan Ingilby.

In addition to giving the general reader an accurate insight into the lifestyle and food of Yorkshire people during the nineteenth century, it is hoped that this volume will prove useful to anyone studying or teaching social history or domestic science. It will also provide an interesting source of menus, recipes and background information for anyone who wants to re-create a meal of the period, whether in the home, in school, in the pub, or in the local church hall. Most of the dishes described here (including seventeen varieties of Yorkshire pudding!) are economical, simple to make, and quite substantial enough to satisfy those Yorkshiremen who still use the old West Riding 'Grace before Meat':

God bless us all, an' make' us able
Ta eit all t'stuff what's on this table!

Chapter 1

The Wool Textile Workers

At the opening of the nineteenth century, the manufacture of wool textiles in West Yorkshire was still heavily dependent on the centuries-old domestic system. Although a few massive factories had been built in the 1790s, and public mills now scribbled the wool ready for processing, the actual spinning and weaving were chiefly carried out in the homes of the smaller domestic clothiers.

Their cottages were of various shapes and sizes, some being enclosed within a few acres of land which supported a cow and a horse, and perhaps also enabled a few oats, potatoes or vegetables to be grown. In its simplest form, the weaver's cottage was a small, single-roomed structure of stone, brick, or turf, roofed with either thatch or thick stone slates. Inside, it had a fireplace built into one of the end gables, while a bed, a chest, and one or two looms were spaced around the walls, leaving just sufficient room for a table with chairs, a winding wheel and a cradle etc., to be arranged in the centre of the stone-flagged floor.[1] Rather more common were the one-up and one-down cottages, perhaps with cellars, which were built either as 'throughs' or as 'back to backs' in terraces. Their upper rooms, frequently lit by long rows of mullioned windows, served as weaving chambers by day and as bedrooms by night, although further beds might still remain in the living room below.[2] The most substantial form of weavers' cottages were built from the late eighteenth century onwards, when the younger members of the family who had formerly prepared wool for spinning were now put on to the loom instead.[3] The accommodation required for the additional looms was provided by adopting a three-storey design, the ground floor being used as living room-kitchen, the first floor as a workroom for spinning, warping and warehousing, and the second floor for weaving, each storey also being provided with beds according to the particular circumstances of each family.[4]

The domestic worker at this period was considered to be 'for the most part blessed with the comforts without the superfluities of life', and certainly this is borne out by contemporary evidence.[5] Take, for example, Griffith Wright's mid-eighteenth century account of the diet in the household of a Leeds clothier; having started work at 5am:

> Ere clock strikes eight their called to breakfast
> And bowls of milk are brought in great haste –
> Good Water-Pudding as heart could wish |Porridge|
> With spoons stuck round an earthen dish.

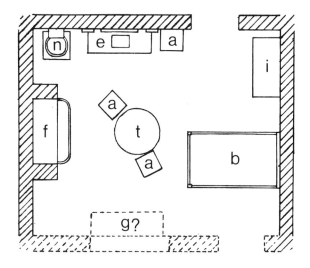

The living room of an early-mid nineteenth century weavers's cottage at Saddleworth. Note the oatcakes hanging on the creel above the hearth, the samplers on the wall, and the family bible on top of the chest. (a). spindleback chairs; (b). bed; (e). chest; (f). fireplace; (g). settle; (i). bureau; (n). mash-tub; (t). table. (see appendix Ij.)

While at mid-day:

> With wooden platter, bowl and ladle,
> All seated round a scoured table,
> Hard oaten cakes, some two or three,
> In pieces fly, with fist and knee,
> Tho' hard, it in an instant doth
> Eat like soft manchet in the broth,
> Ere Tom or Jack have supped their mess,
> With quick large strides comes 'prentice Bess,
> Who, on earthen dish, with leg of mutton,
> As good as knife was ever put in –
> Each cuts a lunch, none care to inch it
> 'First come – first serv'd' – They never flinch it!
> But cram like Capons, while they eat!
> All rise well pleased with their cheer,
> Then march to spicket-pot for beer
> When quench'd their thirst, they quickly go,
> And thro' the web the shuttle throw,
> Thus they keep time with hand and feet
> From five at morn till eight at *neet*!
> Then call'd down e'er the clock gives warning
> Of Broth that is on the fire a-warming...[6]

The broth would undoubtedly be made from sheep's heads, Mr. Hainsworth of Farsley being remembered going 'into the Shambles at Leeds and buying a sackful of

The interior of Timmy Feather's cottage at Buckley Green, Stanbury, near Haworth, appears to have changed very little since it was first set up in 1834. (see appendix II.)

sheep's heads at once and these would be boiled in a large set-pot along with a lot of bacon (not carefully dressed) and thus had a regular and full supply of Golden Guinea Broth for Breakfast and ditto with Pudding and meat for dinner, and those who like old milk to wash the broth down could have it ad infinitum'.[7]

By 1800 merchants such as Gamaliel Lloyd of Leeds were beginning to complain of the clothiers' higher wages, shorter hours, and richer tastes, 'The Manufacturers' wages being nearly triple what they were 40 or 45 years ago, and they work 2 or 3 hours less than they did at that time, being now universally paid by the measure and not by the day which 45 years ago was for a common weaver only 9d or 10d a day from five in a morning till nine at night, deducting the necessary time for meals. At that time and for several years after the Clothiers bought an Ox or a Cow at the Leeds November fair and salted it. This with Water Grewel & Onion & Bacon & Eggs, Oatcakes & salt butter furnished the principal food of the People. They now eat fresh meat, vegetables & a good deal of Wheat bread. This advance of wages opens to make new wants and new desires'.[8]

Some of the more prosperous weavers probably did enjoy the diet described by Gamaliel Lloyd, but these were certainly in a minority. Men like John Wood of Bradford remembered a much plainer regime being common about this time:

Breakfast. Oatmeal water-porridge and blue milk.
Dinner (mid-day). Boiled potatoes, sometimes in their jackets, and fried bacon.
Tea time. Oatcake slightly covered with bacon-dip, with a black pint pot full of mint tea sweetened with treacle *or* a pint of blue milk and oatcake as a substitute.[9]

It is surprising to find that some fifty years later, around 1850, the same diet was still in use:[10]

6–7am. start weaving.
Breakfast. Fire lit, and an ironpot set over the fire. Water was then poured in, with a little salt, and a sprinkling of oatmeal to keep in the steam. When it boiled, more oatmeal was added to make porridge for all the weavers (in some households the porridge can was hung against the loom[11])
12.00
Dinner. Boiled potatoes and a bit of fried bacon, with a small piece of bread if it could be spared. It was then customary to go out of doors for a chat with the neighbours, topics ranging from pig feeding, hen raising and bird catching to the scriptural correctness of infant baptism as opposed to adult immersion, etc.
1.00pm Resume weaving.
Evening. Porridge, with new milk brought in a two-quart jug from a nearby farmhouse.

The only exception to this monotonous diet was that on Sunday afternoon each person had a currant cake, with tea served in half-pint pots.

It would be a mistake, however, to believe that sufficient food, even of this basic standard, was always readily available. The rapid development of textile factories using power looms etc. placed the handloom weaver under ever-increasing financial pressure, as did the great commercial depression which deepened throughout the 1830s and 1840s. In 1844 Samuel Laing's essay on *National Distress* summarised the effects of increasing mechanisation on the working classes, with 'About one third plunged into extreme misery, and hovering on the verge of actual starvation; another third, or more, earning an income something better than that of the common agricultural labourer, but under circumstances very prejudiced to health, morality, and domestic comfort – viz; by the labour of young children, girls, and mothers of families in crowded factories; and finally, a third earning high wages, amply sufficient to support them in respectability and comfort'.[12] The handloom weavers fell within the first two groups, their poverty being only slightly alleviated by the labour of their children in the factories. As there was insufficient trade to keep them in full employment, many were forced to move away to work as navvies on the railways, or to try to start new lives in America or Australia.[13] The population continued to expand, however, as their places were soon taken by the influx of numerous workers from various parts of rural England, by Scottish textile workers (who brought their Clydesdale terriers with them, soon to be transformed into the 'Yorkshire' terrier) and by tens of thousands of poor Irish immigrants driven from their own country by the great famine of 1847. When a skilled weaver did manage to obtain work, his wages might only amount to some 6/6d (32½p) to 15s. (75p) a week, from which a rental of some 1s (5p) to 4s (20p) had to be deducted. This did not leave much for food when potatoes cost 2s (10p) a stone, flour 4/6 (22½p) and oatmeal 2s (10p).[14]

In rural weaving settlements such as Heptonstall Slack the condition of the inhabitants was actually compared to that of Napoleon's troops in their disastrous retreat from Moscow, so great had been the combined effects of low wages, poor diet, insufficient clothing, and virulent disease. Here the midday meal had been reduced to small pieces of suet, fried, and mashed into a partial pulp with water, salt and boiled potatoes. This was eaten with oatcake, even a small piece of bacon now being considered a great extravagance. Tea and supper, meanwhile, were united into a single meal of porridge, oatcake and old milk.[15] About the same time, Thomas Wood returned to Bingley and found his father and mother suffering great want from the scarcity of work and the high price of the absolute necessities of life: 'Father would have died and seen his children die before he would have paraded his wants, or, I believe, asked for help'.[16] Similar evidence of the weavers' chronic inability to buy adequate supplies of food in the 1840s may be found in most parts of the wool textile area of West Yorkshire, particularly in the memories of those who were children at this time. Many could remember there being insufficient porridge to feed every member of the family, others that sometimes there was neither oatmeal nor bacon left in the house, or that children might be seen eating potato peelings off the road.[17] By 1850 a revival in trade brought with it a moderate increase in prosperity, and an end to the worst period of poverty. Even so, the days of the handloom weaver were over. Those who continued to work into the 1870s were only able to earn some four shillings a week, this being less than had been paid in the opening years of the century.[18]

The expansion of the factory system which superseded the domestic industry brought with it enormous changes in household life. It broke up the traditional close family units, in which everyone worked together on a range of domestic and

A reconstruction of a Pennine weaver's cottage of the early nineteenth century. Based on a variety of documentary sources, it shows the ground-floor living room, the first-floor workroom equipped with a spinning jenny, mending table, sizing-trough, creel and bar trees, and the second floor loomshop. The family would sleep on beds, folding beds, or mattresses in each room.

industrial processes. It removed children from the protection and control of their parents, and prevented them from learning normal domestic skills. It placed enormous pressures on wives and mothers, who now had to work long hours in the mills while still raising their families and running their homes. Even though the factories were eventually to bring great prosperity to the textile communities of

West Yorkshire, it is not surprising that many viewed the former handloom weaving days with nostalgia.

The hours worked by men, women and children in the mills were extremely long, 6 a.m. to 8 p.m. throughout the week and on Saturday from 6 a.m. to 4 p.m. (that is some 80 hours a week, less meal times) being quite normal in the 1830s.[19] Due to the combined efforts of Richard Oastler, 'the King of the Factory Children', Michael Sadler, M.P., and Lord Ashley, legislation such as the Ten Hours Bill of 1847 significantly reduced these hours, particularly with regard to the younger children. Even so, by the end of the century the mills frequently worked from 6 a.m. to 5.30 p.m., while some continued as late as 8 p.m. or 9 p.m. on a fairly regular basis.[20]

Having risen around 5 or 5.30 a.m., the workers might clean out the fireplace, light the fire and boil a kettle of water to make a cup of tea before setting off on foot, or perhaps by tram, to arrive at the mill by six o'clock. Any food which was to be eaten during the day had also to be prepared, although this might have been done on the previous evening to save time.

If they lived fairly close to the mill, they might return home to take their meals. In the 1840s, for example, the mill hands used to pour freshly-made porridge into a bottle and leave it wrapped up in the bedclothes so that it would still be hot when they came back at midday.[21]

After working for two hours, there was usually a half-hour stoppage for breakfast. This usually comprised a small bread-cake or slices of bread spread with beef dripping, black treacle or jam, which had been carried to work in a 'jock handkerchief' of the red spotted variety; alternatively, a boy could be allowed out to the local shop ten minutes before breakfast, in order to buy any pasties or tea-cakes which his colleagues required.[22] Tea, also brought from home, was either mashed with water from a boiler in the mill, or, where this facility was not provided, it could be made at a nearby house on payment of 2d or 3d (c. 1p) a week. 'There was generally a spare bit of wall [in the mill] hung with brackets of pint pots. Most of the pots would have gone brownish with age. Some were cracked. Some were honey-combed with a fine network of fine lines, not exactly cracks – due to their natural reaction to years and years of alternate boiling brews and cold neglect. Some were held together around the rim with grimy string. Others were minus handles', remembered one operative.[23]

At noon, dinner might either take the same form as breakfast, or be rather more substantial with pudding basins full of hot sheep's-head broth or potatoes and vegetables, perhaps with meat and topped by a Yorkshire pudding. These were often brought to the mill in the morning and allowed to heat through by being left on top of the steam pipes, a slow but sure method with no risk of burning.[24] In 1849 a visitor to Holdsworth's Shaw Lodge Mills in Halifax noted that 'A sort of small cookshop is established near the furnace of one of the steam engines, and thither every girl who pleases brings her dinner, ready cooked, but disposed in a dish so as to allow it to be readily warmed up again. I stationed myself in the dinner-bar at noon, and so had an opportunity of seeing nearly 300 of the messes prepared, and they were handed out through a sort of buttery-hatch to each applicant as she shouted the number of her carding-machine, her spinning-frame, or her loom. The dinners consisted almost invariably of a portion of baked meat with potatoes, and in a few instances mushrooms. A great number had coffee and tea in little tin flagons. Altogether the dinners seemed substantial and nourishing. I was gratified by the appearance both of the consumers and the fare consumed'.[25] Alternatively a wife or mother working at home would cook the food in the morning, and send it fresh and hot directly into the mill. In the Batley shoddy mills 'the people had their meals carried to them ... meat pies, with thick underbaked crusts, appeared to be the staple dish. The meal was despatched in the most primitive style. I observed one woman helping herself to potatoes with one of the broad-bladed shears used for cutting rags'.[26]

'Folks with 'brass' to throw away, and those who couldn't be bothered to put their own jock up would send out a bobbin-lad at dinner time for a pork pie or a 'penn'orth of each'. In pre-canteen days lads used to stagger back to the mill with yard-high loads of fish and chips.'[27]

In most mills all meals were taken in the 'shed' or 'shop' amongst the machinery, sitting in window recesses or on the floorboards.[28] Here, towards Christmas time, excerpts from 'Messiah' would be sung, following a tradition firmly established in the eighteenth century.[29] In some locations the dust-laden air was so foul that it was necessary to put pieces of paper on top of the pots of tea and keep the food covered to prevent it being contaminated with fine, greasy flocks.[30] Manufacturers such as Sir Titus Salt, who erected a large dining hall for his workforce, where provisions were sold for a trifle above their cost price, were far from common.

One seven-year-old boy who started as a doffer at Salts in 1862 remembered that you could buy a good dinner in the common dining room with beefsteak pie or stew, for 3d (1p). There were also a number of large ovens for heating the workers' own food, each dish being numbered according to the room in which they worked. Men also carried large cans of hot tea or coffee round the mill, where it could be purchased for about a halfpenny a pint. The boy's name was Joe Wright. Later he rose to become one of England's finest scholars, Professor of Philology at Oxford, and editor of the great *English Dialect Dictionary*.

The introduction of canteens into the textile mills was largely a twentieth-century innovation. In the town centres, however, at midday, dining rooms were provided by the Working Men's institutes. A visitor to the Leeds Institute, housed in the former Assembly Rooms above the White Cloth Hall, found more than 150 men and youths in the conversation-room, 'a number of them doing justice to sundry steaks, chops and savoury rashers of bacon, which viands were supplied to them through a trap-door from the kitchen, the recipients paying one half-penny each for the cooking. No intoxicating drinks were allowed on the premises, but any of the members could have tea or coffee on payment of one penny per cup, and bread and butter or muffins at equally reasonable rates'.[31]

Tea time, if taken at the mill, was identical to breakfast, but if taken at home it could be more substantial, particularly in the more prosperous households. Here it could include either sheep's-head broth with dumplings, rabbit stew, fish, or hash, perhaps made with corned beef.[32]

In the latter half of the nineteenth century it was quite possible for a family to

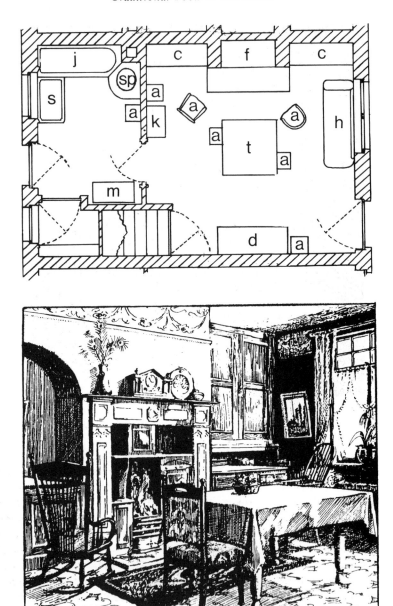

A model City Cottage built in Faxfleet Street by Bradford City Council in 1902-4. The council published these suggested furnishing plans in its promotional brochure.

a) Ground floor plan; a. chairs; c. cupboards; d. dresser; f. fireplace; h. sofa; j. bath; k. sewing machine; m. mangle; s. sink; sp. set pot; t. table.

b) The living room.

c) The scullery, where the set pot provided water both for laundry and for bathing.

obtain a very good income from their work in the mills. 'A large family, instead of being a burden to a man is one of his best blessings,' wrote William Cudworth in 1888. 'It is not uncommon for an overlooker and his family to earn £5 or £6 a week and allow the mother to remain at home. There are few places where home comforts are more enjoyed than in the dwellings of the working classes of Bradford. The women and girls employed in the factories dress in a stylish manner and generally in good taste.'[33] Some of the vast profits being reaped from the world's most important wool textile 'industry were now beginning to come into the possession of the workers on the shop floor. Although many families were to continue living at virtual subsistence level, others were able to make great strides forward in their overall standard of living. This is clearly seen in their housing, as well-built terraces began to be erected in increasing numbers by industrialists, societies, speculators and local authorities. Some retained the back-to-back arrangement of earlier years, while others adopted much more advanced forms, with large cellars in the basement, good-sized parlours, kitchen-living rooms and pantries on the ground floor, and a number of bedrooms on the first floor and attic. Their furnishings were now of good quality, probably even incorporating suites of french-polished mahogany in the best rooms, while their walls were covered in fashionable machine-printed wallpapers. A clear indication of these advances is seen in Bradford City Council's brochure for their Faxfleet Street development of 1902-4, which includes detailed plans, drawings and costings of the most suitable furnishings. At first these may appear rather lavish, but contemporary photographs confirm the accuracy of this standard of interior decoration.[34]

One of the great advances in the Victorian textile worker's house was the inclusion of a cast-iron cooking range, incorporating both an open fire for roasting and boiling, and a hot-air oven. Instead of being largely restricted to oatcakes made on the bakstone and porridge and potatoes boiled in the pot, it was now possible to bake in the oven. This enabled the housewife to produce fruit and meat pies, stews, bread, and a vast range of puddings, cakes and pastries. As the price of foodstuffs fell in relation to wages, a 'golden age' of home baking thus developed, traditional recipes for curd tarts, custards, and fruit cakes etc. descended from country house cookery of the seventeenth century now being joined by new recipes culled from the popular cookery books of the period. Baking day formed part of a regular weekly cycle of domestic chores, where the housewife was at home throughout the week:

Sunday. Hot dinner at midday
Monday. Washing
Tuesday. Ironing, darning
Wednesday
or
Thursday. Brewing or baking. The dough was mixed and left to rise in front of the fire before breakfast. Loaves were made first, then teacakes, followed by pastries and cakes.
Friday. Cleaning and scouring
Saturday. am – finish cleaning, bring out best carpet and tablecover. pm – excursion to shops, to family or friends, etc.[35]

Otherwise it had to be fitted in during the weekday evenings or on Saturdays, when she came back from the mill.[36] To buy bread and cakes from a baker was popularly judged to be a sure sign of poor housekeeping, but in many households it was the only way these essentials could be obtained. It is not surprising that commercial bakeries flourished throughout the region.

Since the family was now separated during the working week, the importance of the Sunday dinner, when they all dined together, was greatly enhanced. After church, chapel or Sunday-School, the family therefore gathered around the table for their main meal. Usually it followed the traditional local practice of serving a Yorkshire or a seasoned pudding with gravy as a first course, before proceeding to a roast with potatoes and vegetables, followed by a pudding. Later in the day, perhaps around 5 or 6 p.m. tea would be served – with cold meats, bread and butter and cakes – thus fortifying everyone against the long working hours of the week to come.

Chapter 2

The West Riding Coal Miners

From the fourteenth century at least, coal has been mined from the exposed West Riding coalfield which extends from the gritstone moorlands of the Pennines in an easterly direction until it disappears beneath the magnesian limestone ridge running from just north-east of Leeds down to Killamarsh. This area included all the major towns of the region – Bradford, Halifax, Huddersfield, Wakefield, Barnsley, Rotherham and Sheffield – whose rapid expansion was largely dependent on plentiful supplies of cheap good-quality coal. By the late eighteenth century coal was being used to power steam engines in textile factories, ironworks, and coal mines, to provide coke for smelting, and to heat homes both locally and at considerable distances as it could now be distributed by the newly constructed canals and navigations. As the nineteenth century progressed, the demand for coal increased enormously, vast quantities being consumed in industry, in coking and gas plants, and in the steam-powered locomotives and shipping which, particularly from the 1840s, carried Yorkshire coal to other parts of Britain and beyond. The following table succinctly demonstrates this rapid growth:[1]

Year	1800	1840	1864	1880	1890	1908
Coal production (in millions of tons)	–	–	9.3	17.5	28.3	34.9
Thousands employed	3.5	13.8	34.5	60.4	107.9	143.9

The early mines were fairly shallow small-scale operations, worked by perhaps eight or ten men in 'day-holes' or drift mines and bell-pits. Where vertical shafts were sunk down to the seams, they were rarely more than a hundred feet deep, both miners and coal being raised either by simple hand-turned winches or 'jack-rollers', or large horse-powered winding drums called gins. These started to be replaced by steam-winding and pumping engines from the mid-eighteenth century, thus permitting deeper and more productive seams to be worked. As the size of individual pits increased and new shafts were sunk in relatively rural and sparsely populated areas, there was a great demand for additional labour, this being filled by men coming into the West Riding from most parts of Britain, but especially from the midland counties, from Somerset and Devon, and from Ireland.[2] Here they soon became established into close-knit mining communities, united by their unique work and lifestyle, yet maintaining a certain degree of independence from their surrounding neighbours.

In appearance, attitude to life, health and diet, the early nineteenth century miners were quite distinct from any other occupational group, being described as

Wearing his traditional white cloth suit edged with red tape, this South Leeds collier carries his 'snap' in a wicker basket hooked over his arm. This illustration is taken from George Walker's *Costume of Yorkshire* of 1814.

'the most ignorant of all workmen ... looked upon by some persons as little better than "white heathens" ... in their blanket coats and dirty faces looking like no other human beings but themselves; and so they will, in all probability, continue to do as long as colliers are colliers'.[3] Their traditional dress, worn on the journeys to and from work, was a gown for women, and a suit of white cloth edged with red for the men, white stockings, low shoes and a very high shirt-neck stiffly starched and ruffled also being worn for best.[4] Except for neck, face and ears, however, they never washed, for it was believed by some until comparatively recent times that water would weaken their bodies, and make them subject to strains. In terms of sheer hard work and physical injury, few occupations were as demanding or as dangerous, the face-workers perhaps spending eight to ten hours a day lying naked in a cold slurry of coal and water while picking away in the narrow seams. At the same time they were constantly at risk from roof falls, explosions of dust or firedamp, and a whole series of accidents, especially around the shaft, haulage and winding gear. The physical conditions in which they worked also brought on serious long-term disabilities in the form of rheumatism and arthritis, back troubles, and the deadly pneumoconiosis and silicosis which totally clogged their lungs with fine particles of coal dust. All these factors combined to drastically shorten the working life of the miner and to permanently change his appearance.

When Rider Haggard came into contact with Yorkshire miners for the first time, he found that 'for the most part they were somewhat pallid-faced men, bent by stooping in the tunnels and wearing heavy wooden-soled boots'. The 1842 Commission on the Employment of children similarly reported that 'after they are

Miners' cottages at Ratten Row, Lepton. Henry Briggs, proprietor of the Flockton collieries described such cottages in 1842 as having 'seldom but one lodging room, and one living room, and a little back kitchen. Where there is a large family there will be a turn-up bed downstairs'. Rent was 15-18d. (6-7p) a week, including a little bit of garden.

The living room of a miner's cottage of the early nineteenth century. Note the stone-flagged floor, the open roof, and the plaster walls which were colour-washed either white, buff, Venetian red, or deep blue.

turned 45 or 50 they walk home from their work almost like cripples, stiffly stalking along, often leaning on sticks, bearing the visible evidences in their frame and gait of overstrained muscles and overtaxed strength...I should have difficulty in finding any work harder than a collier's, take it from first to last'.[5]

Since life was likely to be short, with the constant threat of fatal injury and the virtual certainty of chronic disability for those who survived into old age, it is not surprising that the miners enjoyed their wages while they could. Unlike the weavers, for example, thrift was rarely one of their strong points: 'They live very well, and [Mr Prater has seen] a miner's family with three joints of different sorts of meat on the table at one meal. Within a fortnight the same people were applying for parish relief!' When coal was in great demand, as in the winter of 1871-2, 'working colliers ruled the roost for the time and all sorts of tales were told about colliers' high living, drinking champagne and other expensive drinks, so flush were they in cash. The bulk of the men would only work about half time and then it was said they earned their 3 or 4 pounds a week' when contemporary handloom weavers might expect only 4/6d (22½p) for the same period.[6] Wages at this level were exceptional, however, and periods of depression in the industry brought great reductions in their standard of living.[7] Even so, it is probably true to state that in financial terms the miners were the elite of the industrial working class.

From the seventeenth century at least the traditional workers' housing in this region took the form of one or two-roomed single-storey stone or mud-walled cottages roofed either with thatch or with standstone slates. During the late eighteenth and early nineteenth centuries these were reproduced in large numbers to provide housing for the miners required to work in the new pits. Some are still occupied today, but the fullest account of their original use and furnishing is given in a report of a government commission's visit to the mining village of Flockton between Huddersfield and Wakefield in 1842 (see Appendix 2).[8]

Most of the houses were well furnished for the period, their large living rooms having a number of chairs, including an armchair or easy chair presumably used by the head of the household. A chest of drawers and a 'delf-case' or delf-rack provided storage for domestic utensils, crockery, and clothes, while a clock, probably of long-case design, served both to give the time and as a status symbol. One unusual feature is the number of tables, up to five being listed instead of the solitary tables used in the homes of most working families. It is possible that the additional tables were necessary to seat the large families who sat down each day to their cooked meals of meat and vegetables, in contrast to the contemporary weavers' families, for example, who might stand around their table while spooning porridge from bowls held in their hands. Most miners' houses contained a number of books, of which the bible and new testament were the most common, along with hymn books and other religious works. In the second room of the house, the bedroom, there were usually two or three beds, either four-posters or, more likely, half-testers. These were variously described as being 'neatly' or 'very handsomely' hung with curtains, although it is probable that some of the children in the larger families would be sleeping in dresser-beds or folding beds in the living room.

In the 1840s the collier's day started around 4.30 a.m. with breakfast of porridge and milk, onion porridge, or perhaps milk, water and bread, for oatcake was rapidly going out of use with the mining communities due to the difficulty experienced in making it, and their preference for wheatmeal bread, which they found to be much more nourishing. They then set off to the pit, carrying their lunch of dry bread,

Silkstone Row, Lower Altofts, was built in the mid 1860s by Pope and Pearson to house the workers at their West Riding Colliery. A single row of 52 houses, its three-storey design provided accommodation for large families and their numerous lodgers.

bread and dripping, bread and meat, or bread and cheese wrapped in a cloth within a small wicker basket hooked over their arm. Although the engine might be stopped for an hour or so at midday, there were no fixed or regular lunch breaks underground, some pits near Chapeltown scarcely stopping above a quarter of an hour. Having finished work some time between three and five in the afternoon, they returned home, 'troops of coal-begrimed men and boys returning on foot, or towed along in caravans as grimy as themselves . . . each of them carrying a safety-lamp, these dusky 'mouldy-warps' are a merry lot, and will presently make sad havoc of the breasts of mutton and 'trimmings' which Sarah or Betty has in store for them. And well they earned such a sumptuous repast, poor fellows!'[9] Dinner was a most substantial meal with hot cooked meat and potatoes, probably with a Yorkshire pudding too. This was the final meal of the day for the children but the parents usually had a pot of tea or a little beer shortly before going to bed.

Much of the meat and most of the vegetables were home-grown, the miners usually spending their evenings and any other free time in their gardens, where pigs were reared and sparrows caught for food. They also rented potato plots at the rate of £5 an acre in order to grow further food both for themselves and for their pigs. As a result of the wife's work in the local fields at harvest time, the family also earned the right to glean the corn left in the stubble, this providing a useful source of additional flour for bread-making.[10] As the Yorkshire Sub-Commissioner noted, the colliers were extremely well-fed compared to most other industrial workmen, as evidenced by the 'contrast between the broad *stalwart* frame of the swarthy collier, as he stalks home, all grime and muscle, and the *puny, pallid,* starveling little weaver, with his dirty-white apron and feminine look'.

As the nineteenth century progressed, the collieries became much larger, with still deeper shafts and more extensive underground workings opening up yet more productive seams. Now even greater numbers of miners were required, the colliery companies providing major new housing schemes to accommodate their workforce either in established colliery villages or in completely new settlements often called 'lumps' near the pit-heads.[11] These collections of houses usually clustered around a pub on a knoll and had their own general shop and fish and chip shop. The men would only leave it to go to the pit or to make joint excursions to football matches or popular resorts such as Blackpool. The women too left it very seldom, except to take a day to go with a neighbour or two to do some special shopping in some nearby town. Thus the atmosphere of the lump followed them wherever they went and the inhabitants knew everything about each other. In health or in sickness, in feud or friendship, their lives were the property of their neighbours. Unlike the scattered single-storey cottages of earlier days, the late Victorian colliery housing took the form of long two or three-storey brick-built terraces, the individual units varying in plan and arrangement according to local circumstances. Some were only one room deep, others were back-to-back, while most were 'through' houses with a large kitchen, called 'the house', and a smaller parlour or 'room' on the ground floor, with a cellar below and bedrooms on the upper floors.

The 'house' was the centre of family life, its black-leaded Yorkshire range fuelled with supplies of coal provided by the colliery giving out radiant heat. At its side, a copper or set-pot heated water for the washing and laundry which took place in the adjacent stone or glazed earthenware sink. At the other side of the fireplace the recess was usually fitted from floor to ceiling with cupboards which held food and crockery etc. On the stone-flagged floor lay a number of home-made brodded rag rugs, these being regularly cleaned by having damp used tea-leaves rubbed into them with the foot, before being taken out and banged heartily against a wall. In the centre of the room stood a cleanly-scrubbed square dining table, perhaps covered with American cloth, this being surrounded by a number of sturdy chairs or buffet stools, with a rocking chair and high-backed Windsor chair facing the fire. Arranged round the walls, meanwhile, were an upholstered sofa, a polished sideboard perhaps topped with a pair of vases or ornamental figures in the more houseproud homes,

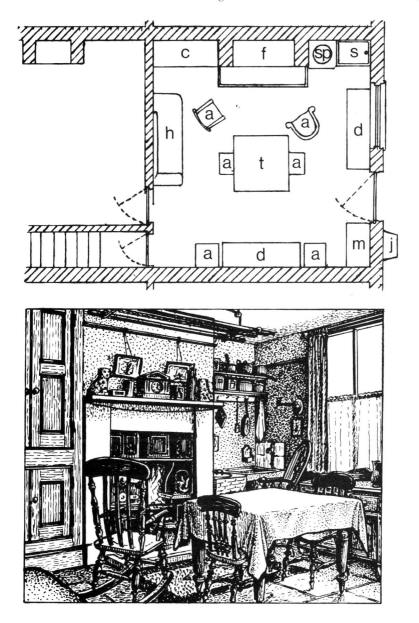

A typical late-nineteenth century West Riding miner's living room. The furnishings include:
a. chairs; c. cupboards; d. dressers; f. fireplace; h. sofa; j. bath; m. mangle; s. sink; sp. set pot.

and a working sideboard topped with a scrubbed working surface and having drawers for cutlery, linen, and miscellaneous household equipment. Most miners' homes followed this general arrangement, but in other aspects they showed marked individuality. Some might be unspeakably dirty and others spotlessly clean, while there was always evidence of some personal enthusiasm. It might be a pedigree fox terrier of a prize-winning strain, or a highly-polished cornet, harmonium or violin, a good piano, a suite of drawing-room furniture, or prizes for garden produce, pigeon racing or rabbit breeding. Then there was almost always a smell of home-made bread, a noble fire, and a sense of welcome.

Up to the 1840s, some miners' wives only went out to work at harvest time, but from 1843, when new legislation prohibited the employment of women and young children underground, the majority of women in the mining communities were full-time housewives. In 1911, for example, 90% of the women aged over ten years were classed as 'unemployed', although their responsibilities in running a miner's home and family were extremely demanding.[12] There was always a constant series of meals to prepare, a constant demand for clean clothes, towels, etc., and constant cleaning duties made necessary due to the smuts and dust which blew in from the smoking chimneys, the black ash of the streets, and the great grey muck-stacks which dominated the local landscape. Jim Bullock has recorded the importance of home baking at Bowers Row near Castleford: 'the basis of our diet was bread, so my mother had to bake every day. At one time there were six men taking six slices of bread and dripping each to the pit, six days a week, plus two slices each for breakfast before they went out. In addition there were three of us still at school and all eating our share. So my mother not only used her own oven every day, but also borrowed the neighbours' ovens [to bake her eight loaves]. Twice a week a different mixture would be kneaded, similar to bread, but flatter and full of currants. These teacakes were really lovely ... Another delicious batch of cakes that my mother used to bake were flat oven cakes. These were like bread, but crusty all round, and were eaten hot, with cheese on'.[13]

In the early nineteenth century most mines had worked for a single shift of perhaps ten hours or more each day, but as the century progressed two or even three-shift working became the general rule. Before setting off to the pit, perhaps in the early hours of the morning, breakfast was eaten in the form of a few slices of bread and perhaps a pot of tea. Further slices of bread wrapped in a cloth and fastened to the back of the miner's belt (or later enclosed in a rat-proof tin) together with a glass or tin bottle of cold tea or water was then carried off to work for 'snap'. If overtime was being worked, they might be given 'pie notes' to a certain value by the management.[14] These could then be exchanged for pies, food or a drink at the pit-head when they had finished the shift, but otherwise they returned home directly, where dinner would be waiting. Having sat down at the head of the table, the miner was served by his wife with the greatest attention, a first course of large squares of Yorkshire pudding being placed before him with a jug of rich gravy, preferably made from rabbit, liver, or perhaps poached game, this being followed by a plate of roast or stewed meat, potatoes, vegetables and gravy. After resting for a while, either stretched before the fire with a pipe, squatting on the doorstep or at the foot of a nearby wall with his workmates, he might then go out to the allotment, join in an impromptu game of football, cricket, or knurr and spell, or go for a drink in the local pub or club, before returning home for supper perhaps made from bread, cheese, and slices of raw onion before going to bed.

This routine was rarely broken except for brief holidays on the main Christian festivals, perhaps a day's 'laking' on a Friday to give an opportunity to rest up for the week-end or do things in the garden or about the house, or a few days holiday in the summer months when the pit closed for the local feast.[15] This was usually preceded by 'Bull-week' when every man worked as long and hard as possible in order to swell his wage packet to pay for the forthcoming festivities. Some indication of the atmosphere of these extremely popular local events is given by the old folksong 'Wibsey Fair':

> I'm collier Jack, thro' Wibsey Slack.
>   am allus praad to tell
> At few fairs in old England can Wibsey
>   Slack excel,
> There's plenty raam for cattle and other
>   sports we hare
> I'm allus praad to go wi' my mates, to
>   t'seets at Wibsey Fair.

Chorus
> So cheer up, my collier lads, an' niver
>   forget to share
> The jolly fun for old and young, at t'seets
>   of Wibsey Fair.

> At Wibsey Fair we gladly share, we've cake an'
>   beef an' ale,
> With strangers too, as weel as friends, we're
>   nivver known to fail;
> There's English, Irish, Scotch and Welsh, an
>   ivvery other mak
> That likes to come and see wer fun at top
>   o'Wibsey slack.

Chorus

> There's Boxing Shows and Comic Shows and
>   swinging boats as well;
> Thes quacks donned up i' the soldier clothes,
>   their physics for to sell
> I'll bet they cure you on the spot, if you
>   believe their tales,
> But ad rather choncea lump o' beef and a
>   drop of good Wibsey ale.

Chorus

B

So here's success to Wibsey Slack, the place
    where I were born,
Ther foolish folks at often tries to run it
    down with scorn;
But I love the birth place and my mates,
    that's honest true and square,
As nivver forget the jolly fun I've had at
    Wibsey fair.

Chorus[16]

Chapter 3

The East Riding Farm Workers

In the decades around 1800, the East Riding of Yorkshire rapidly developed into one of the richest agricultural regions of England as thousands of acres of the high chalk Wolds and the bleak flat lands of Holderness were enclosed and improved. As the population of this region was very sparse, and the villages spaced widely apart, it was difficult to assemble adequate workforces to man the new farms which now appeared across the landscape.[1] To solve this problem, the farmers found it most convenient to have many of their labourers living in the farmhouse where they were always readily available for work throughout every daylight hour, and frequently into the night time too.

At the age of eight or nine the East Riding children began to work in the fields, but usually only between spring and harvest, the months from November to March being occupied in daily attendance at school. Due to a chronic shortage of sleeping accommodation most went into residential service with local farmers when twelve to fourteen years old, although some of the girls became servants in the households of craftsmen and traders in the towns.[2] They gained their employment by attending the 'stattis' or Martinmas hirings held in all the market towns on November 23rd each year. Here they stood in the main street or market place while the farmers and their wives passed amongst them looking for suitable lads and lasses. If, after a brief interview, a mutually acceptable agreement was reached, the servant was paid a 'fest', 'God's penny', or earnest money, usually about half a crown, and was thus legally bound to work on the farm throughout the coming year. Although the servants could borrow from the farmer up to half of what they had earned, they only received their wages at the end of their year's service, just before the next Martinmas hirings. At this time they would pay off their outstanding tailors' and shoemakers' bills etc., and either remain with their current employer for another year's service or return to the hirings to try to find a new place of work. The week following the hirings was their only period of holiday, usually being spent at their own homes, where the greatest family reunion of the year took place. The Sunday of this week was celebrated as 'Rive-kite-Sunday' – literally tear-stomach Sunday – when the mother prepared the best dinner in her power for her offspring. If possible, a goose might be roasted, and a hot ale posset prepared from spiced ale, sweetened with treacle, although some preferred gin, hot water and treacle.[3]

Having carried his box of clothing to his new place of work, the young farm servant found himself in a society where living conditions, hierarchy and discipline were maintained with an almost military strictness. At the top of the structure was the farmer, master, or gaffer, who frequently appointed a foreman or hind to supervise the working of the farm. Depending on the size and wealth of the establishment, either the farmer or the foreman would provide accommodation for the farm servants.

Around 5 a.m. the men would rise and dress in their chamber, a large barrack room with scrubbed floors and a number of double beds, which was entered from the floor below by means of a staircase or a broad-tread ladder with a handrail.[4] After working the stable for an hour, getting the horses ready for the field, the men returned around 6 a.m. or 6.30 a.m. for breakfast in the farm kitchen. This room had a large cooking range at one end, and a long white wood table with benches down each side. Early in the nineteenth century the thick table tops were carved out to provide a series of plate-size hollows about two inches deep into which the broth, meat and vegetables were poured before being eaten with wooden spoons. The whole table was then well washed with hot water and soda, although in some houses wisps of straw were used for the rough cleaning. By the middle of the century these tables had been replaced by the usual plank-topped variety on which wooden trenchers were laid for each man.[5] White earthenware plates had come into use by the 1890s, but cutlery continued to be fairly rudimentary, the men using their own clasp knives at table in preference to the knives and forks used elsewhere.[6]

At breakfast, as at all meals, the head of the household occupied the head of the table, from where he carved and served the meat to the men in strict order of precedence; first, the head horseman, waggoner, or 'wag', then the third man or 'thoddy', the fourth man or 'fowaty', and finally their respective lads. If the carver was really skilful, he would flick the slices of meat from the point of his knife directly on to each plate in turn.[7] Along the table, there would be a number of curd tarts or fruit pies containing jam, apple, dates, figs, plums or prunes according to the season.[8] Each man helped himself to slices of pie, always finishing one pie before starting another, and always cutting the pie in the distinctive East Yorkshire manner. Holding the plate steady with two fingers on the edge of the pie, the first cut was made from the centre to the left side of the fingers, a second cut then being made from half an inch short of the centre to the right side of the fingers. Each succeeding cut was made in the same way, proceeding anti-clockwise around the pie, until the last slice was left with a hexagonal piece at the centre. This method ensured that everyone had the same proportion of crust to filling, and also that no one ever handled anyone else's piece of pie. If a man failed to cut the pie in this way he would receive a sharp crack across the back of the knuckles with the flat side of the table knife, together with a warning not to 'cut all't guts out o' that pie lad!'[9]

By 7 a.m. breakfast was finished and the men and horses were setting off for work in the fields, returning again at noon for dinner. This was a substantial meal of beef, vegetables and puddings, its actual content varying from farm to farm as may be seen in the following table.

In the eastern parts of Holderness a large dish of fried bacon or ham with plenty of rich brown gravy might be set in the middle of the table with a supply of hot 'light cakes'. Pieces of cake were then broken off and dipped into the dish before being eaten with the fingers, although spoons were being used for this purpose by the 1870s. For pudding there could be rice, plum duff or 'spotted dog' with custard, or a very large suet pudding into which a deep hole was cut and filled with treacle. This

EAST RIDING FARM SERVANTS' DIETS

	General view of Agriculture, 1812[10]	Cooper Hall Farm, Skerne, 1840s[11]	Royal Commission Labour, 1893	Mr Jordan's Eastburn, 1920[12]	Farm near Driffield, 1914[13]
Breakfast	Cold meat or fruit pies or cheesecakes, Milk.	Wheatmeal bread, beef bacon, Basin of Milk.	Boiled beef, bacon, bread, cheese, fruit pies and Milk.	Cold beef and bacon, fruit pie, Boiled Milk.	Cold beef, fruit pies, Basin of tea.
Dinner	Hot meat pie or boiled beef and dumplings, Small beer.	Sundays, Tuesdays & Thursdays: beef & bacon, hot rice & apple dumplings sweetened with treacle. Mondays, Wednesdays & Fridays: as above but with meat pies instead of beef & bacon.	Sundays: Soup, suet pudding and roast beef. Weekdays: Beef or meat pie, fruit pies.	Beef pie or boiled beef twice a week & roast beef on Sundays with potatoes, another vegetable, rice pudding & fruit pie.	1st course: basin of broth. Main courses: Sunday: Roast beef, potatoes and turnips, Yorkshire pudding with gravy or treacle. Monday: Cold beef, potatoes and turnips, plum duff and thin custard. Tuesday: Broth of beff, potatoes, turnips and dumplings, boiled together. Wednesday: Roast beef ǀ with veg. etc. ǀ Thursday: Bacon cakes ǀ with veg. etc. ǀ Friday: Beef ǀ with veg. etc. ǀ and duff. Saturday: Hash
Supper	Cold meat or fruit pies or cheesecakes, Milk.	Wheatmeal bread, beef, bacon, & a basin of boiled milk.	Boiled beef, beef, bacon, bread, cheese, fruit pies and milk.	Cold beef & bacon, fruit pie. Boiled milk.	Cold beef and fruit pies

pudding was then cut into portions, leaving the hole containing the treacle intact so that each person could dip each mouthful into the hot molten syrup before carrying it to his mouth.[14] After working from 1 p.m. to 5.30 p.m. supper was served, this being a similar meal to breakfast. Then, once the horses had been fed, cleaned, and bedded down for the night, there might be a little time for conversation, a game of cards, darts, or nine men's morris, or, on summer evenings, some extemporised cricket or quoits before going to bed.[15] Even so, leisure time was almost non-existent, the men working virtually every daylight hour throughout the year.

As Charles Howard noted in 1835, 'there are few countries where [the farm servants] and the labourers work harder'. Long hours of strenuous work demanded a wholesome diet, even though one commentator noted rather peevishly that although 'one cannot grudge good and abundant food to young growing fellows – working hard – yet one cannot disguise the fact that they are sumptuously fed and are frightfully dainty . . .'[16]

The work of the farm girls was just as strenuous as that of the men. Between 5 and 6 a.m. perhaps twenty cows had to be brought up to the farmstead, milked and the dairy work of straining the milk, setting the cream and churning the butter commenced. The fires had to be lit and the ovens made hot enough to bake all the bread and pies required by the household, up to eight stone of flour, a stone of bacon and a whole sheep regularly being consumed each week, with some forty standing pies made at a single baking. Then the potatoes had to be washed and the 'fire-eldin' gathered to heat the copper in which they were boiled. On wash-day work might have to start as early as 1 a.m. in order to complete the laundry for the farmer's family and servants by late afternoon. These duties, together with housework, nursing the children and looking after the poultry were onerous enough, but the farm girls were also expected to play an active part in running the farm itself, pulling and topping and tailing turnips, raking 'wicks', weeding the young corn, and working in the harvest field. It would have been impossible for them to undertake such a formidable amount of sheer hard work without plenty of good, nourishing food, and for this reason they received a similar or identical diet to that provided for their male colleagues.[17]

One of the most important factors in the farm servant's life was the quality and quantity of food provided by his employer – whether he kept a 'good-livin' place' or a 'poor-livin' place'. In the latter, the servants might sing verses about the cook:

> We had an old cook, she was an old snake,
> She baked sike cakes as ne'er you c'n eat.
> Bread made of iron, and cakes made of bran,
> They rattled i' your guts like an old tin can
> To my wa-fa-la diddle-da-la-day.

or, about the quality of her standing mutton pies:[18]

Cold Stringy Pie

Down in Yorkshire a farmer did dwell,
They called him Yaddy 'Ughes, you all know him well.
He keeps four servants it aint any lie
He feeds them up on cow stringy pie
Singing fal-de-diddle-i-do, fal-de-diddle-dee.

He has nine hosses and they're that thin
You can count every bone as it ligs in their skin
There's four thick in't leg and five swung in't back
And he drives them along with a wharve-gee-back
Singing fal-de-diddle-i-do, fal-de-diddle-dee.

He gets lads up at half-past five
To gan to't stable to see if they're still alive
He feeds 'em on oats, an he feeds 'em on bran
And it rattles in their guts like an old tin can
Singing fal-de-diddle-i-do, fal-de-diddle-dee.

One day I hear him to't shepherd say
We had an old ewe died three weeks today
Fetch her up, Bullocky, fetch her up on't sly
It'll make these lads some rare mutton pie
Singing fal-de-diddle-i-do, fal-de-diddle-dee.

They fetched her up and they boiled her in't pot
She came on't table reeking hot
Mawks crawled ower her inches thick,
Owd Yaddy had a lad knocking em off wi' a stick
Singing fal-de-diddle-i-do, fal-de-diddle-dee.

Now if any of you lads 'ud like to learn how to plough
Gan to bold Yaddy's he'll soon show you how
He keeps you at it the live-long day
He expects you to plough forty acres every day
Singing fal-de-diddle-i-do, fal-de-diddle-dee.

The farm servants who lived in were usually young men and women in their late teens and early twenties. When they married they left the farmhouse and set up new homes in cottages situated either close to the farm or in one of the villages. The men now became labourers, being paid by the day, by the week, or, at harvest, by piece-work.[19] If they lived near the farm they might go home for their meals, or carry their food to work wrapped first in a white cloth and then in a red handkerchief.[20] Since many could only find cottages some miles away from their work, the farmers arranged to provide all their meals after deducting about a third of their wages. Where necessary, they could also stop overnight, one Neswick farmer stating that he 'provided beds for the men if they want them, they usually go home on Wednesday and Saturday'.[21]

At harvest time, when a greatly enlarged labour force was required, day labourers from the North and West Ridings, particularly from Richmond, Knaresborough and the western dales, travelled to Malton, where they were hired for work in the Wolds and Holderness.[22] During the harvest, when long hours were worked in the fields, 'lowance' was carried out from the farm around 9.30 a.m. and 3.30 p.m. It could include currant pasty, sad cake, very short, hot, and running with butter, bread and cheese, and bacon or ham cake which was really a kind of pasty:[23]

Ham Cake

1 large slice of gammon
Shortcrust pastry made from 4oz plain flour, a pinch of salt, 2oz lard, 4 teaspoons water.

Roll out the pastry on a floured board, lay the gammon on one side, cover with the remaining pastry, dampen and seal the edges to enclose the gammon, prick the upper surface, and place on a baking sheet. Bake for 15 minutes at 425°F gas mark 7, then reduce heat to 325°F gas mark 3 for a further 30 minutes. Serve by cutting into slices about three inches across.

This was all washed down with home-brewed beer carried into the field in two-gallon stoneware bottles sheathed within neat wicker cases. The usual allowance was 1½ pints for each man, two men sharing a pint mugful in the following manner. The first man drank until he could just see the bottom of the mug, after which he passed it to his colleague, who finished the draught. The mug was then refilled, the second man now drinking first, and so on, until they had consumed three pints between them.[24]

The cottages or 'nooks' occupied by the married farm labourers and their families could be basic in the extreme, being described as very uncomfortable and unwholesome hovels not fit to put cattle in.[25] The older examples were simple cruck-framed structures, with whitewashed walls of mud or chalk blocks and steeply sloping thatched roofs. Half the area of their single rooms was occupied by a hearth large enough to accommodate the whole family around a fire of wood and coal. The wide timber-framed smoke-hood rising above their heads allowed them to amuse themselves by betting odds as to who could see the most stars out of the chimney without rising from their seats.[26]

The later cottages, built from around the mid-eighteenth century, tended to have substantial walls made of brick or sea-cobbles and roofs of thatch or pantiles. From the outside, they presented an aspect of idyllic rural charm, with red-painted woodwork, white-painted window-leads, yellow-ochred doorsills and steps, and bright, colourful flower gardens resplendent with tulips, hyacinths, geraniums and fuchsias.[27] Within, the living room or 'house' and the parlour were floored with brick or a deep layer of beaten cement suitably marked out in rectangles to resemble freestone slabs.[28] The interior decoration and furnishings of one such cottage of the 1840s have been described in some detail by the Rev. Henry Woodcock, who, as a

An East Riding cottage at Routh, near Beverley.

Primitive Methodist minister, frequently lodged with the labourers: 'The house floor, though rough and broken, was washed with rud-coloured water, and tastefully sanded through a cullender, so that beautiful patches, a quarter of a yard apart, adorned the floor, and woe betide the youngster who set his foot on one of these before six p.m. The hearth-stone was as clean as a new pin, and on the whitewashed walls hung pictures of ... Bunyan fighting with Appollyon; Dick Turpin, on his famous mare 'Bess', leaping a five-barred gate; The Rev. William Clowes; Sir Tatton Sykes; a pack of hounds; St. Peter holding the keys; James Hall, esq., of Scarbro'. There was a deal dresser, with a shelf above it, on which all sorts of crockery, ancient and modern, were tastefully arranged. A set of chairs, with high backs and awkward legs, were arranged around the room; a polished chest of drawers, covered with a bright cloth, with two or three plaster images and glass vases. An eight-days' clock, seven foot high, an heirloom for three generations, told exact time the week round. Right overhead were suspended from the rafters bunches of herbs, mint, garlic, sweet marjoram, sage, sides of bacon, a ham (there was a porker fattening in the sty). The table was covered with a cloth of alabaster whiteness and the knives and forks shone in their polished brightness. Upstairs there was one bed.'[29] Additional accommodation was frequently provided by flooring across the upper part of the roof-space to make a 'cockloft' just large enough to house one or two small beds for the youngest members of the family.[30]

Outside many of the cottages lay an allotment. Here the labourer and his family could grow fruit and vegetables, especially potatoes, in addition to keeping a pig or a cow. The pig provided the family's main source of meat, as well as giving a good cash return if the hams were sold off, while the cow gave a considerable level of support, enabling them to 'live much better than such as are unfortunately compelled to be contented with the washings of the tea-pot, rendered palatable by treacle, and perhaps a little gin'.[31] The allotment might also be used for keeping poultry, but this could mean that some of the farmer's corn would be 'borrowed' to provide their feed. As Mr Burton of Linton-on-Ouse commented, 'if they get a little corn out of me to feed them, well, I know nothing about it, but I know that anyone who wants to keep a good man must overlook such small leakages'.[32]

The 1812 General Account of the Agriculture of the East Riding records that 'The labourers who supply food for themselves and their families live comfortably in general comparison with those of many of the southern counties. Their bread comprehends the whole of the wheat, except the coarse bran, and is home-made; this they eat with butter, or bacon and potatoes, and they have commonly one meal in the day of fresh meat, or meat-pie. Barley-cake, or a mixture of barley and wheat, is sometimes adopted when wheat is very dear; this is a very wholesome, nutritive, and not unpleasant food'.[33] Later in the century the labouring family's diet became much poorer, the fresh meat and much of the bacon disappearing from the table completely. In some cottages the family had tea, bread and butter for both breakfast and tea, dinner being either potatoes or bread, with bacon only on three days during the week. In order to sustain his strength, the labourer himself had milk and bread for breakfast and bacon for dinner every day.[34] If any fresh meat was cooked, he alone would eat it at Sunday dinner.

In many East Riding households there was an enormous difference in the quality and quantity of food consumed by the labourer, and that which he could provide for his family. The farmers knew that it was cost-effective to have well-fed labourers, and so kept back six shillings (30p) a week from the man's wages to pay for the food he had at the farm, thus leaving him with only eight shillings (40p) a week to feed, clothe, and house his dependants. As the son of a labourer working on this basis at Nafferton in the 1840s. William Blades could clearly remember his poor and monotonous diet.[35] For breakfast there would be some kind of brown or barley bread and treacle, a basin of water, and possibly an occasional sup of milk. Tea was at a prohibitive price; the nearest approach to it they could ever achieve was when the landlord of the neighbouring inn would give his mother the used tea leaves which produced a drink with the faintest flavour of tea, and might be likened to water 'bewitched' or tainted with smoke. For the children's dinner there would be a kneading bowl on the floor in which were mixed the broth which they got from the farm three days a week, mashed potatoes with pepper and salt, with perhaps a dumpling or two in addition; the children sat round on the floor with wooden spoons and ate away as quickly as they could, and when the meal was ended their mother would come to them with the words 'Say your grace, and away you go'. The evening meal was similar to breakfast, except that they might have a bit of cheesecake or apple pie in addition.

Even though the later nineteenth century saw the gradual improvement of the farm labourer's diet, it still remained comparatively plain and simple up until the recent post-war decades when it finally approached the national norm.

Chapter 4

The Urban Poor

Here, in the dark and dank cellar, including pigs, with broken panes in every window frame, and filth and vermin in every nook, with the walls unwhitewashed for years, black with the smoke of foul chimneys, without water, with corded bedstocks for beds, and sacking for bedclothing, with floors unwashed from year to year, without out-offices, and with incomes a few shillings a week derived from the labour of half-starved children or the more precarious earnings of casual employment, are to be found what seem the dregs of society, but are human beings withal, existing from hour to hour under every form of privation and distress, while without, there are streets elevated a foot, sometimes two, above the level of the causeway by the accumulation of years, and stagnant puddles here and there with their foetid exhalations, causeways broken and dangerous, ash-places choked up with filth, and excramentitious deposits on all sides.'[1] This is not a description of some squalid Third World suburb, but an accurate account of the Bank, an area a few yards from Leeds Parish Church, in the 1830s.

The massive expansion of industry and especially of the factory system in the decades around 1800 brought with it a great demand for cheap unskilled or semi-skilled labour. On asking the workers in a Bradford factory where they came from, Angus Reach received the following replies: 'I'm from Leicestershire' – 'I'm from Devonshire' – 'I'm from Cornwall' – 'I'm from Mount Mellick, in Queen's County'.[2] Many had come into the towns to escape the rural poverty of these areas, together with others from the Yorkshire countryside, with Scots from the depressed textile industries of Clydesdale, and with the Irish fleeing from the famine raging in their country. The towns were quite unprepared for changes of this magnitude, but private landowners, industrialists and speculators soon realised that the erection of small houses for rent produced a very good financial return. As a result, individual plots of land near the town centres were rapidly developed to contain the greatest possible number of dwellings, the lack of any overall control making it impossible to incorporate any effective form of sewerage, drainage, refuse disposal, or water supply. Thus, within a few years of being built, these new houses had degenerated into the most foul, dirty, overcrowded and unhealthy of slums.

Most were built as back-to-backs around small courtyards, this system being adopted from the seventeenth and eighteenth-century housing erected in the narrow yards of the medieval town centres. Each house had a living room measuring from about twelve feet square, around Sheffield, to about fifteen feet square in Leeds. This served as kitchen, scullery, dining-room and wash-room, and on wet days the clothes were hung up in it to dry. The room was usually paved with flagstones, its fireplace being filled with an oven for baking and a side-boiler for hot

In 1879 the *Illustrated London News* sent one of its artists to record the state of the distressed poor in the city of Sheffield. In these drawings he shows one of the small town-centre cottages, the living-room being almost devoid of furniture, except for a table, a chair, and an empty corner cupboard.

water, while there was also a dished slopstone or sink perhaps with a lead pipe leading to a soak-away, a street channel, or a sewer.[3] In the bedroom, or chamber above, a room with a boarded floor and fireplace, slept the whole family, unless this room was required for an industrial purpose such as weaving. In some areas, such as Sheffield, there might also be an attic occupying the roofspace. This formed the sleeping accommodation for the older children and, if necessary, the lodger.

Beneath the house was a cellar. In many cases it was not used by the occupants of the house, however, but was rented out as a separate dwelling. In 1849 Angus Reach visited a number of the virtually destitute rag collectors, matchmakers, rope pickers, rug-makers and out-of-work living in the cellars in the West Yorkshire textile towns. His vivid descriptions of life in these dank and dark surroundings are extremely depressing, as may be seen in the following account of a Halifax cellar.[4] 'Access to the apartment was through a door, or rather hole, not four feet high, broken in the wall, and through this the inmates crawled backwards and forwards. This den – the place was about eight feet by six – was inhabited by a man, his wife, and several children. Filthy plates, and tubs full of foul-smelling scum and slops lying everywhere about'. In a Leeds cellar, about seven feet square, he found the floor 'littered with old bagging, Russia mats, old ropes, and shavings – furnished with rickety deal tables, and two or three chairs more or less dilapidated, and a bedspread on a low frame or rolled up in a corner. The cooking apparatus consisted of a single pot'. One Bradford cellar, meanwhile, was 'a low, dark foul-smelling place, with rough stools, and a broken table or so lying about; coarse crockery, either unwashed or full of dirty water; knives without handles, and forks with broken prongs; bits of loaves smeared over by dirty hands; bundles of rags, buckets of slops, and unmade beds huddled on the stone or earthen floors in the corners'.[5] It is not surprising that the sanitary reformers who began to tackle these enormous problems from the 1830s concentrated much of their effort on closing down the cellar dwellings, then proceeding with the clearance of the old slum property, and replacing it with improved designs of well-built terrace property built according to new local authority byelaws adopted in the 1860s. Even so, it is quite true to say that the conditions experienced by many members of the urban poor were deplorable throughout the entire nineteenth century in terms of housing, health, and food.

When Robert Baker was carrying out his survey of the labouring classes of Leeds in the late 1830s he had the following conversation with a group of Irish factory children:[6]

> 'When have you had flesh meat?'
> 'We never get it' . . . 'sometimes once a week.'
> 'What then do you live upon?'
> 'Coffee and bread – or tea.'

Ten years later Angus Reach found Bradford families barely subsisting on the same diet. 'We live chiefly on bread, I get a stone and half of flour every week, and I bake it on Sundays. Then we have a little tea or coffee, and sometimes we have a little offal meat because it is cheap'.[7] Sixty years later Leeds slipper-makers were living on home-made bread and tea, with threepence (1p) worth of meat some weeks, and plenty of 'working man's beef', 'that is to say onions. There's grand stuff in onions'.[8] Even in 1899 many poor families were still eating bread, butter and tea for the majority of their meals. This is clearly illustrated by evidence gathered by Seebohm Rowntree from a York labourer's wife. She had to provide food for her husband and four young children for about 10/6d (52p) out of their total weekly income of some 18s. (90p):[9]

	Breakfast	Dinner	Tea
Friday	Brown & White bread, butter, tea	Fish, bread, tea	Bread, butter, onions, tea
Saturday	Bacon, bread, tea	Eggs, bread, butter, tea	Bread, dripping, onions, tea
Sunday	Bacon, bread, tea	Potato pie, potatoes, cabbage	Bread, butter, currant cake, tea
Monday	Porridge, bread, butter, tea	Potato pie	Bread, butter, currant cake, tea
Tuesday	Brown & White bread	Meat, bread, tea	Bread, butter, dripping, tea
Wednesday	Brown & White bread, butter, tea	Bread, bacon, tea	Bread, butter, dripping, tea
Thursday	Porridge, bread	Bacon, bread, bread pudding, tea	Bread, butter, lettuce, tea

From this evidence, it is clear that many, if not most, of the urban poor were living almost entirely on bread, butter, tea and coffee for the greater part of the nineteenth century. It had the advantages of being extremely cheap, quick, and easy to prepare, requiring the minimum of fuel, but this was all that could be said in its favour. Nutritionally it was completely inadequate, unbalanced, and quite unable to sustain the body in a good state of health. As early as 1824 the *Family Oracle of Health* had noticed that 'notwithstanding all we have so often said in favour of tea, that the use of it with bread and butter, as the almost *sole* food of the working classes in manufacturing towns, is a leading cause of scrofula among the mass of their population, which the introduction of tea has promoted, compensates little for the loss of vigour of constitution and power of body which have followed its use by that class of the community'. It is not surprising that food of this quality contributed to the enormous spread of deficiency diseases among the poor, particularly when combined with insanitary, overcrowded and poorly ventilated living quarters. The effect is more clearly seen in the life expectancy of the different social groups living in Yorkshire's great towns early last century.[10]

Town	Gentry, etc.	Manufacturers, Tradesmen & Shopkeepers	Labourers & Mill Operatives
Leeds	44 yrs	27 yrs	19 yrs
Halifax	55 yrs	24 yrs	22 yrs

The semi-skilled workers and operatives in regular employment could usually afford a rather more substantial diet, even though it was relatively plain and economical. Detailed evidence of their food was again collected by Seebohm Rowntree from fourteen York families with weekly earnings of less than 26s. (£1.30) in the 1890s. Bread spread with butter, or perhaps dripping or bacon fat was eaten for breakfast in virtually every home, cheese, jam or treacle being used only very sparingly, if at all. Bacon and dry bread might also appear every day, three or four times a week, or even once a week or less depending on the family's means. Porridge and milk, bread and milk, sausages, boiled eggs or fish were only eaten very occasionally. As might have been expected, tea was by far the most popular breakfast drink, being cheap and quickly and easily prepared in comparison to coffee and cocoa, although these drinks were taken to a limited degree.

Dinner, served around noon, was the most substantial meal of the day. The Sunday dinner was of particular importance, for on this occasion the housewife had sufficient time to prepare more substantial dishes which her family could eat together at a comparatively unhurried pace. A joint of roast beef formed the basis of this meal, although some chose mutton or pork, these being served with potatoes, cabbage or cauliflower, and Yorkshire pudding. Over the next few days Sunday's meat re-appeared at dinner times when it was served cold with potatoes and perhaps beetroot or pickles, finally emerging in the form of a hash on Tuesday, Wednesday, or even Thursday. Once the roast had been finished, it was usually replaced by cheaper meat such as bacon, liver and onions, chops, sausages, brawn, or rabbit, with potatoes or bread. In some households, however, more economical dinners were made from fish, stewed giblets, pea soup, or bread and dripping. Puddings were not made on a regular basis, perhaps only once or twice a week in the more prosperous homes, semolina, rice, suet or bread puddings and rhubarb pies being the most common varieties.

Bread and butter and a pot of tea formed an essential part of the light meal eaten at teatime in the late afternoon or early evening, currant cakes, shortcakes, baked custards, and simple salads of lettuce and onions or water-cress might also be served, but for many these simple luxuries were, like jam, reserved for Sundays alone. The last meal of the day was supper, with further bread and butter, cheese, cold meat or fish. Even though this diet was a great improvement on bread and butter and tea, it was still starchy, monotonous, and inadequate, providing only 71% of the protein and 77% of the calorific intake required to sustain good health.

In these circumstances it is perhaps not surprising that unscrupulous employers deliberately used hunger as a means of depressing wages. This was certainly the case in the Leeds tailoring industry, where one girl working in a sweat-shop has recalled how she had 'often been so weak for want of food that she had fainted over her machine. Many of her fellow workers used to beg food off the men in the factory, but she had never cared to do this, as it led to things . . . when they were all very hungry, the foremen told them there were four hundred sailor suits coming up, would they do them at 3d each? They refused as the lowest price was 3½d. The foremen kept them waiting a day and a half (without pay) and at last they were so hungry that they gave in'.[11] In many households it was only the coming of wartime rationing that

'In one of the lowest neighbourhoods in Leeds, I found an old slipper-maker at his tea.
Although it was then past ten at night, his five little children were up and with him. As his
wife explained "They've got to be there, when there's something to eat going. Father chucks
them a bit of bread now and again, and so they like to be there" ...'

eventually enabled them to receive an adequate and balanced diet, even though it
was still extremely sparse.

One of the advantages of urban life was that supplies of ready-made food were
always to hand, although they might not be particularly wholesome, or represent
good value. Take, for example, the meat and potatoe pies purchased from the local
cookshops. Richard Spencer, the Holbeck poet, addressed them thus:[12]

> So tha'rt a meit an taty pie,
> Nay nivver that, it's all mi eye,
> Bud cum, fair play, ah will just try
>   Ta' fin' sum meit;
> It's true ther is sum thear, ah spy,
>   Aw yes, its reight!
>
> If t'scraps o' t'dinner plates they've been,
> It matters nowt, – it can't be seen, –
> Thear's no connectin link between, –
>   An as fer t' gravy
> Ta analize it 'ud puzzle e'en
>   Sir Humphrey Davy.

The contents of these pies was always the subject of some controversy, as witnessed by the story of a Yorkshireman in Wakefield who, having tasted his pie, rose to his feet, took off his coat, and rolled up his shirt sleeves ready 'ter mak these 'ere pertatees tell weer t'mait is!'[13] Hot potato pies were one of the standard dishes served in the poorest eating houses, along with soup made from dried peas, called 'gray pays' and savoury ducks, a variety of faggot made from pig's fry.[14] They were also available in public houses, both for casual customers and for 'footins'. These were the occasions 'when a chap (generally an overlewker) starts at a new shed (and) pays summat t'ard a spree, a lot mor join in, an they hev a 'puttato pie do' at a pub. They awlus sup abaat a quairt o' beer ta ivvery spooinfull o' pie; ha' they finned ther way hooam is a mystery...'[15] Hawkers were permitted to sell their wares around the pubs too, as James Burnley discovered in Bradford around 1870.[16] During the intervals between suggestive songs accompanied on the piano, 'a man with a basket containing sheep's trotters comes in, and keeps asking "Who wants another trotter?" When he goes away a little decrepit old woman steps in, with a large milk can full of hot pies. She places her burden down on the hearth, stands with her back to the fire, and looks round for customers; but she has come at the wrong moment, evidently, for they begin to chaff the poor creature as to the contents of her pies, and, after a while, she gets enraged, and goes out without having disposed of a single pie'. In the streets, the pies were sometimes sold from small carts equipped with ovens, the trader crying his wares:[17]

> Potatoes, Peas and Pies all hot,
> Potatoes Peas and Pies,
> Potatoes, Peas and Pies all hot,
> Potatoes, Peas and Pies

or simply 'Hot peas and pies all hot!'

Hot pea sellers were to be found in almost every town and sizeable village. Over one arm they usually carried a can from which they ladled the hot mushy mint-flavoured peas, although some had large cans, mounted on wheels, full of peas:[18]

> Reeking hot, smoking hot,
> Peas all hot!
> Bring out your pots and get a big lot.
> Peas all hot!

Hot chips, cockles, muffins, roasted potatoes and hokey-poky – a predecessor of today's ice cream – were similarly cried around the streets. Here their value as cheap instant food brought ready sales, even though they contributed little to the dietary needs of their purchasers.

Chapter 5

Fuel and Fireplaces

The domestic fire was always far more than a mere source of heat. It was the focus of all family and social life in the home. Around its warm glow people gathered for conversation, for drinking, for courting, for knitting, and for thawing out in cold wintry weather. Its heat was essential for roasting, boiling and toasting all manner of food, for heating water for washing, for drying and airing clothes and bedding, and, when contained within a range, for baking bread, pastries, puddings and meat dishes. Since the fire played such an important part in sustaining the family, it is not surprising that it retained a certain reputation for magical properties: some practical divination by looking for shapes in the burning coals, for example. Even when flint and steel, sulphur matches, and safety matches were readily available for fire lighting, the technique of kindling a fire by rubbing two sticks together was still remembered, for the smoke from a 'needfire' made in this way prevented the cattle from catching the fatal murrain.[1]

In most parts of the county wood was rather too sparse or expensive for use as a major fuel. Fallen timber could be collected from woods and hedgerows, or driftwood from the shores, but it was only on the farms and country estates that formal arrangements might be made for the supply of firewood to the cottagers. Near Charltons in Cleveland, for example, the woods were opened once every two or three months, when the head woodman would mark a tree for every family with a cross and make a note saying which family was to have the tree. The family would then go and chop down their own tree for winter fuel.[2] In the urban areas, where there was virtually no growing timber, but where it was still required for igniting coal fires, wire-bound bundles of chopped wood called 'chips' were made by traders who then hawked them round the streets.

Throughout the North Yorks Moors, the Dales, and the Pennine hills extending south to the Derbyshire border, the major fuel was peat. In these areas, many of the cottages enjoyed common rights of turbary, the right to cut peat on the moors, this being controlled by the manorial courts leet. Even today Mr Harold Quarmby, Constable of the Graveship of Holm in the Manor of Wakefield is in charge of the peat beds around Holmfirth.[3] In March, when the moors had started to dry out, but before the grouse had begun nesting, an area of heather moorland was burnt off, the remaining dry stalks called cowls being collected in bundles and carried back to the house for use as kindling. The techniques of cutting the peat differed from one part of the country to another, but the following account from Nidderdale is typical:[4] 'The top spit of the peat was cut with a spade with a long bent handle, called the flaying spade, into pieces sometimes a yard long and eight or ten inches wide. These strips were called flouts or fleights. They were not used for burning when peats

42

could be obtained, but blacksmiths used them for heating the tires of wheels. When cutting the peats, a wooden spade with an iron L-shaped blade cut out slices the shape of a thin brick about eight inches or so long, in May. These were called peats. They were laid to dry and harden on the moor a few hundred paces from the place where they were cut. About a fortnight later the cutters 'set' them, one piece standing on its edge leaning towards two others resting endways against it. After another fortnight they 'hut' them, setting another six or eight more peats round them, and laying two or three flat on the top to shoot the rain off. After a time, the peats were piled into tall stacks called 'Ruckles''. Having thoroughly dried in this way, the peats were led in carts or sleds back to the farms and cottages, where they were stored either in a small masonry building called a peat-cote, or were neatly stacked and covered with fleights to keep them dry. Fleights were the long strips of vegetation and roots pared from the surface of the moor before peat cutting commenced.

When Joseph Lucas entered Ling Hall, one of the old cottage farms of Nidderdale, on one December evening in 1871, he found that there 'was no light in the house but that of the peat fire, which was burning upon a flag-stone that stood well out in the room. The night was a very dark one, and the general impression was that of entering a wood shed in the dark in which a man was lighting a pipe'.[5] This scene, with the glowing peat fire smouldering directly on the hearthstone filling the room with the characteristic pungent reek could be found everywhere in the peat-burning areas of early nineteenth-century Yorkshire. In the old cottages, the hearth area, measuring perhaps twelve feet wide by six feet in depth, had sufficient room to seat a few people on the spence, or wooden benches arranged at each side of the fire. As Martha Hessletine told F.W. Moorman, 'We allus used to burn peats on our farm [at Goredale in Upper Wharfedale], and varra warm they were of a winter neet. We'd no kitchen range i' yon days, but a gert oppen fireplace, whear thou ould look up the chimney and see the stars shining of a frosty neet. We liked the ash; we could roast taties in't, and mony's the time we've sat i' the ingle-nook and made our supper o' taties and buttermilk'.[6] Over these hearths, the chimney or smoke-hood took the form of a large open-topped pyramid of wattle and daub carried on a strong horizontal bressumer beam running across the house at head height. In the houses and cottages built in the county during the eighteenth and nineteenth centuries, however, the smoke hood was replaced by rectangular masonry chimney stacks of the usual domestic type still common today.

The other major fuel burned in the county was coal. This had been mined for domestic use in Yorkshire from the fourteenth century at least, and by the early nineteenth century the coal measures lying approximately between Leeds and Sheffield were amongst the most productive in the whole country. Visitors to the area were greatly impressed by the cheapness and quality of the local coal: 'near to Leeds the fuel is so cheap as not to be an object. In the lodging houses they include coal [with the price of the room]. Behind the grate and over the fire a heap of coals is deposited for the day. As they are wanted they are drawn down with the poker; it is very convenient, but its appearance in a genteel appartment is not quite so well'.[7]

In other parts of the county a number of small collieries worked narrow local

In the West Yorkshire Pennines, coal continued to be delivered by teams of donkeys equipped with panniers as late as the 1890s. The one seen here is from a painting made in the Shibden Valley near Halifax (a). From the early part of the 19th century carts were also used for delivering coal both from the pitheads and from the railway coal depots, the strongly-built cart of A.H. Smith of Morley being typical of the vehicles used for this trade (c). The 'chips' of wood required to light the fires were either sold from corner shops or hawked around the streets in urban areas, Mr. Braund operating from Halifax Road, Sowerby Bridge (b).

seams. At Fryup Head, Danby, Blakey and Rudland in the North York Moors, at Tan Hill, at Mossdale, Storth, Arnagill and Thorney Grange in upper Wensleydale, at Bewerley, Thornthwaite, Birstwith and Smelthouses in upper Nidderdale, in Garsdale, and around Ingleton in the Dales, near Gilling and the Howardian Hills, and even between Easingwold and Thirsk in the Vale of York, seams up to a foot and a half in thickness produced coal for local consumption.[8] Their quality and quantity were both of an extremely low order, however, some pits only producing eleven tons of heavy, sulphurous coal each week. In the northern and eastern parts of the county, the only really worthwhile supplies of coal were those brought in from distant coalfields. The coal from the central area of the West Riding was carried by river to depots at York, Malton, Driffield and Pocklington, and by the Leeds and Liverpool Canal to Settle, from where it was carried into the country. Coal from County Durham, meanwhile, was brought by carts and pack-ponies as far south as Thirsk. In towns such as Richmond in North Yorkshire, the rattle of the one-horse coal-carts started at midnight on Sunday and went on for two hours as they set off for the pits of south-west Durham. Having loaded up, they immediately started back, probably stopping for refreshment and a short sleep at one of the wayside inns between Piercebridge and Scotch Corner, then continuing on their way so as to be able to discharge their coals in Richmond by noon on Monday. A few hours rest, and then at midnight or soon after they were on the road again to repeat the journey seven times in a fortnight.[9]

The poor were supplied by donkeys, mules and pack-ponies locally known as galloways. Many hundreds of these animals were employed in conveying small bags or 'pokes', three to a beast, to towns and villages throughout the county.[10] They cost very little to maintain, for there was always plenty of wayside grazing and occasionally, if farmers were so careless as to leave a gate open or unlocked, the animals would 'stray' into a good pasture or even into a field of growing corn. Two or three hours of good grazing at midnight for fifty donkeys was certainly a convenient windfall for the collier donkeyman. They were particularly useful in hilly country where they could use the network of paved pack-horse tracks established in the medieval period, and where wheeled vehicles were completely impractical. Often they were grossly mistreated by their owners. In Pudsey in the 1830s, for example, some had their backs in a most horrible state from wounds made by the coal, whilst others had sores on their legs caused by the bites of dogs kept to drive them along. Then it was quite common to see the poor animals fall down under their load, and in wet weather the roads were such that their feet stuck in the clay and mud, so that they constantly stumbled and fell.[11] Although the coal was usually carried in sacks placed over the donkeys' backs, a painting of a team being driven up the Shibden Valley on the outskirts of Halifax in the 1890s shows each donkey equipped with a pack-saddle fitted with two panniers. These were made from spelks, strips of oak about three inches wide and under a quarter of an inch in thickness woven together to form light, strong baskets ideal for carrying coal.[12]

On arriving at the customer's house, the coal could be left in the street just by the house door, for coal cellars and coal houses might not be provided in workers' houses in the early nineteenth century.[13]

Along the coast, coal supplies were obtained from the collier brigs which regularly carried their cargoes down from the north-eastern parts to London and beyond. In the 1850s small fishing villages such as Robin Hood's Bay owned about eighty coal brigs and schooners sailing as far as Edinburgh, France, and even to America.[14] If delivering coal to the Bay itself where there was no harbour, but an expansive rocky scaur exposed at low tide, vessels such as *The Success* or *Temperance Star* would come in near Ness, so that carts could go out into the sea alongside. The cart ruts are still visible in the scar even to this day.[15] Similarly at Sandsend, vessels would ground themselves on the firm, level beach at high tide so that the coal carts could drive up to them when the water receded. In Whitby, meanwhile, where there was an excellent harbour, the brigs tied up at the quays to be unloaded. The *Whitby Times* of November 25th, 1887, advertised:

Good and Cheap!

Best Household Coals are now selling on board the brig 'Ebenezer' lying at the New quay, at 14/- per ton, cash, or 11d per bag. Orders received at the ship or James Ward, Schooner Inn, Whitby.

It is interesting to note that George Chambers, the marine artist, started his working life here around 1813. His job, as a boy of under ten years old, was to hold open the mouths of the sacks on board the collier vessels until they were filled by the shovel men. For this he was paid two shillings and the sweepings of coal dust drom the decks for a week or more's work.[16]

With the expansion of the mining industry and the spread of an efficient railway network across the country in the 1830s and '40s, the coal transport industry was completely revolutionised. The old system of carts, pack horses and canals had been extremely expensive, coal costing 8s6d (42p) at the pit head actually costing 15s (75p) at York, 17s (85p) at Malton and £1.4s (120p) at Thirsk, these increases being entirely due to transport costs.[17] The new railways combined in some cases with the canals, could now carry coal quickly, cheaply and efficiently from the major Durham and West Riding pits to depots in virtually every major county town, thus forcing most of the small rural collieries out of business. The opening of the Leeds and Thirsk Railway in 1848 brought the price of coal down from £1 (100p) to 10s (50p) a ton in Knaresborough, for example.[18] Some of the old coal carriers, such as Willie Garbutt and John Patty of Guisborough, felt the sudden change very deeply: 'What sal we dea now, when there's nea coals te lead, when t'railway brings 'em plenty of coals, wese ha' nowt te dea an' beeath us an' hour hosses u'll starve te deeath'.[19] Most of the coal carriers did go out of business as they predicted, but others began to cart coal both from the railway depots and the pit yards, distributing supplies to all the surrounding areas. The typical Yorkshire coal cart was a development of the agricultural tumbrel, being a strongly-built two-wheeled vehicle which could tip a complete load of loose coal directly into the street or yard where it was required. Those who got a cartload of coal at a time seldom knew what weight they got. Some carriers had carts made small to make a little load look like a big one. Others had bags of coal on top, which they sold to customers on the road, but did not deduct them when delivering the rest, although all were weighed together at the pit.[20] In the late nineteenth century some of these problems were solved by hawking the coal in sacks from a four-wheeled flat cart or lurry which carried a set of sack scales and weights as part of its regular equipment.

In some parts of the county, particularly on the East Riding wolds where there was little or no peat or timber for fuel, and where transport costs made coal extremely expensive, some alternative form of fuel had to be found. The only available material was cassons described by George Meriton in 1685 as:

> Stride Tibb, & clawt some Cassons out o'th Hurne
> Than geay they wayes and fetch a skeel of Burn
> And hing the Pan o're the fire i'th Rekin-Creauk.

The 'hurne' was a hole behind the chimney where the fuel was stored ready for use.

It would appear that this fuel had been used here for many centuries, the similarity between the northern English expression to *clap cassons*, the Danish *klapkassen, klappinger*, the Norwegian *klafsa*, used of kneading a wet, peaty mixture, and the Swedish *klappertorv*, kneaded turf, suggesting that the Viking settlers in Yorkshire were familiar with the use of dung as fuel.[22]

J.R. Mortimer remembered that in the 1830s the cottagers' wives at Fimber on the Wolds collected sun-dried cow-plats from the surrounding lanes and pasture lands. They also collected them in a soft state and clapped them in lumps on the sunny walls of their cottages, there to remain until perfectly dry, when they were removed and replaced with a fresh supply.[23] Alternatively the dung was spread in a layer two or three inches in thickness on a level piece of ground and cut into squares, oblongs, diamonds and other shapes. When dry, it was stacked or stowed away ready for use.[24] Clay was sometimes mixed in with the dung, or it was burnt with chalk stones, to make an excellent fire, long lasting, giving off great heat, little smoke, and a pleasant perfume.

Hob Grates

During the eighteenth century the hob grate, with its wrought-iron firebasket mounted between two low masonry hobs, had come into almost universal use throughout Yorkshire. In this elevated position, about a foot and a half or two feet above the hearthstone, the fire was ideally placed for cooking. Kettles and pots could be hung over it from reckon-hooks, bakstones could be mounted on iron brigs placed across the firebars, while the glowing coals at the front were available for toasting and grilling. In order to give the fire sufficient air while still retaining a warm atmosphere in the kitchen, draught-holes might be pierced through the back of the fireplace, out to the open air. These were known as 'worral holes' in North Yorkshire, while in West Yorkshire they were 'drate hoils'.

The only places where the hob grates were not used were the peat-burning areas, where the fire had always burned directly on the hearthstone, and homes of the very poor, such as Robert Hartley of Bedale:[25]

> He kept his pig, likewise his horse,
> All under the same roof,
> At stable door, his dunghill worse!
> The mire above the hoof.
> Eight persons they in family,
> And only one fireside!
> 'Twas on the hearth, no range had he!
> The fam'ly had no pride.

Hob grates were used in virtually all Yorkshire farmhouse and cottage kitchens of the early nineteenth century. These examples are from (a) Coverdale; (b) West Yorkshire, after Walker's *Costume of Yorkshire*, of 1814; (c) a cottage at Croft, Teesdale, 1839; (d) the home of Julius Caesar Ibbotson at Masham in Wensleydale, 1809; and (e) Crackpot Hall, Swaledale. Note the hooked end of the bars which tied the grate back into the surrounding masonry.

Kitchen Ranges

In the prosperous town and country houses of mid-eighteenth century England the demand for excellent bakery and puddings brought with it a need or much more efficient ovens. The old stone beehive ovens, with their dirt, smoke and ashes, their inability to maintain a constant temperature, the difficulty of loading and emptying their deep, dark chambers and their dependence on brushwood as a fuel made them quite unsuitable for the new style of cookery. The solution to this problem was soon found by adapting the materials of the emerging industrial revolution to culinary use as ovens began to be made of cast iron and thin iron sheet.

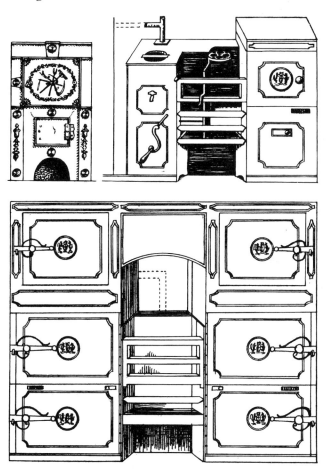

Examples of the high quality ovens and ranges made in South Yorkshire. The oven (top left) with its own firebox and ashpit, was probably first produced in the late eighteenth century by Walkers of Rotheram. The two ranges, meanwhile, were illustrated in an 1825 advertisement for Green & Pickslay of Sheffield's 'Patent Oeconomical kitchen ranges' which 'With one small open Fire will Roast, Steam or Bake for a Family of from five to fifty Individuals, and afford a constant supply of hot Water.'

At this time the ironmasters of South Yorkshire were amongst the most prominent in the whole country. In Masborough in the Parish of Rotherham Samuel Walker's iron works, founded in 1746, was developing rapidly, making wrought iron bars, sheets or rods, tinplate, steel of every kind, and cast iron ranging in scale from flat irons to cannon of the largest calibre. They also made the longest iron bridge in the world, erected across the Wear at Sunderland in 1793–6. Here also was the Rotherham Foundry of Messrs. Clay, Young, Swallow, Cotton, Shore and Elliott, which made all manner of cast ironware, including frying pans, for the domestic market. Well before the end of the eighteenth century these and other South Yorkshire manufacturers were using their plentiful local supplies of cheap coal and ironstone to make first-rate ovens and ranges distinguished by the high quality of their design and by their finely detailed castings.

Some of their earliest products of this type appear to have been ovens which, like the beehive ovens, were quite separate from the kitchen fire, having their own independent source of heat. When built into the wall of the kitchen, their cast-iron facades had a central firebox fitted with a door to control the draught, beneath which there extended a deep ashpit. The oven itself, either made of cast iron or fabricated from sheet iron, lay behind a polygonal or rectangular door near the top of the facade. Inside, a series of narrow ledges was provided along each side to support moveable oven shelves, while a hook sliding on a rod fixed across the roof of the oven allowed joints of meat to be suspended over a dripping tin, just as it had been when roasting in front of an open fire. In January 1750, the Rev. John Lister installed an oven of this kind at his home at Shibden Hall near Halifax, paying for a 'Perpetual Oven and setting £4.4.0 (£4.20), Smith work 9s (45p), Lime 3s (15p), bricks 1s (5p), Plasters' work and colouring 3s 5d (17p)'[26] About the same time the Wentworths of Bretton Hall installed a similar oven, which was illustrated and described as the 'old oven' in a modernisation scheme of 1780.[27] The foundries also made other fittings for the kitchens of large houses, including hot plates, stoves, boilers, roasting ranges, hot cupboards, and series of capacious steam-heated kettles. Their most useful and popular fitting, however, was the range.

By the late eighteenth century the development of practical kitchen ranges had been largely completed. Their great advantage was that they could carry out a number of cooking operations utilising a single central fire. In front of the range, meat could be roasted, behind it, cast iron tanks supplied hot water or steam, flues to the sides carried its heat to ovens for baking, while even the smoke rushing up the chimney could be utilised to operate a mechanical jack which turned the spits in front of the fire. As with all innovative kitchen technology, from roasting jacks to gas, electric and microwave cookers, there was a considerable lapse of time between the use of the range in the wealthier homes, and its adoption throughout society as a whole. During the Napoleonic wars many of the major British foundries had concentrated on making cannon, cannon-balls and similar supplies for the great European campaigns. It is possible that they turned to making small kitchen ranges in the post-war years, when they were relatively short of work.

For the working family, the acquisition of a range involved a considerable outlay of precious funds, but its convenience, economy of fuel, attractive appearance and its

These oven doors demonstrate the high quality of design found in the late eighteenth century ranges made in Rotheram. The upper door, made by Walker & Co., was supplied as far afield as Bilsdale and Nidderdale, its decoration being ideal for rural areas. Clay & Co., who made the lower door c. 1780-1800, had Ebeneezer Elliott, senior, father of the Corn Law Rhymer, as one of their partners.

value as a status symbol made it highly desirable. It is probably for this reason that miniature cast-iron fireplaces were extremely popular as chimney ornaments and doorstops about this period. Between the 1820s and the 1840s most families managed to obtain a range, evidence for this being provided from a number of documentary sources, including Poor Law inventories. In 1832 the handloom weavers in Ossett had the individual castings of their ranges listed separately – '1 oven 1 range, facings, 1 grate, 1 fender' – while the lead miners of Arkengarthdale

These ovens were built on to the sides of existing fireplaces, and were heated by new flues cut through the intervening masonry. The upper example was made by William Walker of York sometime after 1853, while the lower example was made for Butterhills' farm, Knaresborough, by Robert Gott in the 1820s-40s. Note its arched stone 'sooker.'

had theirs simply described as 'Iron and ovens'.[28] At exactly the same period the York artist Mary Ellen Best showed cast-iron ranges in her highly-detailed paintings of cottage interiors in central Yorkshire. By the time Mr Reach carried out his survey of the social conditions of West Yorkshire in 1849, he found that even in the poor urban cellar-dwellings 'good cooking-ranges are abundant'.[29]

Many of these ranges were made by the small country town ironfounders who had sprung up in the early to mid-nineteenth century. Now that coal and pig iron could be cheaply transported to their works by rail, they were able to make all manner of ironwork to meet the needs of the surrounding community. In this way localised patterns of range became established, each usually bearing the name either of the

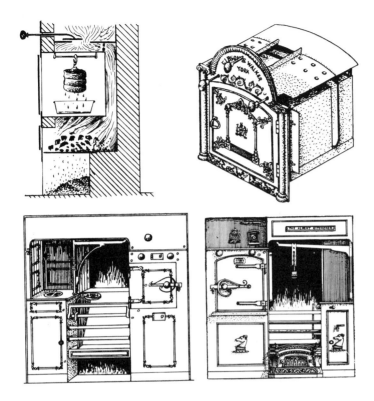

The Walker ironfoundry flourished in York from c. 1825 to 1923. Their oven (top) of c. 1823-37 shows how the heat from the fireplace was controlled using the upper damper, and also the operation of the soot scraper. Below is seen one of their ranges of the late 1830s (left), and their 'Albert Kitchener' of the mid 1860s (right).

founder himself or of the ironmonger who had commissioned and fitted the range, but had no casting facilities of his own.

Where hob grates were already in existence, the founders could supply ovens which were heated by flues cut from the fireplace, through the side of the chimney breast, into a new masonry sheath surrounding the oven. Examples of this type have been recorded near York, where they were made by the Walker foundry from around 1825, and from Knaresborough, where they were made by R. Gott from the early 1820s to the mid–1840s.[30] Similar ovens could also be supplied with their own fireboxes and ashpits, so that they could operate quite independently of the main fire. This feature was particularly characteristic of the founders serving the North Yorks Moors, including Mary Candler of Scarborough, Isaac Hartas and the Rickabys of Wrelton Works, the Carters of Kirkbymoorside, the Robinsons of Loftus, and the Dobsons and the Fletchers both of Pickering.[31] Their ovens usually stand in one side of the fireplace, the remaining space being occupied either by a normal coal-burning grate or by a turf-plate. Since the Moors were a predominantly

North Yorks Moors ranges were specifically designed for peat burning. The first fireplace (top left) shows the characteristic turf plate hearth and low L-shaped boiler. The second (top right), made by Dobson of Pickering, shows both turf plate and an oven with its own firebox. Installed at the Wagon and Horses Inn at Saltersgate, it made batches of hot turf cakes for travellers going across the moors to Whitby. The third (bottom left) was collected from the Moors by Dr. Kirk of Pickering, while the fourth is in the living room of Harome cottage, Hutton le Hole.

peat-burning area, the turf-plate was designed to make the best use of this fuel. It consisted of a heavy iron plate surrounded by a low rim and supported a few inches above the hearthstone by short round legs. A rectangular hole pierced through its centre was fitted with a series of loose firebars to provide both a slow draught to the burning peat and a means of removing the powdery peat ash. Directly on top of the turf-plate, forming a combined fireback and a low side-hob, was an L-shaped cast-iron boiler, the top of the hob having a hinged lid into and from which water could be baled as required. Ranges of this type were still being fitted in the moors even as late as the 1930s.

In the Yorkshire Dales the first generation of cast-iron ranges were supplied in the 1820s and '30s by foundries such as Hird, Dawson, Hardy & Field of Low Moor near Bradford, Ingram of Ripon, or R. Gott of Knaresborough. Their hobs were

In the dales, the ranges installed in the 1820s and '30s had hobs almost equal in size to house either a pair of ovens, or an oven and a boiler. The upper example, at Melbecks, Winterings, Upper Swaledale, has a particularly fine 'sooker' which effectively lowered the fireplace opening to prevent smoking. The lower fireplace, at Lightfoot Hall, Redmire, in Wensleydale, is typical of those installed in the latter half of the nineteenth century. Note its side-oven, low hob, and plain sooker fitted with a reckon-bar and hooks.

usually similar in height and width, incorporating either two ovens or an oven and a boiler, separated by the central grate. The decoration was usually confined to a number of rectangular panels with concave quadrant corners enclosing radiating patterns or closely hatched lines marked in narrow raised ridges. When ranges of this type were installed in the large rectangular openings of Dales fireplaces, They

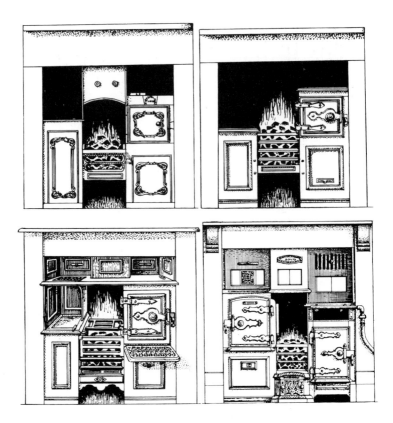

This group of Yorkshire Ranges from the industrial West Riding include; (top left) a mid nineteenth century range made at Kirkstall Forge, Leeds; (top right) an open-fire range made by the Rotherham Foundry, Effingham Works, Rotherham, and; (bottom left) another Foundry example. This shows the fully-developed form of the Yorkshire Range, described in the Pattern book as having 'Flanged Oven and Hob Boiler, Wrought Bars, Fall Barr and Fall Crows; Flanged Oven with Bright Hinges, Latch and Knob, Draw-out Fret. Continuous Plate Rack and Covings.' The fourth range (bottom right) was made by W.H. Micklethwaite & Co. of Clough Road, Masborough, Rotherham, about 1890. It is a combination range, incorporating a gas oven and boiling rings in its right hand hob.

tended to smoke badly. This problem was solved by erecting a 'sooker', a wide slab of stone which entirely blocked the upper quarter or third of the opening, causing the fire to 'draw' much more effectively.

The majority of ranges installed in the Dales during the later nineteenth century were supplied by local ironmongers such as Todd Brothers of Summerbridge, Manby of Skipton, Iveson of Hawes, Spence of Richmond, or Kendall of Ripon, whose names they bear. Their ovens, placed to one side of the grate, occupied the full height of the fireplace opening, and had three knobs over their doors to control the heat and operate the soot scrapers. The hob on the other side was usually level

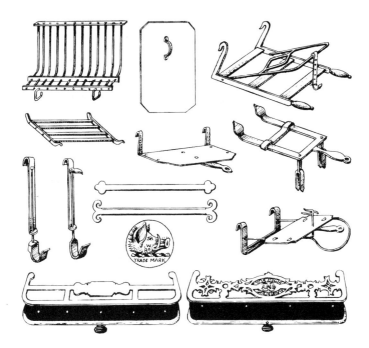

Established in 1830, the firm of Joseph Woodhead, Vaughan Street Works, Bradford, made a series of accessories for use on the kitchen range. Taken from his late 19th century catalogue, these illustrations (not to the same scale) show (a) a wrought iron coal saver; (b) a wrought false grate; (c) a blow tin; (d) a sad iron heater; (e) a brandery, used to hold the Yorkshire pudding in its tin beneath the roasting meat; (f) briggs; (g) a draw plate with fork; (h) – (k) reckon hooks, and the reckon bars from which they hung; (l) fender with stamped top; (m) fender with cast top.

with the top of the grate, and incorporated a boiler, while above a sooker of stone or iron was fitted with a horizontal reckon-bar from which kettles could be hung over the fire.

In the industrial areas of the West Riding, the foundries of Rotherham and Sheffield continued to be the main producers of kitchen ranges, although they were also made in other towns such as Leeds and Bradford. They were usually quite simple in design, with an oven in one hob, and either a boiler or a mass of solid masonry in the other. Since they only occupied the lower two-thirds of the fireplace, it was usual to construct a sheet-iron canopy above the fire to conduct the smoke directly up into the chimney. From around the 1860s the upper parts of the range were completely re-designed, the brick fireback now being completely sheathed in moulded cast-iron panels, while a broad shelf or plate rack was fixed across the fireplace at the level of the oven top. This greatly improved the appearance and usefulness of the range, providing space for plates, pans and kettles. About the same time additions were made to the grate, including a fall-bar which enabled the top two or three fire-bars to hinge down to a horizontal position, and a falling crow which bridged over the fire to provide more accommodation for pans and kettles. Some of the better ranges incorporated a draw-out fret, a broad shelf which pulled out in front of the firebars to heat still more pans or plates. In front of the oven, a bright bracket table pierced in an elaborate pattern was also added to hold dishes and tins when they were being placed in, or removed from, the hot oven. This improved 'Yorkshire' range soon acquired an excellent reputation for its convenience, practicality and design. It certainly looked extremely handsome with its gothic hinges, banjo latch and sharply-detailed mouldings in bright cast steel contrasting with its black-leaded panels. Kitchen ranges of this pattern were soon being made in foundries far distant from Yorkshire, including the Carron Ironworks in Scotland, but their main centre of production remained in Rotherham and Sheffield, where some twenty companies were listed as stove, grate and kitchen range manufacturers in *Kellys Directory* of 1901.

Many of these firms, along with small manufacturers, ironmongers and blacksmiths in other parts of the county, made a whole series of accessories for the ranges. To save coal, grilles with narrowly-spaced bars were made to fit directly behind the main firebars, for example, while small 'false grates' could effectively halve the size of the grate. The firebars could also be used to support either briggs, which held pans, kettles or bakstones over the fire, sad-iron heaters, branderys, draw-plates, or toasters. On the hearth itself, ornamental 'tidy-betties' were provided for masking the front of the ash-pit and preventing the fine dust and cinders from spreading, while strong steel fenders effectively retained any hot coals which fell from the fire, which providing a convenient rack for warming plates, slippers and feet.

Another important accessory was the blow tin, a rectangular sheet-iron plate which was propped between the firebars and the plate rack when lighting or reviving the fire. This caused a rush of air through the coal, rapidly drawing it up to a flaming mass. In some households the place of the blow-tin was taken by a coal shovel propped up on the firebars and surrounded by a sheet of newspaper. This was quite effective, but could be extremely dangerous if the paper caught fire, as it frequently did.

Chapter 6

Oatcake

From time immemorial up to the opening years of the nineteenth century, oatmeal formed a major element in the diet of the labouring classes in most parts of the county.

Although relatively small quantities were grown in the corn country in the southern parts of the Vale of York, it was chiefly associated with the upland farming economy. Here it could withstand the harsh wet climate found around the 600–800ft. contours even though it might still be in the field in mid-November when the first falls of snow lay on the ground.[1] In the North York Moors crops were successfully raised in the higher parts of the more fertile dales, but in the upper reaches of the Pennine dales, such as Swaledale, the arable land was exceedingly cold 'and although sown with oats every second year, there were obliged to be cut for cattle without ripening'.[2] The inhabitants of the milder, sweeter limestone country of Craven 'all grew oats, which formed the principal article of their subsistence', while on the sour gritstones of the South Pennines small fields of oats, cut with the toothed sickle up to about 1870, played an important role in the dual textile/farming economy of the region.[3]

By 1800, however, the rapidly expanding population of the textile area had so vastly outgrown its own meagre agricultural resources that it now had to bring in five-sixths of the corn required to support its inhabitants.[4] Most of this came from Ryedale, a broad, fertile valley running in an easterly direction between the shelter of the Howardian Hills and the North York Moors. Here two or three successive crops of oats, frequently yielding 64 or 80 bushels per acre, were quite normal, although some tenant farmers could raise six or seven consecutive crops without depleting the rich soil.[5] Having been sown in April, the harvest usually commenced in early to mid-August, teams of perhaps six men, all working in perfect time, each taking nearly three feet in depth by eight feet in width with each stroke of their scythes.[6] In this way they were able to cut up to three acres apiece working from 5am to sundown.

Unlike other grain crops, which were stacked in the yard ready for threshing during the winter months, the Ryedale oats were always threshed as soon as possible, either in the harvest field itself, or in the stackyard. On some farms four men threshed the sheaves on a cloth spread over the ground, while on others the opened sheaves were spread in a thirty-foot circle, heads towards the centre, on a level area of fine greensward. Eight or ten men then proceeded to thresh the oats with flails, the sheaves being turned over halfway through this operation. The straw was then stacked and the grain winnowed to remove the chaff and dust before it was scooped up into sacks ready for carting off to the corn factors in nearby Malton.

Here it was loaded on to sailing barges and carried down the Derwent, along the Ouse, and up the Aire and Calder Navigation to arrive in the industrial towns of the West Riding. The speed with which the oats could be delivered was of the greatest importance, for new oatmeal produced the finest oatcakes, and thus commanded a much higher price for the farmer.[7] 'New Oats were sold in our market on Tuesday last [August 12th]', reported the *Leeds Mercury* in 1800, when prices ranged from 3/9d (19p) to 6/3d (31p) a bushel.

In addition to these home-grown supplies, oats were also imported from Holland in large quantities, perhaps 3,600 bushels per week during the season being shipped into Hull. Much of this superior grain was purchased as seed-corn by the Ryedale farmers, who used it to maintain the excellent quality of their crops.[8]

Whether home-grown or purchased from dealers, the oats had to be converted into meal before they could be used for food. They were therefore carried to the kiln at the local mill, unless a communal kiln was available, as in the village of Linton in Craven. Here it also served as a sort of village coffee-house, where the politics of the day and of the place were discussed as the oats were dried.[9] The kiln itself took the form of a raised masonry platform heated by a fireplace fuelled with coke, charcoal or 'shillings', the waste husk of the oats.[10] Great care had to be taken in gently turning and drying the oats at this stage, otherwise they were 'fire-fanged' and took on an unpleasant scorched flavour.

By passing the dried oats through a pair of shilling stones and winnowing the grain, the inedible husks were fractured, detached and separated to leave only the groats. These were then finely ground between a pair of gritstones which reduced them to oatmeal, which after being sifted, could be taken back to the house for use. Most households stored the meal by packing it tightly down inside a meal ark or chest.

In some parts of Wharfedale men put on white stockings kept especially for this purpose and, climbing into the ark, proceeded to stamp the meal down as it was poured in by the sackful.[11] The West Riding arks often had sloping lids, one example from the mining village of Wibsey having its deal planks fitted with artificial drawer-fronts and elaborately grained to give the superficial appearance of an expensive mahogany bureau.[12] It is remembered that 'Old John Mealy-Face' of Topcliffe near Thirsk used to leave the imprint of his sharp features in the top of the meal in the ark before leaving the house. He could then check it exactly for size on his return, just to make sure that his wife had not used any during his absence.[13]

Inside the ark a small wooden spade, called a spittle, was provided to enable the oatmeal to be removed as required.[14] Perhaps this implement developed into the large square spittle used in making thrown oatcake.

There are numerous references to the importance of oatcake as the staple diet of the majority of Yorkshire's working population. At the opening of the nineteenth century oatcake was made in the North York Moors, in the Pennine Dales extending down from the borders of County Durham and Cumbria to those of Derbyshire, in the industrial conurbation of West and south Yorkshire, and in the agricultural flat lands of Holderness. Some indication of its widespread use is given by the range of names by which oatcake was popularly known. In Sheffield, for example, virtually the same article might be called snap-and-rattle, knap cake, scrapple cake, reed bread, havercake, flannel, slammak, flat-dick, jonta, or even 'tooa clate' (i.e. toe-rag).[15] In general, however, there were just two main varieties of oatcake. The first, made from a stiff dough rolled out into a thin cake and called clapbread, haverbread or havercake (from the Old Norse *hafri* meaning oats), was common to the area north of a line running approximately from Bowland and the Three Peaks area and down the North Riding boundary to the plain of York. South of this line, riddlebread, oatcake, or havercake were made of a liquid batter poured or thrown on to the bakstone.

Bakstones

Whichever type of oatcake was to be made, it had to be cooked on a smooth, flat heated slab called a bakstone. As this name suggests, it was first made of thin slabs of any locally available stone which could withstand the heat of the fire. From the twelfth century at least a variety of outcrop sources were utilised, variously known as Bakstone Gill or Backson Edge etc., but even though these sometimes remained in use up to the 1870s, by the sixteenth century the major centre of the bakstone-making industry had become established at Delph, near Saddleworth.[16] Here large blocks of mudstone, called 'fly-wings' although they might weigh several hundred-weight, were carried from the pit on the back of one of the workmen. As the stone rapidly deteriorated when exposed to the atmosphere, it was submerged in the Hull Brook when not actually being worked by hand. Sitting by the side of this stream, the bakstone makers proceeded to shape the stones using the implements described on the rhyming signboard of the Bakestone Inn:

> These bakestone makers are brave men,
> They take a pot here now and then!
> Be not in haste, come in and taste
> With these ingenious gentlemen!
> For it is the axe, the pick, the shave,
> that make the bakestones look so brave.

Each stone was split into half or three-quarter inch slabs measuring up to some two feet square. The upper side was then scraped down to give a perfectly flat surface, while the underside was left with long parallel runs of chisel marks. The edges having been neatly worked to a smooth convex finish, the stones were allowed to remain in the stream for a few weeks before being fired. This operation involved stacking the stones vertically around a fire of wood burning in a pit within a small drystone hut. Two dozen made up the load of a horse or donkey when the bakstone men went round the towns and villages of Lancashire, Cheshire and Yorkshire crying their 'Havercake Backstones'.

Although Delph bakstones continued to be made up to 1928, they were being replaced by iron from the seventeenth century at least. These were circular in shape, usually with a vertical looped handle rising above their working surface.

In use, both the stone and the iron bakstones were supported across the firebars of the range by a brigg, crow, or branderi.[17] This rectangular iron frame had two short front legs with forked ends which sat directly on the top firebar, while the two rear legs rested on the deep ledge or hurne where fuel was stacked at the back of the fire. In some areas a sliding bar was provided, so that the briggs could be adjusted to receive any size of bakstone.

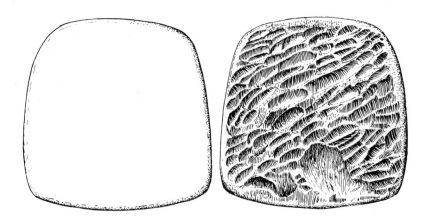

Bakstone. This product of the quarries at Delph near Saddleworth shows the typical smooth flat baking surface on its upper side, with shallow concave chisel or scraper marks on the underside. (Halifax Museums, ex Ling Roth collection, AH 706.)

By 1800 large built-in bakstones were already being constructed in farmhouses and cottages in the West Riding dales where oatcakes were made with a liquid batter. One clearly seen in George Walker's *Costume of Yorkshire* of 1814 corresponds exactly to the following description of cottage interiors in Pudsey. The bakstone is 'built in bricks. Some have double bakstones on which two cakes can be baked at the same time. On these sometimes the neighbours bake in turns, taking their meal tubs and coal to heat the bakstone'.[18]

Invariably these bakstones were built to one side of the main fireplace, so that the smoke and fumes from the small firebox could be carried away up the chimney after they had been used to heat the stone. They were probably introduced to accommodate a new method of making oatcakes in which the liquid batter was forcibly thrown on to the bakstone instead of being slipped off a wooden reeling board. To hurl a pool of batter on to a twelve-inch diameter iron plate standing over the fire would be a virtually impossible feat of skill, whereas it was quite feasible to do this when the table-height bakstone measured up to two feet by four.

Before the bakstone could be used successfully, its surface had to be treated or 'proved'. John Leach of Skipton used to burn oatmeal on the bakstone before rubbing it off vigorously, while one Addingham maker rubbed in a mixture of brown sugar and suet.[19] A little bacon or mutton fat might also be rubbed over the stone before each cake was baked, but this tended to make the oatcakes rather heavy and tough.

Rolled Oatcake

Oatcake made from a stiff dough rolled out and baked in large thin, crisp discs was characteristic of Bowland, the Three Peaks area, the North Riding dales and Holderness.[20] There were two main varieties, one being about a quarter of an inch in thickness, while the other was almost paper thin. Through the researches of the late Dr Bedford it is possible to give recipes for both types.

M. Harker from Muker in Swaledale used to make up to fifty thick cakes ready for the haymakers to eat either with cheese, to put into the soup, or to eat along with the soup.[21] To make them, the following recipe was used:

Thick Havercake

6oz fine oatmeal
pinch salt
4 tablespoons water

Mix the ingredients in a bowl, and knead to make a firm dough. Turn out on to a board sprinkled with meal and roll out to about a quarter of an inch in thickness. Using a thin board or spittle place on an iron griddle over a moderate heat and allow to bake until the edges begin to curl, then turn over and cook the other side. The baking should be slow and gentle, 'they were very pale when done, more a matter of drying than baking'. The traditional method of finishing the oatcakes was to toast them on a cake stool, a wooden easel which supported them in front of a clear fire, preferably of ling.[22] Today a similar effect can be obtained by placing the cakes under a grill at a moderate heat for a few minutes. When perfectly dry, the cakes can be stored for future use.

Making the thin oatcakes was a rather more complex operation, as may be seen from the following recipe used by Mrs Jane Woof of Morthwaite near Sedbergh.[23]

Thin Havercake

2 lb fine oatmeal
1 pt tepid water
1 dessertspoon bicarbonate of soda
1 dessertspoon salt

Stir the soda and salt into the water in a deep bowl and continue to stir while sifting in some 8 oz of the oatmeal, thus forming a soft dough. Knuckle this mixture down into the bowl until it forms a level, compact mass, and allow to rest for a few minutes.

Place a large tablespoonful of the mixture on a handful of oatmeal spread on a piece of coarse cloth or hessian, and knead it into a flat round cake about four inches in diameter by half an inch in thickness. Sprinkle more dry oatmeal on to a baking board, and proceed to roll out the dough, turning it over by hand from time to time and dusting it with more oatmeal. When the cake is too thin to turn by hand it may be rotated or reeled by lifting the board in both hands and giving it a few clockwise jerks. The oatcake can then be turned over using a turning stick, a narrow rolling pin measuring about an inch in diameter. After easing one edge of the cake off the board with a knife, proceed to roll the cake around the stick. Dust the board with more oatmeal, turn the stick round, and unroll the cake on to the board again so that the upper side now faces downwards. Dust with oatmeal again, and roll the cake still thinner, reeling it to make sure that it does not stick to the board. After brushing away all the loose meal, the cake can be slid off the board on to the bakstone and allowed to cook.

Mrs Woof stored her cakes in a chest. Often these chests were divided into two compartments, one for meal and the other for oatcakes. There were competitions for cakes of this type at the local agricultural shows, the winning points being awarded for shape: a perfect circle; colour in baking; thinness; and crispness, due to the skill in kneading.[24]

Yeasted Oatcake

'Havercakes were big, wet, oval things. They would be put over winterhedge or up on t'creel to dry and then you lugged them wi' pork dripping'.[25] Unlike the crisp, rolled type of oatcake, the West Yorkshire variety were large and soft, their appearance often being described as resembling lengths of wash leather. This was achieved by using a batter made from finely ground oatmeal lightened with yeast, sourdough, or, later, bicarbonate of soda. The technique is clearly described by the Rev. Easther of Almondbury: 'First get your nakit (knead-kit) a sort of small tub to mix the dofe (dough) in. Two persons are generally employed. Warm water is poured into the nakit; then one of the operators puts the meal in by handfuls, whilst the other mixes with hand and arm, yeast being added, until it is considered thick enough though able to be poured out. It is then left for a night to 'sour'. Next morning more meal is helted in to make it rather stiffer; it is then ready for baking'.[26]

Montagu noted the alternative sour-dough method as used near Bolton Abbey in Wharfedale in 1838 'The cakes are made of oat-meal and water or buttermilk, or, what is termed blue milk – that is, milk after the cream has been skimmed off. The meal is generally mixed the night before baking in the kneading-tub, one hand continually stirring the mixture to prevent lumps, whilst the other is employed in putting in the meal. This tub, which is kept expressly for the purpose, is rarely ever cleansed with water, but merely scraped out with a knife. The particles adhering to the sides ferment, and cause the next quantity of meal put into the tub to rise more speedily – the proportion of meal to moisture is one pound to a pint'.[27]

Before the oatmeal batter was ready for use, additional meal was helted in to adjust its consistency. If the oatcake could not be baked successfully, the fault was often attributed to the influence of witches during this process. In one case recorded in the Almondbury area of the West Riding around 1823, the batter refused to thicken until it was stabbed with a pen knife, and more meal added. It then thickened immediately, but next day the supposed witch came into the house with her arm bound up, proving that she had been responsible for causing the problem.[28] In the Craven region at the same period, it was customary to 'cross the witches out' by making a cross with the finger on the surface of the batter, the baker even crossing every finger in turn to ensure the success of the charm.[29]

Once the dough or batter had been mixed it could be prepared for baking in any of the following ways:

Poured Oatcake

Probably the simplest method of making oatcake, but one which produced relatively thick and tough results, was to pour a pool of batter directly on to the hot bakstone. This technique appears to have been in use in the mid-eighteenth century, but was not very common in nineteenth-century Yorkshire.[30] The 'turn down cake' of Nidderdale was of this type, being made by employing the back of the ladle to spread the batter, after it had been poured on to the bakstone. As Lucas recorded, it did not rise like other oatcake.[31]

In Sheffield and the nearby hills of Derbyshire an almost identical form of oatcake was made by mixing fine oatmeal, salt and water with either brewer's yeast or a basinful of sour dough from a previous baking. After an hour or an hour and a half a ladleful of the batter was poured on to the centre of a hot bakstone greased with bacon fat, the centre of the twelve-inch diameter pool being pressed down with the back of the ladle. When baked on one side, the edge was raised with a knife, a wooden spittle pushed underneath, and the whole cake turned over. After a short time the cake was allowed to 'soak' for a while on a cooler part of the bakstone in order to ensure that it was thoroughly cooked throughout its thickness. Having cooled on a deal table covered with about three thicknesses of tablecloth, these round cakes, up to a quarter-inch in thickness, were finally wrapped in a piece of clean cloth and kept for use.[32]

Reeled Oatcake

It was possible to make thinner, lighter oatcake by using a bakbrade or riddling board. This was a thin, smooth wooden board measuring some eighteen inches square one side of which was carved with a diagonal grid of incised grooves. The manner of its use was first described and illustrated in George Walker's *Costume of Yorkshire* of 1814, but Mrs Ingleby of West End in the Washburn valley was still making her oatcakes in the same way up to the 1890s.[33]

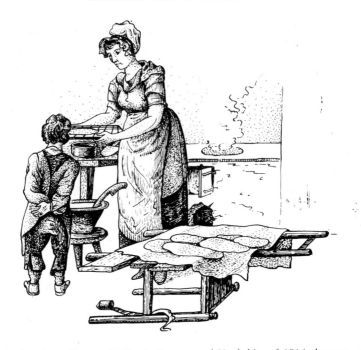

This illustration from George Walker's *Costume of Yorkshire* of 1814 shows a woman making reeled oatcake. A ladle-full of the batter from the bowl or pancheon is being swirled round on the riddling board, which has been prepared with a layer of fine oatmeal shaken from the seive seen in the background. The batter will then be slipped off the riddling board on to the the hot bakstone, allowed to cook, and then cooled off on a piece of cloth resting on a few planks laid across the back of a chair.

In brief, a layer of oatmeal was sprinkled or 'smithen' over the face of the riddling board, the hand moving around the board in a circular direction. A ladleful of the batter was then poured on to the meal, and the whole board, gripped with both hands, was swirled or shaken in a rotary motion to run the batter out to form a shallow rounded pool. This was then slipped or tossed on to the bakstone, allowed to cook for a few seconds, then cooled off on a cloth before being hung up on the creel to dry. In the Huddersfield area this was known as a leathercake, since it was much thicker, and presumably tougher, than the finer thrown oatcake.[34]

Thrown Oatcake

The oatcake which was the most palatable was also the most difficult to make. To produce a thrown oatcake which might measure over two feet in length and yet be under an eighth of an inch in thickness required a degree of skill which was a matter of great pride both to the housewife and to the professional baker.

The first stages of making thrown oatcake were identical to those which were used for the reeled variety, but instead of slipping the pool of batter directly from the riddleboard on to the bakstone, it was slid on to a sheet of cartridge paper or, perhaps more commonly, on to a piece of linen or flannel.[35] Then, to quote a newspaper account of Mrs Marsden baking in the West Riding in 1880, 'she lifted the cloth with both hands, holding opposite corners, then, with a rapid movement, she threw the batter in a longer oblong straight on to the heated iron plate, dropping the lower corner of the cloth as she did so. In less than half a minute the oatcake was ready to be skimmed up with a spatula and hung across a wooden rail. The rapidity with which the operation was performed showed the fruits of long practice'.[36]

Throwing a pool of liquid batter from a piece of cloth was an extremely difficult and precarious manoeuvre, and so, from the early nineteenth century at least, it was much more common to support the cloth on a spittle. The use of this thin board, measuring some ten inches square, with a short projecting handle, is clearly described in Frederic Montagu's *Gleanings in Craven* of 1838: the pool of batter is transferred from the riddleboard 'to a piece of thin linen, or at times cartridge paper, called the "turning off", resting on a smooth board called a spittle, very similar to the backboard in shape, having the addition of a handle and an edge of iron; the cake is then with a strong jerk thrown laterally upon the backstone and the linen is taken up: this movement requires great dexterity, as the length of the cake proves the efficiency of the baker. After baking for one minute, the spittle is used to turn it over. Another minute completes the baking, and the cake is placed on the bars of the "fleeok", its shape being oval and from half to three quarters of a yard long; it is much eaten, and considered very wholesome'.

This was the standard technique of the commercial oatcake bakers throughout the later nineteenth and early twentieth centuries.

Scrape Bread

From about 1850, a new system of making oatcakes was introduced which had the advantage of being quicker, more efficient, and much less skilful than the traditional methods of reeling and throwing. In the Pennine hills from Sheffield northwards to Bentham, Settle and Upper Wharfedale, the batter was now poured directly onto the bakstone and formed into a thin flat cake by the use of a scraper or 'machine'.[37] This wooden implement had a long straight edge supported just above the surface of the bakstone by a small screw or nail-head at each end. Mr Hesleton of Holly Tree Farm, Mewith, Bentham, remembered that the batter was made from fine oatmeal, yeast and salt mixed with milk and water and allowed to rise overnight in the usual way. The mixture was then poured just in front of the scraper as it travelled forwards across the heated bakstone, which had been lightly greased with mutton fat. After being eased off around the edges with a knife, an iron-shod spittle was passed underneath the oatcake, which was then turned over to complete its baking.[38] Commercial oatcake makers such as Walter Inman of Silsden might make scrape-bread without the use of the scraper, pouring the batter from a ladle held in the left hand while using a spittle in the right hand to spread it forward with one

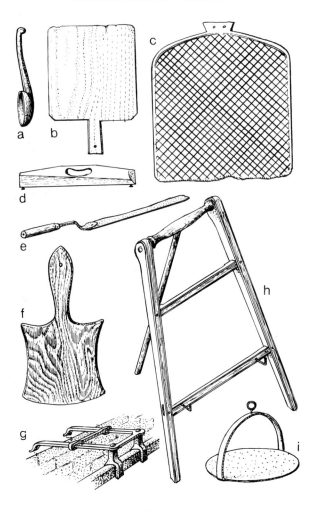

Oatcake Equipment. a). Ladle, from the Halifax area; b). Spittle for thrown oatcake, from Skipton; c). Riddling board or bakbrade, from Lane Ends Farm, Upper Saltonstall; d). Scraper or 'machine' for scrape-bread; e). oatcake knife, from Lane Ends Farm, Upper Saltonstall; f). Spittle for rolled oatcake, from Ripon; g). Branderi or brandreth, resting on topmost firebar of the range, from Nidderdale; h). Cake stool for drying rolled oatcake, from Cote Moor, Kirkby Stephen; i). Iron bakstone from the Halifax area.

stroke.[39] Most bakers regarded scrape-bread with a certain amount of disdain, however, for it was tougher and not so light as the thrown variety.[40]

The Commercial Bakers

Although the making of oatcakes was essentially a domestic process, commercial makers had operated in the county from the seventeenth century onwards.[41] By the

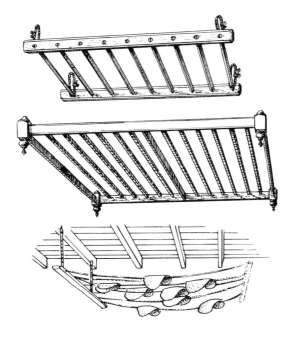

Bread Flakes or Creels. Hung from the ceiling directly over the hearth, the creel provided a convenient rack on which to hang the oatcakes for drying out and for storage. They came from Nidderdale (top), Ripponden, Calderdale (middle), and probably Airedale (bottom), the corded example being illustrated in Walker's *Costume of Yorkshire* of 1814.

mid-nineteenth century skilled ladies such as old Polly Slater or Betty Simpson of Barnoldswick had opened public bakehouses to serve those families who had neither the time, the skill, the equipment nor the fuel to make their own oatcakes.[42] A family might send seven to fourteen pounds of their own meal to one of these establishments, every week, paying around 4d (1½p) to 6d (2½p) per stone for it to be made up into batter and baked.[43] Oatcake had also been baked for sale, and in 1814 George Walker was recording that the standard price for a single cake was one penny, the size of ladle used to measure the batter being varied according to the market price of the meal. As the mining communities in the Wakefield area could afford to indulge their preference for wheaten bread, and frequently retained a strong tradition of home baking, the last oatcake baker in the town had closed down by 1846.[44] Throughout the remainder of the industrial West Riding, however, the trade appears to have flourished and expanded up to the 1880s, when Easther was able to state that 'Oatcake is seldom made by any but public bakers'. This was particularly the case in the areas to the west of the county, where the collapse of the domestic textile industry forced most working women out of their homes and into the mills. Working from 6.30am to perhaps 5.30pm on five days a week, together with Saturday mornings, they had little time for their former duties, and so relied increasingly on ready-baked foods. The exact number and location of oatcake bakers

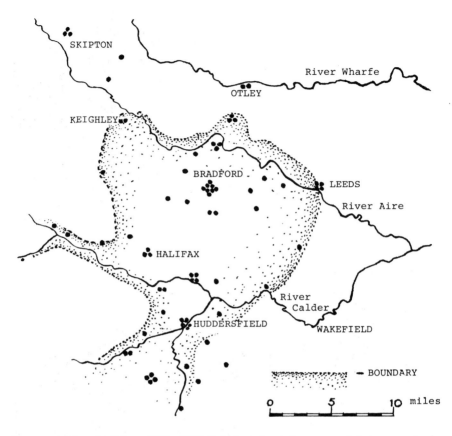

Commercial Oatcake Bakers 1880 – 1900. Relatively few bakers entered their names in the local directories, but the distribution of those which were listed clearly shows the relationship of their trade to the major industrial textile area. Note that there are none in the mainly coal mining and agricultural areas to the south and east of Leeds.

is virtually impossible to determine, since they were frequently very small-scale operations, and were not comprehensively listed in local directories, but by plotting those mentioned in Kelly's directories and other sources a clear pattern emerges. With the exception of one group in the city of Sheffield, they all lay in the industrial textile centres of the Pennine dales.

Most bakers made thrown oatcake, the liquid batter being mixed and reeled in the normal way. From this point, however, the technique could differ a lot, some bakers, such as James Leach of Skipton, using a piece of flannel and a spittle to throw the batter, while others used a mechanical device for the same purpose. Writing in 1894, I. Dickinson remembered 'the ingenious mechanic who invented the baking of havver cake by machinery. He has a small bogie carriage running on a railway over the bakestone; as it runs, an endless web of cloth revolves with the motion, and the gruel deposited on this web is transferred to the bakestone with never a mishap'.[45]

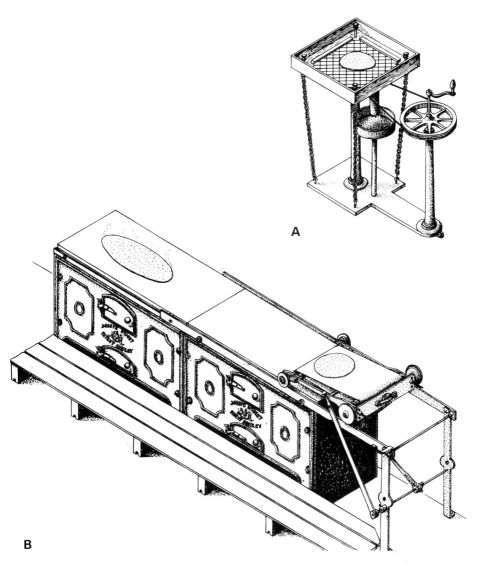

The Patent Bakstone and Riddling Board. Registered on March 3rd, 1864, by Joseph Wright, oatcake manufacturer, of Briggate, Shipley, this equipment attempted to speed up the process of making thrown oatcake. The riddling board, rapidly rotated on an eccentric cam and with a container beneath to catch the surplus oatmeal, is only known from the patent drawings, and probably never went into production. The bakstone, however, enjoyed widespread use by the commercial bakers, the example seen here being used by Mr. L. Feather of Haworth up to 1968. The oatcake batter was slipped from the riddling board on to a canvas roller at the right-hand end of the bakstone. A quick jerk on the lever caused a crank and a leather strap to send the trolley speeding along the stone, spreading the batter as a very thin sheet in the course of its progress. Having cooked, the oatcake was then removed to the cooler left-hand bakstone to finish off.

Probably the 'ingenious mechanic' was Joseph Wright who appears as an oatcake manufacturer of Briggate, Shipley, in the local directories of the 1860s. The cast-iron bakstones he patented in 1864 have the inscription 'JOSEPH WRIGHT PATENT, SHIPLEY' and 'EVIL BE TO HIM THAT EVIL THINKS' in raised lettering at each side of the coal-burning firebox.

Having cooked, the oatcakes were removed to a cooler part of the bakstone with a specially designed long-bladed knife with a cranked handle, seventy or more being made every hour in this way.[46] They were then hung on a creel or flake to cool before being either sold directly from the bakehouse, or covered in white cloths, placed in an oval basket, and hawked either on foot or by horse and cart around the neighbouring streets and villages.[47]

Oatcake in the home

'Oatcakes . . . butter, milk and eggs, and a toughish cheese, made of skimmed or 'blue' milk – the produce of the farm, are the ordinary viands', wrote the Rev. Thompson in his *Sedbergh, Garsdale and Dent* of 1910. The crisp rolled variety certainly formed the basis of the staple diet of the Yorkshire Dales, being eaten either on its own or as a major part of most meals. At High House, Firbank, Sedbergh, for example, it was served on the table in a special wickerwork basket and appeared at 'drinkings' at 10am at dinner and at supper.[48] This practice is recorded in Wordsworth's story of the shepherd Michael and his son who

> When day was gone,
> And from their occupations out of doors
> The son and father were come home, even then
> Their labour did not cease, unless when all
> Turned to their cleanly supper-bard, and there
> Each with a mess of pottage and skimmed milk
> Sat round their basket piled with oaten cakes
> And their plain home-made cheese.[49]

At harvest great quantities of oatcake had to be made for the additional labourers who arrived to reap and mow. Ralph Daykin, who farmed Ballowfield in Wensley-dale, remembered when the farmers' wives would make up to fifteen dozen oatcakes at a single baking weeks before haytime. These were then served to the men with white cheese and light beer, both of their own making.[50] For long journeys, similarly large quantities of oatcake were baked. When the leadminers David and Ralph Fawcett left Crag Hall Farm at Angram in Swaledale to take part in the great Californian gold rush of 1844 they, like most of their fellow countrymen, took several apple barrels full of oatcake to provide sustenance throughout their transatlantic voyage.[51] When soft and fresh, the yeasted oatcakes were eaten with butter spread with the thumb or spread with treacle and rolled up, this moist, succulent delicacy being a great favourite with the children.[52] For a more savoury dish, they could be made into 'sops', portions being soaked in the gravy tin under the roasting beef.[53] In Leeds, all the public houses which provided meals always gave oatcake and dripping free, the dripping generally being fresh and warm from the joint.

Alternatively, the oatcakes could be hung on the creel or flake mounted on the ceiling above the hearth, where they soon dried to a perfect crispness. In this state they might be eaten just as they were, used to accompany a meal, or be broken up and sprinkled into soup or broth. Dry oatcake could also be converted into brewis. In most parts of the West Riding this was 'made by teeming hot water upon it to soften it; then some sort of fat or 'greease' [poor quality butter] is poured over it, and all seasoned with pepper and salt. There is another kind called 'water browis' but this is very poor, having no fat'.[54] Brewis was traditionally served during the morning of the annual Cutlers Feast in their great hall in Sheffield, while the churchwardens at Ripponden used to retire to the Bridge Hotel for brewis once they had ensured that all their parishioners were properly seated in St. Bartholomew's.[55] A pleasant supper dish, and one which was supposed to be good for a cold, was prepared by toasting the oatcake by placing it directly across and in contact with the embers. It was then dropped when sizzling hot into a basin of cold new milk, and slowly sipped. A rather more intoxicating version was made by crumbling the hot toasted oatcake into home-brewed ale.[56] In a completely different direction, the strong association of the yeasted oatcake with the people of West Yorkshire made it an appropriate symbol or rallying standard for their region. Thus the 33rd Regiment of Foot, raised in the Halifax area during the American War of Independence, were known as the 'Haver-cake Lads'. Their recruiting sergeants traditionally held aloft a haver-cake impaled on the point of their swords whenever they visited the area.[57] Similarly Benjamin Wilson 'headed a mob with an oatcake upon a stick exciting them to riot' during a period of high food prices in 1800, but he was thrown into Wakefield Gaol for his trouble![58]

Chapter 7

Porridge

Porridge, together with oatcakes and potatoes, formed the basic diet of the working communities of North and West Yorkshire. Being relatively cheap, quickly and easily made, hot, nourishing and filling, it provided an ideal meal for the poorer sections of society during the early nineteenth-century decades of low wages and high food prices.

Despite the various acts of Parliament which prohibited the payment of wages in kind, oatmeal for porridge etc. continued to be distributed in exchange for work throughout the 1830s and 1840s.[1] In this way landlords and manufacturers organised the reclamation of moorland for agriculture and the construction of access roads to their outlying properties. In 1826 the men of Saddleworth were allowed to carry out this work for two days in the week and receive 12 lb. of meal per day as wages.[2] Within a few years, however, this had been reduced to as little as 8 lb., Edward Winterbottom of Delph recording this event in his song of the Meyl (Meal) Roads:

> When aw started o'th Meyl Road
> Aw sang like a lark!
> Aw'd a peck a good meyl
> Every day fur mi wark;
> But neaw its eight peaund–
> Un thi gi'e it wi' scoff,
> Un if aw dunnot like it
> Aw contak' misel' off.[3]

The easiest way of preparing oatmeal for the table was to make it into crowdy by mixing it with either hot milk or water and allowing it to swell and soften. 'Crowdy Billy' of Sedbergh, whose 'faculty for consuming this article of diet unknown at modern dinner-tables had won for him the proud title which took precedence of his baptismal name, upon one occasion, in his eagerness to gain a wager, he swallowed his meal and hot water before the maximum point of expansion had been reached, and subjected himself to consequences which were alarming and all but fatal'.[4] This dish was sometimes enriched by pouring the fat from the broth into a hollow made in the crowdy, into which every spoonful was dipped before it was eaten. Similarly it could be made as 'stirabout' by adding a mixture of meal and water to the frying pan after the bacon had been cooked.[5]

Although crowdy was widely used, a few porridge were generally preferred, these always being referred to in the plural. Cooking this apparently simple food could be

74

This cast-iron gallon porridge pot from Haworth and its accompanying thible or stirring stick from Halifax are typical of those used in mid nineteenth century West Yorkshire.

quite difficult, however, as Catherine discovered one evening at 'Wuthering Heights', where she came on the old skilled servant Joseph peering into a large pan that swung over the fire, a wooden bowl of oatmeal standing in readiness on the settle close by. As the water came to the boil 'he turned to plunge his hand into the bowl; I conjectured that this preparation was probably for our supper, and, being hungry, I resolved it should be eatable – so crying sharply – "I'll make the porridge!" I removed the vessel out of his reach ... Joseph beheld my style of cookery with growing indignation. "Thear!" he ejaculated, "Hareton, tha willn't sup they porridge tuh neeght; they'll be nowt bud lumps as big as maw nave (i.e. fist), Thear, agean! Aw'd fling in bowl un all, if ah were yah! Thear, pale t'guilp (i.e. handle) off, un then yah'll hae don wi't. Bang, bang. It's a marcy t'bottom isn't deaved aht!"'[6]

Usually the oats were gradually sprinkled into the boiling water in the iron cauldron or kale pot while a flat wooden stick or thible kept the whole mass in agitation until it was thoroughly cooked. The porridge was normally cooked to such a firm state as to allow the spoon to stand perpendicular in it, such descriptive titles as pandewaff, thick-hots, or thick-uns giving some indication of the consistency.[7] It was even said that you could stand on your head on the porridge without creating even the slightest impression. For variety, lumpydicks could be made by dropping tight handfuls of meal into the boiling water, which seared over its surface to produce a lumpy mixture.[8]

The manner in which the porridge was eaten varied from one household to another, but some of the earlier references suggest that it was usually spooned from a communal bowl during the eighteenth and early nineteenth centuries. In the 1730s the Leeds clothiers were woken by the blast of a horn, then:

Ere clock strikes eight their call'd to breakfast
And bowls of milk are brought in haste–
Good Water-Pudding as heart could wish
With spoons stuck round an earthen dish.[9]

Similarly John Wood of Bradford recalled that around 1810 'The porridge ... were served up in one large dish or bowl, and placed in the middle of the table, the family placing themselves around, some sitting and some standing, each one being supplied with a spoon or a knife, without the use of a fork or plate. They proceeded to help themselves in the best way they could, the most active getting the best share. I just remember a bright youth who, in order to secure the use of the largest spoon, was in the habit of carrying it all the day, stuck into one of the button holes in his jacket'.[10] Even in the 1880s families in Gildersome always took their porridge standing up, a habit which had probably been acquired in earlier years when there was still insufficient furniture for the family's needs.[11] In other homes the porridge was poured out into individual plates, each person taking a spoonful and dipping it into a bowl of skimmed milk held in the left hand before eating it.[12] Back at 'Wuthering Heights' Catherine had been appalled when Hareton had seized their gallon pitcher of new milk, drinking and slavering it from his expansive lip. Informing him that he should have used a mug, since she was unable to take her basin of porridge with milk which had been treated so dirtily, she was merely told that he was 'every bit as wollsome' and that she should not be so conceited![13] As an alternative, the porridge might be mixed into the milk before serving it out in the usual modern manner. For a particularly rich and creamy dish called 'bull-jumpings' the porridge could even be made with beestings. This, the product of the first or second milking of the cow after calving, was often distributed by the farmer to his neighbours, the jug in which it was contained always being returned unwashed to avoid ill-luck.[14]

Whenever possible the porridge would also be sweetened with a generous helping of treacle. This was usually kept on the mantle-shelf where it would remain warm and relatively fluid in its tin or jar. Specially designed treacle-pots made of blue patterned white earthenware were produced in some of the South Yorkshire potteries, their flat lids screwing down tightly to exclude all dust, dirt and flies.

Oatmeal porridge was certainly held in high esteem, 'some proper owd stick-i'-yo'r-ribs, wi' a pint of new milk at will stand th' inspector lukkin' at it. A mixture o' this sooart turns aght chaps like th' Black Watch: nooan o' yo'r tallow-faced factory lads, reared on th' frying pan an' th' teah-pot.'[15] The main problem, however, was that even as a starvation diet, particularly in the declining handloom textile areas of the 1830s, '40s and '50s, there was seldom enough to feed the entire family.

In his poem on 'The Good Old Days' Daniel Eastwood remembered his boyhood days in the 1850s. The seventh child of ten brought up in a small cottage in

Made in blue transfer-printed white earthenware, treacle pots such as this incorporated a screw-top lid to prevent the entry of dust and flies. They were probably made in the potteries of South Yorkshire during the latter half of the nineteenth century.

Wadsworth in the upper Calder valley, he recalled how the whole family lived on porridge alone:

> But that was a sight, when our work began,
> And porridge was made in a big kilp pan,
> Some water, some salt, and a handful of corn
> For breakfast we had, each day, and at morn.
> it wasn't a lot that was given to each,
> Not hardly enough to silence our speech,
> For barley-pan scrapings was said in a tick,
> While another said nay, let me have a lick.
> When dinner time came 'twas the same o'er again,
> Some water, some salt, and same kilp pan,
> And barley pan scrapings another would say,
> Thou had it at morn, its my turn today.[16]

Another Yorkshire writer, J. Keighley Snowden (1870–1932), had similar grim memories of his childhood in Bingley: 'When I was a little lad,' he wrote, 'I found a penny once. There were seven of us lads in the family, and we took daily turns at scraping the porridge pan. I went to my father and told him about this penny, and I said I would give it him if I might scrape the pan three times running. And that way I would have wared it. We had nought but "porridge and stop" then, and sometimes we had not that. I can tell of my mother fainting one morning when she had served us all round and left herself none, and that morning I had scraped the pan'.[17]

Over the last half-century enormous changes have overtaken the Pennine hills, much improved transport facilities into the region and the vastly higher standard of living having virtually eliminated oats both as a crop in the fields and as a dish on the table. Whenever porridge is made now it is quickly boiled up from rolled oats and tempered with treacle, sugar, or milk as in all parts of the country. Even so, real porridge made from slowly cooked coarse oatmeal, served piping hot, remains one of the most satisfying defences against the black ice and swirling mists of a Pennine winter.

Chapter 8

Bakery

As ovens were to be found only in the most prosperous houses in Yorkshire, the primary baking tradition was firmly baked on the bakstone. Although it was extremely simple, it was also extremely versatile and economical on fuel, especially when used in combination with a 'chover', 'chaumin dish', or chafing dish. This was a small firebasket about six to eight inches in diameter usually supported on three tall iron legs and having three projections rising above the rim to hold the bakstone over the gentle heat of a burning peat. In this way, baking could be carried out quite easily without having to use the main fire, a particularly useful facility during the long, hot days of summer.

Baking in the turf-burning areas of the North Yorkshire Moors was also undertaken in a yetling, a cylindrical cast-iron vessel perhaps a foot in diameter and five inches in height which hung over the fire from a reckon-hook. Heated from below by the fire, and from above by further smouldering peats heaped over its convex lid, it was essentially a small temporary oven. Occasionally a deep frying pan could be converted into a yetling by clipping a broad sheet-iron cylinder on to its rim, thus extending it upwards to provide sufficient room for cakes, pies and loaves.

Of all the bakery produced by the old-established bakstone method, the most common was a cake of flour, fat and water. Its name and the proportions of its ingredients varied considerably from one area to another:

Fatty-cake, in the West Riding, was a round short cake made with flour and butter, dripping, or lard, which was served at tea or breakfast.[1]

Gayle Bannocks, in Wensleydale, were made by rubbing a pound of lard into two pounds of flour, mixed with a little water, sometimes adding currants. It was once the staple diet of the local quarrymen, being filling and satisfying, since it 'stayed with you'.[2]

Girdle, Flap, Mell, Nodden, or Turf Cakes, in the North Riding were made by rubbing three ounces of butter or lard into eight ounces of flour and a pinch of salt, then mixing it to a stiff dough with a little water. For richer versions, milk could replace the water, and two ounces of currants and a tablespoon of sugar could be added. Later recipes also include a teaspoon of baking powder to improve the lightness. These were traditionally baked in a yetling, and were carried into the fields at harvest, especially when the last sheaf had been cut. They were also served with ham and eggs for tea in the farmhouses and inns of the region.[3]

Sad Cakes, in the West Riding, were made by sifting a dessertspoon of baking powder and a pinch of salt into a pound and a quarter of flour, before rubbing in eight ounces of lard and making into a stiff dough with half a pint of milk. Having been divided into six, a hole was

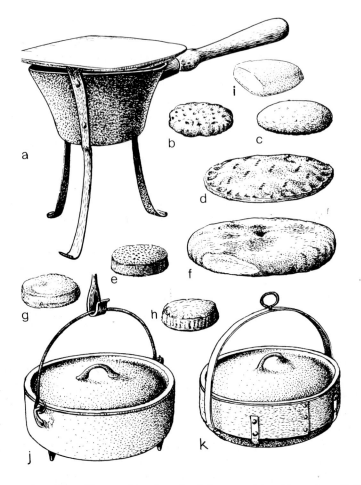

Bakstones and yetlings. The combination of a bakstone with a 'chover' or chafing dish containing a burning peat provided a simple economical and effective means of baking (a). On it could be made suet cakes (b); parkins (c); pasties with sweet or savoury fillings (d); pikelets (e); oven cakes (f); muffins (g); girdle cakes (h) and 'scufflers', the irregularly shaped bread cakes of south Yorkshire (i). In the North Yorkshire Moors yetlings made from cast-iron (j) or by extending an iron frying pan with a sheet iron ring (k), were used for baking.

made into each portion, into which was inserted part of two ounces of currants and two ounces of sugar. When the hole had been sealed, the cakes were flattened to about half an inch in thickness.

Suet Cakes, in the West Riding, differed from the other cakes, since they were raised with yeast. They are still made for sale in Haworth:

1 lb flour	4 oz currants
4 oz suet, chopped	1 oz yeast
4 oz lard	⅓ pint warm milk and water
Pinch of salt	

Rub the lard into the flour, mix in the suet, salt and currants, and the yeast dissolved in the milk and water to make a dough. Form into eight round cakes about half an inch thick and leave to rise on a baking sheet in a warm place until doubled in size.

Water Cake, in the industrial West Riding, was simply a cake made of flour and water, probably with the addition of a little salt. 'Mi granny could ony get meal an' sho ust ter mix it up wi' watter, an' a bit o' plaster, an when sh'od popped t' iron plate i' front of t'foire (for sho 'adn't a back-stooan t' her cottage as most on 'em had them days) sh'd power t' meal an' water on t' plate to bake. Sh's telled me as them little uns wor that clemmed [hungry] they couldn't keep ther hands off'n meal till it wor cooked, but 'ud snip bits off'n it as they crinkled up at t'edges wi' t'heat, an gobble 'em up.'[4]

In all these forms, the cakes were finally baked to a light brown on each side on a bakstone or yetling, the plainer varieties occasionally being split and buttered before being eaten fresh and hot.

One of the other major products of the bakstone was the pasty, two dinner-plate sized rounds of short-crust pastry enclosing a variety of fillings. Having been cooked on one side, it was then turned over with a baking spittle and cooked on the other. It provided a very economical and filling snack or meal, either hot or cold, and was often included in the 'jock' taken to eat at the mill, for pasties were a speciality of the textile areas of West Yorkshire, where they are still made today. The town of

The yetling was used for all kinds of baking in the Moors, where it was hung over the peat fire, with further burning peats piled on the convex iron lid. Here it is seen in use at Stingamires in Bilsdale early this century.

Yeadon near Leeds even acquired the by-name of 'Pastyland' from the size of its pasties which, it was said, 'were so big that when one end was in the oven, the other had to be propped up on a chair back in the middle of the room.[5]

Currant pasties have been made for at least three hundred years in the West Riding, where they were variously known as Dewsbury cakes or transparent tarts. In other parts of the county they were called either sly cakes or secret cakes, since their pastry disguised the rich, sweet filling.[6] A recipe of 1741 includes:

1 lb flour	[4 oz] currants
12 oz butter	[1 oz] sugar
1 beaten egg	

Melt the butter and allow to cool, without setting, then mix in the beaten egg, and pour into a well in the flour, and work in to form a dough. Turn out on to the floured board, and roll very thin. Cut into circles, spreading half of them with a thin layer of currants and sugar, before covering them with the remaining circles, and rolling them out thinly again. If using an oven, glaze with water and sprinkle with sugar before baking at 400°F, gas mark 6, for 20 minutes.

The later currant pasties were made with shortcrust pastry, each large round being filled with some 3 oz of currants and 2 oz of sugar.

Mint pasties included:

2–3 tablespoons chopped mint	2 oz sugar
3 oz currants	2 oz butter

Fruit pasties, of rhubarb, apples, or other fresh fruit, were baked without any sugar, since the syrup it produced would make the pasty heavy, moist, and impossible to turn over. The usual method was to cook the pasty, on both sides, then slide it off on to a plate, cut round the edge, lift the lid, and sprinkle in the sugar. It is remarkable that even today, some 150 years or more since fruit pasties were largely replaced by pies, the old-established households of East Yorkshire still bake their fruit pies without sugar, cut the edge, and put in the sugar after baking. Although there is no reason for this, it is continued simply because the habit has been passed down from mother to daughter over the passing generations.[7]

Egg and Bacon pasty is made by chopping the bacon into small pieces and laying it over the bottom of the pasty, the raw egg being slipped in before the lid is closed down. Alternatively the egg and chopped bacon could first be beaten together.[8]

Onion pasty has either very finely chopped raw onions mixed with butter, pepper and salt, or the onions might first be parboiled, peeled and sliced.[9]

Onion and apple pasty has coarsely chopped onions mixed with a rather larger quantity of chopped apple, and about an ounce of butter and an ounce of sugar. This was popular in the Horton-in-Ribblesdale area.[10]

Cheese and onion pasty is made by mixing two parboiled, peeled and sliced onions with two chopped boiled potatoes, three ounces of grated cheese, salt and pepper.

All the above require twelve ounces of shortcrust pastry, and are baked for 15–20 minutes on a bakstone or in the oven at 400° F, gas mark 6. They may be glazed with egg and milk, and should have their upper surfaces either pricked with a fork or slashed with a knife to allow the steam to escape while baking.

Pikelets were also made on the bakstones, the yeasted batter of flour and water either being poured directly on to the stone, thus producing a thin, somewhat irregular cake, or else poured into a number of tinplate rings arranged on the stone. By confining the batter in this way, the pikelets were made in a perfectly circular form about half an inch in thickness. They were produced in large numbers by the commercial oatcake makers from the mid-nineteenth century, and from that time were only rarely baked in the home, since they could more easily be bought from the men who hawked them around the towns and villages. Toasted before the glowing red coals of an open fire and eaten hot, dripping with butter, they provided a delicious, cheap, succulent and satisfying dish when served any time between autumn and spring:

Pikelets

½ oz yeast	1¼ lb flour
1 pt. or more warm water	1 oz salt

Cream the yeast in a little of the water, sift the flour and salt, make a well in the centre, pour in the remaining water, and stir to form a pouring batter, mixing in the yeast. Cover with a cloth and leave to rise in a warm place for an hour. Having heated and lightly greased a bakstone or griddle, pour a ladleful of batter either directly on to the stone, or into a number of rings, and leave to cook until the upper surface is a mass of tiny holes and has begun to set. Then free the pikelets from the stone with a spatula, turn them over, and allow them to cook until the second side is very slightly browned.

From the seventeenth century at least wheaten bread had been baked on the bakstone, round cakes of very light yeast-risen dough being baked first on one side and then the other to produce something like a light, spongy muffin.[11] By the early nineteenth century breads of this type had become firmly established in three main varieties. The muffin, often made by the commercial bread or oatcake baker and hawked around the streets with the cry 'Come buy my nice muffins', was carried home toasted before the fire, then torn open and buttered:

Hot muffins, hot, and crumpets too,
For breakfast and for tea,
I've only left a very few,
In basket you may see.[12]

Muffins

1 lb flour	teaspoon sugar
1 teaspoon salt	½pt warm milk and water
2 oz butter	1 oz yeast

Rub the butter into the flour and salt, and make a well in the centre. Cream the yeast with the sugar, add the milk and water, pour into the flour, and knead to a soft dough. Cover the bowl and leave to rise in a warm place for about half an hour then divide into small rounds which, placed on a floured board or baking sheet, are allowed to rise once more. The muffins are then placed on a hot bakstone and baked to a light brown first on one side and then on the other. To serve, cut around the edge with a knife and toast each side in turn. The two halves are then pulled apart, buttered, put together again, and placed on a hot dish.

The teacake measured about four to six inches in diameter and rose to about an inch and a half in thickness. As the name suggests, it was mainly eaten at tea, sliced in two, and spread both with butter, if it could be afforded, and perhaps a filling such as potted meat. It was also one of the basic forms of bread eaten for breakfast, for supper, or for the 'jock' or 'snap' carried to work. Covered with 'mucky fat', the brown flavoursome layer at the bottom of a basin of dripping or lard, with cheese, meat or jam, it provided a cheap, substantial and satisfying meal. The following recipe shows how the same batch of dough could be prepared to make both plain and currant teacakes:[13]

Yorkshire Teacakes

1 lb plain flour	1 oz yeast
6 oz lard (rubbed in)	Warm new milk
1 teaspoon sugar	[about ½pt]
A little salt	

Mix all well together, and finish beating up with your hands. Sprinkle a little flour over and put down on the hearth to rise in a warm place. When risen take out three plain teacakes, and add to the rest of the mixture 3 oz sugar, currants, and a little candied peel. Mix and let the dough rise again. When ready, roll our and put on baking sheets, and again rise *well*. [Bake at 450°F, gas mark 8, for 15 minutes.]

The oven-bottom cake was eaten in a similar manner to the teacake, but was much larger, measuring anything up to a foot across. Once the bakstone had started to be replaced by the cast-iron oven in the 1830s, the housewives found that the best way of continuing to bake this extremely popular cake was to place the dough directly on the bottom of the oven, hence its present name. This cake was usually made from about a pound of ordinary white bread dough cut off after its first rising. It was often enriched by kneading in two or three ounces of lard cut in small pieces before being formed into a cake, allowed to rise until doubled in size, and baked at the bottom of the oven. [425°F, gas mark 7, for 20 minutes.] After baking, the cakes would either be propped up by the doorstep to cool, or be torn open and eaten steaming hot with butter, as one of the most succulent and delicious of all Yorkshire delicacies. Such pleasures were not to be enjoyed without suffering considerable physical discomfort, however, as Mr. Crowther of Bankdam found to his cost:[14]

'So you've gotten t'wind again, have you?' said Mrs. Crowther grimly. 'You get it every time you eat hot oven-cake. Hurry up, lass . . . no, t'copper Kettle'.

The sufferer sipped the steaming water, had a further supply and then belched freely. He, holding up his hand, anticipated the coming scolding.

'Alreet, alreet, it's my own fault. But I fair can't resist your oven-cakes, Lydia.' From the nail on the wall he removed the large key. 'Get your shawl on, lass,' he said, belching again, 'while I go down to the privy to get shut on the rest o' this.'

'That reminds me, Simeon,' said Mrs. Crowther. 'You must see about getting the cesspool cleared out. What with one thing an' another I forgot to mention it.'

'Stinks, does it?' nodded Mr. Crowther. From a shelf he took a stubby, clay pipe, the mouthpiece of which was bound with cotton thread, and filled it with shreds of black tobacco he cut from a bar he held in the palm of his hand. Lighting a spill he applied it to the bowl, and sucked out the strong fumes.

'Get out of here wi' that,' cried Mrs. Crowther, coughing.

Her husband laughed. 'I'll noan be able to niff the stinks in the privy with this wi' me.' he said. 'You should start smoking, lass.'

He snatched a piece of old newspaper, climbed the steps into the wash-kitchen, clumped across the flagged floor, and opened the back door . . .

In most parts of the county, except the Pennine areas of West Yorkshire, the housewives living in the farmhouses and more substantial cottages had been able to bake in their own ovens from the seventeenth or early eighteenth centuries. Their ovens were fairly uniform in design and consisted of a beehive-shaped dome of brick or stone measuring two or three feet across built within the masonry of a chimney stack or bakehouse wall. Their doorways were small and rectangular, their sills usually projecting a few inches forward, while the jambs and lintels were recessed slightly to receive simple slab doors. When the oven was to be used, a fire of fast-burning timber was kindled within its chamber, the resulting smoke issuing in clouds from its open doorway. Where the oven was built into a chimney stack, these fumes were quickly sucked up the main flue, although a small smoke-hood might be constructed just over the lintel to carry away the smoke through a purposely-built shaft running up through the thickness of the wall. As the fire died down a 'fruggin' was used, this being 'a Pole to stir in the Oven when it is heated to stir the ashes up', so reducing any flaming pieces to glowing embers. The food was then inserted using a long-handled peel, the door sealed in place with 'dittin' or mud, and then left for a period while the cooking continued using heat retained in the surrounding mason-ry.[15]

The smoke, dirt and inconvenience of the beehive oven were only tolerated so long as there was no alternative method of baking loaves of bread, pies, cakes and puddings. The first iron ovens, heated by their own fireplaces, began to be built into

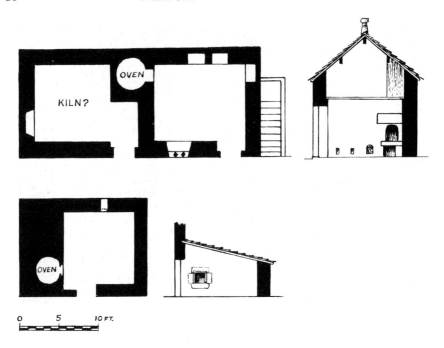

In West Yorkshire the ovens were often incorporated into purpose-built bakehouses as seen in these examples from the Calder Valley. The upper bakehouse stands on the outskirts of Hebden Bridge and appears to have been combined with a corn-drying kiln, while the lower example stood at Lane Ends Farm, Upper Saltonstall.

the prosperous kitchens of the gentry in the mid-eighteenth century, but it was not until the 1820s and '30s that they came within the reach of ordinary working families. Once they had been installed, however, they enabled the variety of bakery made in the home to increase dramatically. In some cases the foods formerly made on the bakstone and yetling were now baked in the oven, without any major change in their shape or constituents, but in others new forms were adopted, as pasties turned into pies for example. The greatest change brought about by the availability of the new iron ovens was that they permitted everyone to bake a whole range of dishes which had previously only been made by the professional bakers and by the cooks employed in the wealthier households. When girls left domestic service with the gentry, clergy, farmers and tradesmen to marry and set up their own homes, they could now acquire the essential piece of equipment required to bake the foods they had learned to make for their former masters and mistresses. Thus the great English bakery tradition built up in the kitchens of the medieval royal household and spread by the ladies of the Tudor and Stuart courts to great houses throughout the country finally entered into most Yorkshire homes. Many of the cakes, pies and pastries now popularly considered to be essentially local in origin really spring from the international cuisine of the great European courts. The period from around 1850 up to the Second World War can now be seen as a 'golden age' of home baking, when almost every housewife took a great pride in baking all the bread, cakes and

'A little bit O' baakin!' Based on a painting by Elizabeth Brockbank, this illustration gives an excellent impression of baking day in a Craven farmhouse, with apple pies being made on the table, tarts about to go into the oven, and the bread rising in pancheons before the fire.

puddings eaten by her family, instead of relying on mass-produced convenience foods.

It had always been possible for families living in the towns and larger villages to have their baking undertaken by a professional baker. Even in the 1890s some families found it inconvenient to cook at home: 'Those who have ovens usually prefer sending their dinners to the public bakehouses of which [at Robin Hood's Bay] there are three . . . the bakers not only bake dinners, but make up to order pies, tarts, or any other confections, wholesome or rich, and this at a reasonable rate'.[16] Having prepared the food for baking, perhaps marking the bread etc. in a particular way so that its ownership was beyond dispute, it was carried to the bakers, baked, and then carried home again, once the appropriate fee had been paid. This process was not without its difficulties. One Bedale apprentice proceeding to the bakehouse one dark night slipped off the pavement and allowed the bread to slip off its board into the 'necessary'. On returning it to his mistress, she proceeded to cut off the unclean part with a knife before sending it back for baking, thus displaying the economy for which the county is quite famous.[17]

Of all the foods baked in the oven, the most important by far were the breads made from rye, maslin, barley, and wheat.

Rye Bread

Sourdough rye bread is still a great German, central European and Scandinavian favourite, and perhaps it is not surprising that it once formed part of the staple diet of Yorkshire, particularly in its eastern parts, where both place-names and dialect still retain a strong Scandinavian influence. By the opening of the nineteenth century rye was being grown to a limited extent in Cleveland, on the flat lands around Doncaster, and in the Moorland dales.[18] A good account of its use is given by John Tuke[19]: 'Formerly a very black, heavy, sour bread was made of rye, and it is not yet entirely out of date, among the lower orders of the country; it is made in the following manner; a large tub, called a kimlin, is provided; this being only scraped, and not washed out each time of using, the paste which remains on the sides becomes sour; in this vessel about one half of the meal intended to be used is mixed with the water in the evening; This is covered up with some dry meal, and lies in sponge till morning; in that time, the tub has communicated its acidity to the whole mass, which causes a fermentation similar to that of yeast; it is then worked up with the remainder of the meal; this is often done with the feet, the dough being covered with a coarse cloth; after it has thus been well worked, it is made into large loaves, and put into the oven, where it remains about ten or twelve hours. As this kind of bread will keep a considerable time, it is made in large quantities at once; three bushels at a baking is frequent, which quantity is made into seven or eight loaves: many farmers do not make this bread more than four, or six times in the year'. Loaves of this type, weighing up to 18 lbs each, were being baked in large tins in iron ovens up to the late nineteenth century, but then passed completely out of fashion as wheaten bread became readily available.[20]

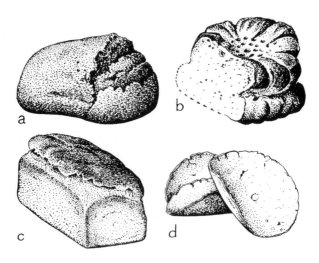

In her paintings of Yorkshire scenes made before the 1830s Mary Ellen Best of York included a number of different forms of bread such as the wholemeal cob (a), the cottage loaf (b), the tin loaf (c) and the crisp, rolled oatcake (d).

Maslin Bread

In the South Yorkshire version of 'Jones' Ale':

> The next that came a miller was he,
> His millstones turned when the stream ran free,
> But he closed his shuttle to come on the spree,
> When he joined our jovial crew.
> Said he, bring me your wheat and rye,
> For your maslin bread that never goes dry,
> And I'll toll you as light as a maiden's sigh,
> While the good brown ale is new.[21]

Maslin, a mixed crop of wheat and rye, threshed, winnowed and ground into meal, was the most common household or brown bread used by all sections of the community. Without exception, the agricultural writers of the late eighteenth and early nineteenth centuries praised its wholesome and nutritional qualities, its moisture and its resistance to going stale.

Barley Bread

> On Yorkshire Wolds we mostly barley eat
> For there they grow but very little wheat;
> We lived on barley bread and barley pies,
> And oats and peas the want of wheat supplies.

Writing in the early nineteenth century, Captain Anderson of Kilham was recording a practice which was fast disappearing, for the improvement of the Wolds had already made them into one of the county's finest wheat-producing regions.[22] 'The valleys and declivities of the hills wave with plentiful crops of wheat, and neither servants nor labourers will eat barley bread,' wrote John Bigland in 1818.[23] Perhaps he was being rather optimistic, for Henry Blades was receiving barley bread and treacle, and a basin of water or milk for his breakfast when working for the Turners at Danesdale in 1854.[24] The continued use of barley meal for feeding farm servants was clearly recognised as a sign of poor housekeeping, however, Edward Atkinson of Monk Fryston remembering their repeated chant of:

> Barley bread, barley pies
> Mouldy bacon and cheese with eyes![25]

Wheaten Bread

Around 1800 wheat was being grown on all the arable land in the eastern half of the county, most of the country to the west of a line running approximately from Sheffield to Ripon being too high, cold and damp to produce economically viable crops. The main areas of production lay in Cleveland, Ryedale and the vale of York, where it formed part of a three or four-year rotation with fallow, turnips, clover, or beans or peas. Vast new acreages of rich wheat land were also coming into cultivation on a similar rotation on the Yorkshire Wolds, where the old sheepwalks were being enclosed and intensively ploughed for the first time. In spite of this increased production, wheaten bread remained a luxury in many homes throughout the first half of the nineteenth century, the only areas where it was eaten to any extent being the town centres.

Even here it was extremely expensive and could be of very poor quality, particularly in years of bad harvest such as 1817–18, 1829–31, and 1838–41. At these times flour costing some six shillings (30p) a pound would not even hold its shape in the oven, but turned into a thin liquid which trickled down the front of thin cakes, but these emerged extremely hard on the outside and so black and soft within that they had to be eaten with a spoon.[27] Further problems arose from adulteration, samples of bread taken in Hull in the 1850s containing as much as five per cent of silex or flint.[28] Pure flour was available to some sections of society, however, such as the agricultural workers in the corn-producing areas.

Here the cottagers were able to provide themselves with an important supply of wheat flour by gleaning after the harvest. When the fields were ready for reaping, the people were organised in teams called 'yans' who took all the corn from one furrow to another along a single ridge. After the shearers, binders and men setting up the sheaves there followed the gleaners, the children of the reapers, who picked up the ears of corn which had escaped the attention of the binders. There was often great contention between the reapers and the more miserly of the farmers as to the number of gleaners each yan should have. On the Wolds, the gleaning was undertaken by the women and children, the former wearing an apron called a 'laggin' which had a large pocket to hold the ears of corn. When full, they were emptied into large sheets which were folded up at the end of the day and carried home on the women's heads, although the children would often play their part by carrying little bundles in their hands.

At night the gleanings were spread around the cottages – on the bed, under the bed, on tables, chairs, shelves, the mangle, suspended from ceilings, etc. – until they were thoroughly dried and ready for threshing. This might be undertaken either by a neighbouring farmer, or at home using a flail, or even a rolling pin. Having been winnowed in the open air, every grain was carefully garnered, measured and sacked ready to be taken to the local mill to be ground into flour. Where a family could send forth two or three gleaners, it could, in a good season, expect to acquire two to four or even more bushels of grain, a very significant amount of food to help keep the wolf from the door throughout the coming winter.[29]

In the towns, cheap and wholesome flour began to be produced by setting up co-operative mills, such as the Union-Mill Society's windmill established in Whitby in 1800.[30] By 1850 many of the larger towns, including Halifax, Leeds and Hull had similar institutions, the Leeds Flour Society founded in 1847 being particularly effective. In return for the payment of a guinea (105p) entrance money, each of the 3,000 members could purchase enough flour to feed his own family at such low rates that the entire subscription was recouped within the first year of membership. The other great advantage was that there was no adulteration, the flour all being of the purest quality.[31]

The widespread use of wheat flour for baking was only made possible after the repeal of the corn Laws in 1846, when increasing quantities of wheat began to be imported from America, Canada, Australia and the Argentine:[32]

Annual Average imports of wheat

Year	tonnage
1801–1810	7,500
1840s	23,750
1861–5	1,732,600
1871–5	2,524,750
1891–5	4,829,650
1911–13	5,983,300

This increase was also accompanied by a great drop in prices:[33]

Year	price per quarter		
1813	120s.	(600p)	
1822	53s.	(265p)	
1855	74s/8d.	(373p)	|Crimea|
1873	58s/8d.	(243p)	
1893	26s/4d.	(132p)	

Given these circumstances, it is not surprising that wheat became the county's major bread corn during the latter half of the nineteenth century, rapidly displacing the oats, rye, barley and maslin eaten by previous generations.

Now that the housewives had ovens, cheap coal and wheat flour at their disposal, they could undertake all their families' baking in their own homes. Baking day became a major weekly event, usually starting early on a Wednesday or Thursday morning in many households, although some would prefer another day. In the East Riding farmhouses baking could prove necessary on virtually every day of the week, for example, while in textile and fishing families baking had to take place in the evenings after the wife had already worked a full day either at the mill or at baiting lines and mending nets.[34] After tending the fire to bring the oven up to full heat, the flour was sifted into large earthenware mixing bowls or pancheons and kneaded with warm water and yeast before being covered with a cloth and placed on the hearth to rise. Early in the nineteenth century the bread might still be leavened by a sourdough technique, mixing each batch with a piece of old dough that had been saved long enough to turn sour. Such bread, baked on the hot hearth under an iron cover in Holderness, was substantial, with a slightly sour flavour which was not unpleasant.[35] Liquid yeast was also available from neighbours, or from a local brewhouse, great care being taken in its selection. To keep it fresh, it could be poured into an earthenware jar or 'barm-pot', sealed carefully, and then be buried in the garden, this crude method of refrigeration being the best that was available at that time.[36] From the 1840s these traditional forms of yeast were largely replaced by a solid compressed variety produced by the Dutch distillers and imported into this country in large quantities.[37] Rather confusingly, it was popularly known as German or dried yeast, as may be seen in the following advertisement published in Whitby on July 25th, 1849:

GOOD BREAD

THE CELEBRATED DRIED GERMAN YEAST

This yeast will be found much superior to any other; bread made with it is never bitter; the colour and quality is improved; and its quantity considerably increased. The dried German Yeast is free from any pernicious Ingredient.

ONE PENNYWORTH

is sufficient for a Stone and a half of Flour, and can be used with as much convenience, and in a manner exactly similar to common Yeast.

DIRECTIONS FOR USE

Dissolve the Yeast in a cup of cold water, mix the Flour with warm water, then add the Yeast, and set to rise in the usual manner.

SOLD BY

T. HALL, Grocer & Confectioner, CHURCH STREET, WHITBY.

When the dough had risen once, it was knocked back, divided into portions, and formed either into cobs, and oven bottom cakes, or into loaves contained in sheet iron tins or salt-glazed stoneware baking dishes. At this stage pieces of the dough could be made into shilley cake by kneading it up with lard and perhaps currants, rolling it out, and baking it on the bottom of the oven.[38] This ate well when eaten hot, split and spread with butter. Pieces of the dough could also be plunged into a pan of water boiling on the hob to make dumplings called water whelps or dog whelps, presumably from their resemblance to small puppies. Sweetened with jam or treacle, they provided a simple and satisfying meal for the children when their mother was particularly 'throng' with baking.[39]

After the bread had been made, it was time to make the cakes and pastries, including all the traditional bakery described elsewhere in this book, together with a vast range culled from experience gained while in service, from friends and neighbours, and from some of the popular recipe books of the period. Sponge cakes, seed cakes, bible cakes, Jordan cakes, chocolate cakes, coconut cakes, pound cakes, date and walnut cakes, fruit cakes, Sally Lunns and feather cakes were all regularly made, the latter featuring in the West Riding version of 'Billy Boy':

Can she cook and can she bake,
  Billy Boy, Billy Boy
Can she cook and can she bake,
  Charley Willy.
She can cook and she can bake
  Aye and make a feather cake
But she's young and she can't leave her Mammy.

Feather Cake

8 oz flour	4 oz butter
8 oz sugar	3 teaspoons baking powder
3 eggs	

Mix the dry ingredients, rub in the butter, and stir in the well-beaten eggs. Pour into a greased dripping tin and bake for 30 minutes at 350° F gas mark 4. Cut into squares when cold.

Then there were the pies of apple, bilberry, plum, prune, rhubarb, gooseberry and elderberry, the tarts containing jam, lemon cheese, ground rice, treacle, and custard, together with curd cheesecakes, rockbuns, scones and macaroons. To buy any of these items from the commercial bakers was seen as a sure sign of poor household management, and even as a risk to health: 'Aw tell yo' what, folk, there's some weary rubbish amoung bought – bread, for 'baat recknin' th' alum and puttates, etc., its a varry common thing to finnd buttons, an blackclocks [cockroaches] an' oddments o' allsooarts in it'.[40] Even so, many families had neither the time, the skills nor the energy to bake all their own food, and small bakehouses flourished in virtually every town and village.

The greatest display of home baking came at the Yorkshire high tea, an early evening meal at which meats and pies were followed by the most impressive mass of cakes and pastries which the wife could muster, especially at feast – time or other major gatherings of relations and friends. To have been offered anything as meagre as the polite south – country tea would have been taken as a gross insult by every guest, and the family's reputation would have been irretrievably ruined.

To close this chapter, we can visit a 'tea drinking' held by Miss Maffin in her small Wharfedale cottage about the 1860s. The round cricket table in the centre of the room, although barely a yard across, had been laid with her best china, a seed cake, bread and butter, ham sandwiches, and a salad of lettuce, cress, radishes and onions. Tea cakes regularly replaced the lid of the kettle, to become hot and moist in its steam, while muffins were toasted on a toasting – dog before the fire.

When her friends arrived, they arranged themselves around the table.[41] It was *de rigueur* on state occasions like this for the ladies to sit fair and square to the table in the ordinary manner; but the gentlemen were allowed more latitude. Indeed, among the old generation, the correct claim to dignity seems to have been to sit with your chair sideways to the table and your back to your hostess, your bread and salad or your ham sandwiches on your red spotted handerchief spread across your knees, and

Toasted teacakes, pikelets and muffins formed an important element in any traditional Yorkshire tea. To hold the bread before the fire toasting forks were used, these examples being made by John Atkinson the Killinghall blacksmith (and my g-g-g-frandfather) in 1855 to celebrate his daughter's marriage to John Boucher, estate joiner at Ripley Castle, who made the handle (left), the other example being used by the Pearson family in the Groves, York. The toasting bull (top) was used at Råstrick in Calderdale, while the slipware toast dish (bottom) was made at the Burton in Lonsdale potteries near Bentham.

your cup and saucer on the edge of the table. Seated in this manner, the assembled company then proceeded to do full justice to the fare set out before them, the conversation flowing just as freely as the hot tea laced with rum. Even on this modest scale, the Yorkshire tea provided a great source of enjoyment and satisfaction to all its participants.

Chapter 9

Meat

The amount of meat eaten in nineteenth-century Yorkshire varied enormously from one section of the population to another. The inhabitants of the poor town-centre slums might taste meat only a few times each year, for example, while at the same time the East Riding farm servants enjoyed meat three meals a day.

Beef was by far the most popular meat, the 'roast beef of Old England' which had been praised as 'a good meate for an Englysshe man' from the sixteenth century at least.[1] This was the meat for all celebrations, from Christmas dinners to feasts and fairs, in addition to being one of the most favoured meats with the prosperous traders, craftsmen and hard-working miners. The country offered large areas of good grazing which were extensively used for raising cattle. In Craven and the upper reaches of the western Pennine Dales the long-horned breeds flourished in the relatively cold wet climate, while in all other regions the shorthorns predominated. As Mr Cleaver noted in 1800, the principal encouragement given to the short-horned breed of cattle arose from the coal-trade, the mining areas consuming large quantities of coarse beef.[2] Shorthorns from the western areas were therefore sold at the Skipton, Wakefield and Rotherham markets, those from the east being bought either by the butchers from the industrial West Riding who attended the market, or by the graziers of South Yorkshire and Lincolnshire.

In addition to locally bred cattle, immense numbers were driven down from the Highlands of Scotland. After being fattened for a year or two on local pastures, they were sold either to the butchers or at the spring and autumn cattle fairs held in all the major towns, where they always attracted higher prices than any of the native breeds. In the eighteenth and early nineteenth centuries families who could afford to buy an entire beast did so at the fairs, driving it home, killing it, salting it, and hanging it up in the smoke of the chimney to dry.[3]

Although salt beef continued to be eaten throughout the nineteenth century, it was largely replaced from around 1800 by fresh beef purchased from the rows of butchers' shops or shambles situated in the centre of most market towns.[4] In addition to the medieval Shambles in York, excellent purpose-built examples can still be seen in Wetherby and Settle. As the urban population exploded, the increased demand for meat could not be satisfied by the traditional series of fairs, etc., and so weekly cattle markets began to be established on the outskirts of many of the larger towns. Neatly paved and equipped with rows of permanent pens, they could efficiently handle thousands of animals every week, much of the stock now arriving by rail. Some indication of the enormous growth in this trade is given by the following extract from the records of the Wakefield cattle market.[5]

Market place in Settle, these arched shambles or butchers' stalls date from the seventeenth century, the houses above being reconstructed in the late Victorian period.

Year	Cattle	Sheep
1805	5,527	100,626
1817	10,444	151,980
1824	12,333	258,750
1835	13,519	170,912
1868	50,289	190,662
1901	73,456	

Up to 1842 all the meat consumed in Britain was home-produced since the government maintained a total ban on imports. In that year, however, the ban was lifted and live animals began to arrive in vast numbers, some 309,000 a year coming mainly from northern Europe by 1854. In the 1860s dried 'Hamburg beef' from Germany and canned boiled beef from Australia and the great American cattle towns were also being imported in large quantities. These were joined in the 1880s by frozen beef from Australia and the Argentine. Due to their methods of preservation, these products were certainly inferior to the fresh home-grown beef, but since they cost barely half as much, they provided a most acceptable alternative, being incorporated into pies and stews or sliced and eaten cold.[6]

Most of the cattle sold at the markets were bought by butchers who then drove them back to the shambles or to their own private slaughter houses where they were killed with a pole axe. At Skipsea in Holderness the villagers used to leave basins containing a sixpence at the butcher's when they knew he was killing, these then being delivered back to their homes full of offal such as the lungs, kidneys, liver, brains, etc., sufficient to feed a family of four.[7] The butcher might then prepare the tripe for sale, although in the industrial towns this work was undertaken by specialist tripe dressers who sold it in pre-cooked form either in their own shops or at one of the local markets. From the stomachs of the cow came several distinct varieties of tripe, such as seam, honeycomb and reed, shag or 'dark tripe'; from the udder came elder, while the feet provided calves feet for jelly or ox and cow heels which were put into stews, meat and rabbit pies, and potted meats. The pre-cooked tripe could be eaten directly, seasoned with salt, pepper and vinegar. It could also be fried in dripping with onions, or boiled:[8]

Boiled Tripe and Onions

1 lb tripe	$\frac{1}{2}$ pt milk
2 large onions	1 oz cornflour
1 oz butter	Pepper & salt

Slice the onions and cook slowly until they are almost enough, then strain off the water. Wash and cut the tripe into neat pieces and place it in the saucepan with the onions. Mix the cornflour with the milk, add this to the tripe with the butter and cook for about 10 to 15 minutes. Season with pepper and salt. Serve very hot with mashed potatoes.

Having divided the remainder of the carcase into suitable joints, the butcher either delivered them to his major customers, probably using a yard-long wooden tray carried over one shoulder, or offered them for sale in his shop. Other butchers might sell their meat from carts and specially-designed horse-drawn vans such as those made by Billy Wright of Rothwell Haigh towards the end of last century.

Up to around 1850 many families, particularly in the industrial West Riding, still salted down large joints of beef for use throughout the winter, the traditional local method being detailed in Ann Peckham's *Complete English Cook* of 1773:

To Make Dutch Beef

Take eight pounds of a buttock of beef without bone, rub it all over with a quarter of a pound of coarse sugar, let it lay two days, then wipe it, take a pint of common salt, a pint of salt-petre, and six ounces of bay-salt beaten, rub it well into the beef, and let it lay three weeks, turning and rubbing it every day; then sew it up in a cloth, and hang it up in a chimney where wood fire is kept for a month, turning it upside down every day; when you use it, boil it in pump water.

The joints of salt beef were usually stored by being hung from hooks driven into the joists or rafters, the Rev. Easther recalling the distress of one weaver whose piece of beef fell from the roof and broke the warp in his loom. To prevent such an expensive mishap recurring, he put a bottle of his own urine up the chimney to deter further witchcraft![9] Beef could also be wet-pickled and pressed, this method of cooking being retained long after salting had gone out of use as the essential method of preservation, since it gave the meat a particularly fine flavour:[10]

Pressed Salt Brisket

3 lb rolled brisket	10 lb water
1½ oz Demarara sugar	1 pearl garlic
1 lb salt	2 bay leaves
1½ oz saltpetre	

Boil up all the ingredients (except the brisket) allow to cool, skim and strain. Immerse the meat in the liquid in a stone jar or wooden bucket, not metal, for four days in a cool place. The meat should be stabbed before introducing into the liquid. It should also be trimmed. Finally boil the meat with one bay leaf and 1½ oz Demarara sugar until tender, then press.

In the poorer households joints of fresh beef were usually boiled, this simple and economical method also producing a good broth which might be further enriched with vegetables and dumplings or thickened with crumbled oatcake.[11] Stews were also popular, one farm at Chapel Allerton near Leeds regularly using a ten-gallon iron cauldron to make sufficient for their labourers.[12] When ovens came into widespread use from the 1820s and '30s they greatly simplified the roasting, or rather baking, of joints of beef, in addition to enabling meat pies to be baked. From this period the traditional Sunday dinner of roast beef, Yorkshire pudding and appropriate vegetables became firmly established in all but the poorest households. Having been served hot, and perhaps again cold at a subsequent meal, the remains of the joint were finally served in the form of hash. Originating as a fashionable French dish introduced into English country-house cookery during the seventeenth century, hash had slowly descended the social scale. Writing to her sister Emily on December 1st, 1843, Charlotte Brontë: recalled how she would like to be in the kitchen at Haworth Parsonage 'cutting up the hash, with the clerk and some register people at the other table, and you standing by, watching that I put enough flour, not too much pepper, and above all, that I save the best pieces . . . for Tiger [the cat] and Keeper [the dog] the first of which personages would be jumping about the dish and carving knife, and the latter standing like a devouring flame on the kitchen floor. To complete the picture, Tabby blowing the fire, in order to boil the potatoes to a sort of vegetable glue!' The hash was usually simmered on the hob in an iron saucepan, but alternatively it could be cooked in a pot in the oven, or placed in a dish, covered with pastry or potatoes, and baked as a pie. This was often made on baking day or wash-day, since it provided a good, hot, filling meal with the minimum of effort, as may be seen in this recipe from Miss Taylor of Ambler Thorn, Queensbury:

Wash-Day Pie

1 oz dripping	Any kind of cold cooked meat
2 onions	Mashed potato
1½lb tomatoes	1 egg
Salt & Pepper	

Melt dripping in a pan, then add the chopped onion, when onions have cooked a little, drain off the fat. Then add skinned tomatoes cut up. Allow to cook a little while, then add meat cut up small or put through mincer. Add salt and pepper. Put the mixture in a pie dish, cover with mashed potatoes, brush over with egg and cook for 20/30 minutes in moderate oven.

Two other popular beef dishes were potted meats, used as a sandwich filling, and beef roll, a West Yorkshire speciality:[14]

Potted Meat

1 lb stewing beef   Salt & pepper
1 cow heel

Cut the beef and cow heel into small pieces, put into a stew jar, cover with cold water, and stew for four hours. Remove the bones, pour into a mould, and allow to cool.

From Coxley Valley, Middlestown, Wakefield.

Beef Roll

1 lb minced raw beef   2 eggs, well beaten
8 oz minced boiled ham or bacon   nutmeg
3 oz fresh breadcrumbs   Salt & pepper

Mix the ingredients and form into a roll. Tie tightly in a cloth | or a greased basin | and boil for three hours. When cool take out of the cloth and roll it several times in browned bread crumbs.

From Triangle, Halifax.

Mutton and lamb were both extensively eaten in Yorkshire, but this is not surprising considering the nature of the landscape. The South Pennines produced the Penistone or white woodland breed which fattened splendidly in the lowlands, the Dales produced Swaledales, Wensleydales and Scotch Blackface, Cleveland and the Vale of Mowbray the Durhams or Teeswaters, while in Ryedale, the Howardian Hills and the southern parts of the country the Lincolnshires predominated. Only the sheep kept on the wastes and commons by the poor cottagers could be described as the most miserable imaginable, but these soon disappeared due to the combined effects of the enclosure movement and the improvements in breeding which took place during the opening decades of the nineteenth century.

In many ways the development of the sheep trade paralleled that for cattle, the traditional sheep droving and fairs slowly being replaced by improved road and rail transport to large urban markets where they were sold to the butchers. Like beef, joints of mutton or lamb might be salted for preservation, or eaten boiled or roast, roast and stuffed shoulder and breast of mutton being prepared for special occasions. In the East Riding mutton pie appeared regularly at the farm-servants' tables, this being the 'cowd stringy pie' reputedly made from old dead sheep on some farms. Perhaps this was not far from the truth, for sheep infected with the rot in Holderness around 1830 were neither killed nor allowed to die, but were rapidly sold off at the local markets.

In the Yorkshire Dales smoking hot mutton pie was cooked for the haymakers at the Hill Inn, Chapel-le-Dale, while at the Buck at Buckden they had roast mutton served with salad and rice pudding. As Walter White enviously exclaimed on seeing these 'sunburnt rustics' enjoying their dinners, 'Who would not be a haymaker!'

Legs of mutton were sometimes taken to sea by fishermen joining the fleet, the meat being towed behind the trawler for a few days to keep it fresh and give it a good brining. It was then cooked and served up with enormous supplies of vegetables in a tin dish placed either on the floor or a table from where it was pronged by the crew using their own forks.[15]

In the north-western Dales the farmers used to combine together in groups for sheep washing and shearing and thus proceed from farm to farm until all their work was completed. To celebrate the end of their labours at each house it was customary to serve a much superior variety of mutton pie, combining the meat with fruit and sugar in the fashionable sixteenth or seventeenth-century manner.[16] It was described as 'a sweet pie, that is a huge pie of legs of mutton cut small and seasoned with currants, raisins, candied peel and sugar covered with a rich crust, accompanied by another favourite dish of fresh fried trout and collops of ham succeeded by gooseberry pasties and curd cheesecakes, strong drink in plenty, with a fiddle and a dance to complete the entertainment'.

At a much more mundane level mutton was also prepared as hot pot, with perhaps best end of neck cooked with sliced potatoes and onions, or as hash. In most parts of the county, but particularly in the textile towns of West Yorkshire, sheep's head broth provided one of the most satisfying, warming and economical winter dishes: 'There's a lot of meat on a sheep's head – it makes a real meal'. Usually the head was cleaned, chopped in two, and the brains, tongue and eyes removed, although one informant remembered how 'Aunty always left the eyes in so it would see her through the week!' After soaking for a few hours in strong salt water, the head was then simmered for two hours with potatoes, vegetables, pearl barley or lentils, and perhaps dumplings. The brains were enclosed within a cloth bag and suspended in the water by means of a string tied on to the saucepan handle.[17] It was sometimes possible to buy a pot-posy which included most of the required ingredients: 'I can remember fetching pot-posies for my mam when I was a lad, and you could get something for your penny then, there was marjoram, thyme, sage, a bit of celery and a carrot and turnip. It makes my mouth water to think what grand broth we used to have in them days, and what suet dumplings and sheep heads'.[18] Around Yeadon the first meal taken from the broth consisted of meat picked from the head and served with potatoes, vegetables and a brain sauce made by mashing the brains with a fork and seasoning them with a little vinegar. The remaining broth was re-heated for further meals, when it might be poured over diced bread in a basin.[19] In some households the brains were eaten separately on toast, cream, butter and herbs being added for a luxurious version of this simple dish.

Of all the meat animals raised in Yorkshire, the pig was by far the most useful as it readily converted a wide range of scraps into really good food. The old Yorkshire pig was one of the largest breeds in the kingdom, weighing up to half a ton. In formation and quality, however, it was one of the worst. It had long lop ears, tall legs, weak loins, and a very long narrow back, its colour being chiefly white with long rough curly hair. The meat it produced was of little value, being coarse and flabby.[20]

By the opening of the nineteenth century the more progressive breeders were

From the 1840s Keighley became established as one of the country's major pig breeding centres. Here are two fine examples of the new Yorkshire breeds, "Parian Duchess", a Large White (above) and "Miss Emily", a Middle White (below).

trying to improve their stock by introducing Chinese, Leicestershire and Berkshire pigs, but the major improvements were made by Joseph Tuley and by W.B. Wainman in the 1850s and '60s. The former was a weaver who, with his wife, earned only eighteen shillings (90p) a week in the Keighley textile mills. Having kept and fed first one pig and then a greater number, they lavished all their care on their animals, watching them, exercising them, scratching and combing them during the dinner hour, and bathing them each Saturday night in the master's bath water. His influence was so great that the weavers in the Keighley area began to take a keen interest in improving the local breed, gaining notable success in the show ring. They swept the board at the Royal Show between 1848 and 1850 with their Yorkshire Large White pigs, and the prize lists for several subsequent years had a preponderance of Yorkshire addresses. Keighley, it was said, 'reserves its most touching sympathy for the pig'.

The improved Large White had considerable advantages over the old Yorkshire pig, with a long head, forward-pointing ears, muscular loins and long, wide hindquarters. It was very prolific, grew quickly, had a quiet disposition, and produced meat with a higher proportion of lean to fat. In addition, its white skin gave the bacon and ham an attractive uniform colour, which made it far more

OLDROYD'S
CELEBRATED
Yorkshire Pig Powder

Makes Pigs Healthy,
Thrive and Fatten.

Directions for Use.—In all cases of Inflammation, Coughs, Colds,
Wheezing, or Falling-off Eating. &c., dissolve one powder in water,
then mix in the food twice a day. *Sows*, one three times a week
for a month before pigging; one every other day after, as they seem
to require. *Feeding Pigs*, one powder given twice a week keeps
them in health, and makes them active. thrive, and fatten quicker
with same quantity of food. A small Pig half powder.
Prepared only by **GEORGE OLDROYD**. Chemist & Druggist,
PELLON LANE, HALIFAX. Sold in 1d. packets; 13 for 1s.

The outlay of these Powders is
saved tenfold, as they arrest disease and save life.
Butchers, Farmers, and Large
Pig Owners should always keep
these Powders in readiness.

Advertisement for Oldroyds Pig Powders.

saleable, some bacon curers actually paying a premium for white pigs.[21] As a breed, it became one of the most popular both in this country and overseas, large numbers being exported to France, Germany and the United States. The weavers certainly benefited from these improvements, eventually being able to sell their young pigs at five guineas each, and obtaining from ten to twenty guineas for each of their sows. Joseph Tuley meanwhile, enjoyed substantial prosperity, the sale of a single litter from his famous sow 'Matchless' enabling him to build a new cottage in the Gothic style – appropriately named 'Matchless House'.

At the 1851 meeting of the Keighley Agricultural Society the judges and stewards withdrew a number of Large White pigs, including Tuley's 'Sontag', 'Matchless' and 'Jenny Lind', on the grounds that they were too small for this class. Since they were of a very superior quality, however, they established a new class for Middle Whites, which subsequently developed as an independent breed. Although smaller than the Large White, they were just as heavy due to their relatively small bones and the lightness of their offal and head. They were also one of the gentlest of pigs, and could be turned out into pasture without fear of breaking down the fences. For these reasons, they were the ideal small man's pig, and by the end of the century had spread from their home in the central Aire Valley throughout the country and beyond.[22]

In the textile towns of the West Riding the pigs were kept either on garden plots or allotments, or within the narrow courts and alleys of the closely-packed town-centre slums. Here they were frequently turned loose every day to scavenge on the rubbish thrown into the streets, consuming the liquid slops, tea leaves, cabbage stalks, oyster shells and potatoe peelings, and rooting up the unpaved streets. One visitor to the eastern suburbs of Leeds in the 1840s 'plodded by the half hour through streets in which the undisturbed mud lay in wreaths from wall to wall, and across open spaces, overlooked by houses all around, in which the pigs, wandering from this central oasis, seemed to be roaming through what was only a large sty, Indeed . . . pigs are more common in some parts of Leeds than cats and dogs are in others'. Although it must appear almost beyond belief today, the inhabitants of the cellar dwellings in Leeds actually shared their kitchens with their pigs, the animals occupying one corner of the cellar, all the excrement having to be carried up the steps and thrown out into the street.[23] It was not until the medical officers began to fight dirt and disease in the 1870s and 1880s that these nuisances were finally removed from the town centres.[24] Pig-keeping remained popular wherever pigs could be housed in healthy conditions, however, each family saving every scrap of household waste to help fatten up their sow. Even the skipping songs of the young girls record this activity:[25]

> Dearly beloved brethren
> Isn't it a sin
> When you peel potatoes,
> To throw away the skin?
> The skin will feed the pigs
> And the pigs will feed you,
> Dearly beloved brethren
> Isn't this true?

In the rural area, pigs were kept by most farmers and agricultural labourers, bacon and ham forming a most economical and satisfying part of their diet. The labourers usually purchased a weaner from the farmer, and fed it upon kitchen scraps, small potatoes from the allotment, and grain gleaned after harvest. If possible, it was used to breed a litter, keeping one back, selling the rest, and killing the sow for food. The income recieved from the sale of the weaners, and probably the hams too, provided an important cash return which could be used for unexpected emergencies, such as doctor's bills, etc.[26]

In the farmhouses where numbers of pigs were killed either for household use or for sale, the refreshments provided for the neighbours could be lavish, including

> Such cakes, scones and biscuits, such pastry and bread,
> A cold joint of beef for the men of the party
> A pair of roast fowls and a nice rabbit pie.
> As Bet said, 'The frost gives them appetites healthy–
> We'll show our respect for the boys in the sty'.
> A pile of fat rascals, deliciously creamy,
> For ladies were asked and had promised to come;
> A dish of 'rough robins', jam sandwich most dreamy,
> While mince pies and cheesecakes were flavoured with rum
> At last all was finish'd, the lifeless pigs hanging,
> Their foot to the joists of an outhouse made fast . . . .
> Then talking, and laughing, and stamping and banging,
> The farmers came in to their well-earned repast.

Pig-killing was quite an event for the community, for everyone who had helped to feed the pig, or who had given its owner some of their pig when it had been killed, now expected a return on their investment. The killing usually took place in the winter months, but never on a Friday, which was unlucky, or when the moon was on

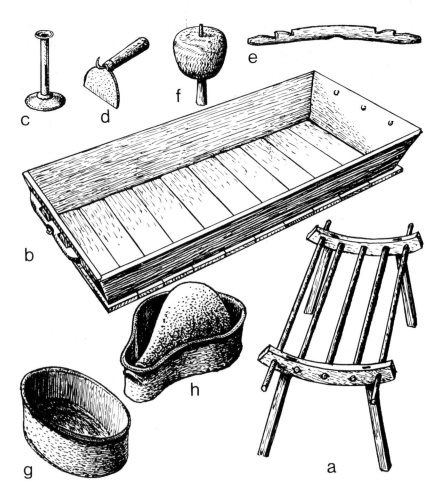

Equipment for pig killing, including (a) pig-stool, for holding the pig; (b) tub for scalding the pig; (c) a sheet iron candlestick, the round base providing an ideal tool for scraping off the pig's hair; (d) a pig scraper, incorporating a hook with which to pull off the toes; (e) a cammeril or hanger, which was inserted through the back legs of the pig so that it could be hung up; (f) a bacon mallet, used to beat the side of bacon into a tightly-rolled flitch; (g) this black lead-glazed redware pot, made in the Halifax potteries, was used for pickling pork; (h) made in similar materials, this pan was specially designed for curing hams.

the wane, for then the meat would not keep.[27] The operation was carried out either by the local butcher or by some amateur with the necessary experience. In some cases, the pig was lifted on to a block or pig-killing stool, being held there by half a dozen volunteers while its throat was cut with a sharp knife. One Wharfedale killer is remembered for his gentle reasurring manner, scratching its ears while murmuring 'Now then, hold they din!, Nobody's going to hurt thee!'[28] Alternatively, the pig's head would be held firmly in position by ropes passed round its snout or through the ring in its nose, while the killer swung his pole-axe into the centre of its forehead. Its throat was then cut and the blood collected for making the black puddings which were either baked in dishes in the oven or boiled in skins. Black puddings were usually eaten grilled, fried, or warmed in a Dutch oven.[29]

As soon as the bleeding had stopped, the pig was placed in a large wooden scalding tub which had probably been borrowed from a neighbour. After boiling water had been poured over the pig to loosen the hair, it was scraped off using either a purposely-made scraper or the rounded base of a sheet-iron candlestick, the latter being preferred since it was much gentler on the skin. When the pig had been cleaned, its carcase was hung up from a notched wooden cammeril or hanger inserted through the hind legs, remaining there until it had cooled and was ready for cutting up.

The offal and some smaller joints were often given away, or rather exchanged, being known as pig favours, pig cheer, or pig fry:[30]

> My wife's sent tha, an' ah've browt tha,
> Pork pie, crappins, spare-rib an' chine,
> An' when thoo kills they pig,
> We shall look for t'same o' thine.

Pig's fry could also be prepared as a hot richly-flavoured dish, eaten either with vegetables or with Yorkshire pudding:[31]

Pig's Fry

1 lb fry (heart, liver kidney, sweetbread, pork, cut in small pieces)
1 teaspoon each of sage & thyme
1 lb onions, chopped
1 pt water
Salt & pepper to taste
Cook in a covered dish for 1½ hours at 350°F gas mark 4. The fry can be thickened with a white sauce if necessary.

Alternatively, the fry could be cooked in the form of a round loaf called haslet, which, when cold, was sliced thinly and eaten like meat:

Haslet

1 lb fry, finely chopped or minced	1 pig's caul
1 lb minced pork	2 oz lard
1½ lb onions, finely chopped	1 teaspoon sage
Salt & pepper to taste	

Mix the ingredients thoroughly and wrap tightly within the caul, place in a greased dripping tin and bake for 1½ hours at 350°F gas mark 4.

Of the other offal, the intestines were either cleaned to make sausage skins or cooked ready for eating as chitterlings with salt and vinegar. The tongue, trotters and pig's cheek were made into brawn, or the trotters might be cooked separately to be eaten as pettitoes at tea. The spare ribs were roasted or made into spare-rib pie, while the fat was rendered down into lard which was stored in jars or in the pig's bladder, and the remaining scratchings or crappins eaten for supper with bread and salt.[32] Any small pieces of pork remaining might be made into polony (alias Bologna) sausage, their traditional bright red skins being a major feature of any Yorkshire pork butcher's window. Every part of the pig was used, including, it was said, the squeal, which was sold to the Scots to make bagpipes!

Fresh pork was eaten in the form of roasts and chops, but one of the specialities of the East riding was stuffed chine, a joint taken from the back of the pig, stuffed with parsley, tied in a cloth and boiled. The most important cuts were rarely eaten fresh, however, for they were much more useful in their preserved form.

In Craven, pork and mutton were preserved by being cut into small pieces, salted and placed in a crock in the oven. The fat then melted and sealed the contents. Every month or so the crock was heated up afresh, meat from a pig killed in autumn being kept through to harvest in this way.[33] [N.b: this method should not be used today, since it could easily lead to food poisoning.] For bacon and the smaller cuts, salting took place either on a stone slab in the cellar or outhouse, or, in the east Riding cottages, on the brick floor of the front room:[34]

To Salt a Pig

12 oz common salt
12 oz crushed saltpetre

Lay one flitch of bacon on a stone slab sprinkled with a little salt, and rub the salt hard into the skin. Turn the flitch flesh side upwards, cover it with a thick layer of salt, and spread about 4 oz of saltpetre on top. Do the same with the other flitch, and also with the face and hamkins, using only a little saltpetre, if any, on the latter. Let the pig remain in salt for three weeks, packing hessian bagging around it to keep the salt from wasting, and add more salt about the eighth day, then wash the bacon and hams, dry them well and hang them up in the kitchen for three weeks, then put them in calico bags and hang in a cool airy place.

One of the county's most famous products, the York ham, was reputedly first smoked over the oak chippings produced by the joiners building the Minster. Various recipes survive, most of them using a dry salting method rather than wet salting in brine, the local potteries at Heworth near York and around the Halifax area both producing special pear-shaped ham-pans in which the meat was cured. Usually the hams were smoked, as described in the following recipe in Thomas' *Housewifes Guide* of 1830, but in some parts of the county unsmoked hams were preferred.

To Cure Hams

Hang them a day or two; then sprinkle them with a little salt, and drain them another day; pound an ounce and a half of salt petre, the same quantity of bay salt, half an ounce of saltprunel, and a pound of the coarsest sugar. Mix these well and rub them into each ham, every day, for four days and turn it. If a small one, turn it every day for three weeks, if a large one a week longer, but do not rub it after four days. Before you dry it, drain and cover with bran. Smoke it ten days.

A thick slice of ham fried with eggs provided an excellent high tea, especially after a long walk across the moors, a popular late Victorian recreation. The Bradford millworkers and engineers returning home across Ilkley Moor on a Saturday or Sunday afternoon could look forward to the famous ham and egg teas served at Dick Hudson's or at the British Temperance Tea Rooms at Eldwick above Shipley Glen. Boiled ham was accepted as the main dish at any funeral tea, great pride being taken that the deceased had been 'put away' with ham. It was also served at other significant meals ranging from church and chapel functions to small private tea-parties.

In many parts of Yorkshire, particularly on patches of sand in the lowlands or on the light soils of the Wolds, Howardian Hills and the northern edge of the Vale of Pickering, rabbit farming produced a good return for the landlords.[35] Here, particularly during the early eighteenth century many large warrens had been established, their average size being around a thousand acres, all surrounded by sod walls and wooden palings, and under the control of a hired man. His major tasks were to prevent the escape of the rabbits into the adjacent farmland, to tend the sheep which grazed the warrens, and to catch and kill the rabbits as required. This might have been an extremely difficult job had it not been for the widespread use of the tipe. This device was described by George Young as 'a trap sunk in the ground between two fields, furnished with a trap door over which the creatures must pass in going through the wall from one field to another. The axle of the trap door works on a wheel, one tooth or pinion of which is turned at each fall; by which ingenious contrivance the trap can be set so as to take only a given number. Without this precaution, the rabbits might be caught in such numbers as to smother each other in the trap. The taking of them commences at the 5th November, and continues till Christmas, or sometimes Candlemas. Towards autumn, and in the winter, they are fed with turnips etc., and often, during frost and snow, with the branches of trees'. After slaughter the carcases were sold for meat in local towns and in the industrial centres of the West riding, transport being by means of covered carts containing from six to eight hundred couples strung on rods suspended across the cart one tier above another. In towns such as York the rabbit man tied a dozen or more rabbits to his belt and then proceeded to cry his wares around the streets. Whenever a customer was found, he deftly skinned the animals on the spot, presenting the carcase to the purchaser while retaining the skin for sale to the hat makers.

During the first half of the nineteenth century the warrens went into a decline largely as a result of the actions of improving landlords who found it difficult to establish hedges and adequately protect their crops in the presence of such large numbers of rabbits. Even so, the rabbit stew and rabbit pie remained welcome dishes on many tables, whether they were purchased, poached, or bred on the allotment garden, or backyard.

The Rabbit Man from Kendrew's 'Cries of York' published in the early 19th century.

'Rabbits! Rabbits
  Pray will you buy a couple?
Or if you choose to buy a leash,
  I'll not quite charge you double'.

Rabbits, along with perhaps pheasant, pigeons, chickens, beef, bacon, and any other meat which might be available, formed the basis for some of the best stews ever made in Yorkshire. Having been simmered very slowly in a black iron cauldron, the vegetables were put in last, and in order, so that each thing was done just right. These stews were not to be found in the country-house kitchens, however, for they were the speciality of travelling people, such as horse dealers or the itinerant Wolds Rangers who cooked their meals in the open air or disused cottages. The Rangers or tramps were so proud of their culinary skills that they actually held 'Drumming Up' competitions to prove who was their finest cook.[36]

Today, when most wild birds are protected by law, it is perhaps surprising to discover how widely they were used as food up to comparatively recent years. The natural history collections of the Leeds City Museum provide a particularly rich source of information for this practice, for quite a number of its ornithological specimens were purchased from Leeds Market, where they were offered for sale as meat. In the 1880s, for example, the market supplied water rail, corncrake, plover, curlew, redshank, snipe, knot, ruff, black-headed gull, blackbird, brambling, jackdaw, and greenfinch, in addition to established game birds such as grouse, ptarmigan and partridge. Even more surprising are the quantities of starlings killed in Scotland which were sold there during the 1940s. It is still possible to buy rooks for pie-making from shops in Malton, but with this exception, the eating of wild birds has now virtually ceased.

Perhaps the most popular of the birds traditionally eaten in Yorkshire was the sparrow. Agricultural workers would catch them in the evening by beating the sides of hay and corn stacks with large sieves, the sparrows being caught by the mesh as they flew out. One enterprising informant used to leave corn on the floor of his greenhouse for a week, so that the sparrows would become accustomed to entering through the open windows. Then, on Friday evening, the windows were closed so that he could kill the sparrows trapped inside by beating them in mid-flight with an old tennis racquet. The usual method, however, was to prop up one end of a sieve or a shallow box with a short stick, a scatter of corn or crumbs beneath the container soon attracting a number of birds. Using a long cord, the hidden catcher then pulled away the stick so that the birds were securely trapped ready for killing.

The mining communities were particularly fond of sparrow pie, and there are memories of songs relating how their grandfathers never went hungry as they always had sparrow pie to rely on. Since they worked on a shift system, the miners could spend many daytime hours in catching sparrows while tending their allotments, an opportunity denied to the neighbouring weavers who were always at work from early morning through to the evening. In Churwell a row of miners' houses officially called Primrose Walk was popularly known as 'Sparrow Barracks' by the local weavers who apparently viewed the eating of sparrows as something not quite respectable.[37] Sparrows were readily available to the gamekeepers, the following rather superior recipe coming from the family of Jim Grass, gamekeeper on the great Wentworth estates in South Yorkshire:[38]

Sparrow Pie

12 sparrows	Parsley & sweet herbs
Fat bacon	Pepper & salt
Mushrooms	Nutmeg
Shortcrust pastry	Mace
Egg for glaze	Good gravy

Pluck, singe, and draw the sparrows, then stuff with a little bacon, the mushrooms herbs and spices all chopped finely. Cover the bottom of a pie dish with bacon, sprinkle with herbs, salt and pepper, add the birds, and cover with fat bacon, herbs, salt and pepper. Roll out the pastry, cover the pie-dish, and glaze with beaten egg. After the pie has baked raise the crust, remove the fat bacon and pour in the gravy. Replace the crust, warm up, and serve.

The same family also made rook pies:

Rook Pie

Skin and draw six rooks, cutting out the backbones (for these give a very bitter taste). Season with salt and pepper, place in a deep pie dish with half a pint of water and a piece of butter on them. Make a tight crust, cover it with a piece of buttered paper and bake for two and a half hours.

Rooks were formerly eaten in large quantities, one poulterer in Southgate, Halifax often receiving five hundred at a time from local farmers. They sold at 4d(2p) each in 1918.[39] A lady from Halifax has told me that her father used to net rooks whenever company was expected. Twenty-four were required for a sufficiently large pie, the breasts being removed with the thumbs and the remainder thrown away.

The keeping of poultry in farms, rural cottages and urban tenements was always the responsibility of the woman of the house, providing her with a useful source of pin-money and a supply of eggs for her family. Since the hens stopped laying through the winter, various methods of preservation were employed, the eggs being immersed in deep earthenware pots full of water glass or lime kept in the cellar. This recipe was used by Ellen Bulmer of St. Mark's Villa, Leeds, in 1878:

To Preserve Eggs

Pour 2 gallons of water boiling hot on 2 quarts of quick lime & 25 lb salt. When quite cold mix into it 1 oz of Cream of Tartar. The following day put the eggs in.

Along the coast at Flamborough, Bempton and Speeton seabirds' eggs were collected for food from the 300 ft. chalk cliffs.[40] From early May to mid-June teams of four men proceeded to the top of the cliffs with all the necessary equipment. First a 300 ft. hand rope was secured with a clove hitch to a stake driven into the ground, and thrown over the edge. On this rope, the 'climmer' would pull himself up and down the cliff face as necessary. A 300 ft. waist rope was then passed through a pulley fastened to a further iron stake, one end being tied to the climmer's breeches harness, and the other passed around the waist of the anchor man. Then, equipped with a collecting bag over each shoulder, the climmer walked backwards over the cliff edge, descending to the nesting ledges where he began to gather the eggs of guillemots, razorbills, fulmar petrels, and kittiwakes. Gulls' eggs were usually destroyed, since they were bitter to the taste, and numerous gulls only brought further depredation on the more useful seabirds' eggs. Having cleared this section of the cliff, the climmer gave a single tug on his waist rope as a signal, and partly climbed, and was partly pulled, back up to the cliff top where the eggs were placed in wicker baskets before the whole operation was repeated further along the cliff. Some of the eggs were sold directly to egg-collectors as specimens, but the greatest number were either sold locally or passed on to dealers for sale at the markets in Bridlington or Leeds. Guillemot and razorbill eggs were the best for eating, being boiled or fried just like hens' eggs, but having a much firmer white. They could also be made into baked custards, known as 'sea-bird pies', or be sold for industrial use to a variety of manufacturers such as curriers, leather breeches makers, or the Hull sugar refinery.

Compared to today, poultry was eaten on relatively few occasions, a roast chicken or boiled fowl being served only when company was being entertained or when there was a family gathering. In many households chickens only appeared on the table at Christmastime, when they made a more economical substitute for the traditional roast goose or goose pie.

Geese had always been kept by farmers and those cottagers who enjoyed commoners' grazing rights, but around the early 1790s they began to be extensively farmed in upper Wensleydale.[41] Towards the end of August the farm servants or daytal men bought up all the geese they could obtain and drove them down in large flocks of about a thousand into Lancashire and the industrial West Riding where they were bought by farmers and fattened up on the stubble after harvest. Since the manufacturers were extremely fond of good roast geese, and did not begrudge paying for them, this trade brought a rapid rise in the price of geese in Wensleydale, a lean goose costing around three shillings (15p) in 1805, whereas they had cost only sixpence (2½p) or tenpence (4p) a few years earlier. By the end of the nineteenth century geese from Dent, Sedbergh, Garsdale, Swaledale, Mallerstang and Wensleydale were being driven by dealers down to the markets at Richmond and Darlington, this being a very slow business, for the drove could only move at half a mile an hour, with half an hour's rest every mile. Seven miles a day was good going, starting at 4 a.m. and finishing at 6 p.m. After the First World War the trade in geese largely declined, for families tended to be smaller, tastes were changing, and more economical dishes were preferred. As a result, relatively few geese are eaten today, even at Christmas, their place being taken by plump turkeys from Norfolk.

Whichever kind of meat was being served, it was always accompanied by the appropriate sauce or pickle. Pickled onions, mustard and horseradish enjoyed widespread use, as they did in the remainder of the country, but other pickles had a much greater regional significance. The usual accompaniment for beef, for example, was pickled red cabbage:[42]

To Pickle Red Cabbage

Cut off the stalks and outside leaves, and shred the remainder into a cullender, throw salt upon it in the shreddings; after it has drained two or three hours, put it into a jar, and then make a pickle of vinegar, cloves, mace, ginger, and sliced nutmeg; boil it and when it is cold, pour it over the cabbage, and it will be fit for use in twelve hours. Add salt to the pickle, if required.

For mutton, there was samphire, *Crithmum maritinum*, a fleshy-leaved plant which grew along the banks of the Humber, especially between Sunk Island and Stone creek. Having been gathered in August, it was washed two or three times to remove the sand, drained, and packed into jars. Malt vinegar was then boiled with pickling spice, about a quarter of an ounce to a pint, allowed to cool, and poured over the samphire. After leaving the covered jar for a few days, the samphire was then ready for eating.

For goose, mutton and veal, greensauce was made from sorrel, *Rumex acetosa*, otherwise known as 'saar grass'. Only the juice was used, this being extracted by crushing the leaves with a heavy ball rotated within a large bowl:[43]

To Make a Sauce for a Green Goose, 1741.

Take the juice of Sorrel, a little Butter, and a few scalded Gooseberries, mix them together and sweeten it to your Taste; you must not let it boil after you put in the Sorrel, if you do it will take off the Green. You must put this Sauce into a Bason.

Chapter 10

Fish

The area of the North Sea lying between the Dogger Bank and the Yorkshire coast was one of the most productive of all the fishing grounds surrounding these islands. From the sixteenth century at least it was visited each week between March and October by local fishermen in their 'five-men boats' or 'farms'.[1] Around 1800 these 58-ton clinker-built vessels measured 46ft. long by 16ft. 8in. broad, and had three masts carrying lug sails, their crew being made up of five men who all had shares in the fishing gear, a cook who had half a share, and a boy who received a small wage.

Since most of the fishing was carried out by series of hooks and lines, it was necessary to gather plentiful supplies of bait before setting off to sea. This was the responsibility of women such as the flither-girls who collected limpets along the rocky scaurs, some even going hand-over-hand down stout ropes stretched between the clifftop and the foreshore at Flamborough in order to obtain the required supplies.[2] These, together with mussels, crabs and sand eels, were used to bait common lines about 400 yards long furnished with from 280 to 400 hooks attached to the line by the same number of 'snoods' each one yard in length and spaced at equal distances. As the lines were baited they were carefully coiled up on flat oval wickerwork skeps, the hooks being laid regularly at one end. Stronger lines used in taking the larger fish were wrapped around wicker 'swaitches'. Known as 'haavres', they were just the same length as the common lines, but had only 90 to 100 hooks, these being baited at sea with pieces of herring or haddock just before they were shot into the water. Having set off to sea on Monday mornings during the season, the boat arrived at the fishing grounds and dropped anchor. Its two cobles, open boats about 25ft. long, then shot the lines across the current, fastening one to another and sinking them with small anchors or perforated stones. When the lines were hauled back into the cobles twice, or perhaps only once a day, their catch was removed and transferred to the five-men boat. Using this method, great quantities of cod, ling, halibut, turbot, haddock, coal-fish and skate were caught, together with whiting, pollack, thornback, sole, plaice, flounder, dab, gurnard etc. At the end of the week the whole catch was brought back to shore on Friday night or Saturday morning, when it was sold, the profits shared, and preparation started for the following week's fishing. Pairs of cobles also worked independently of the five-man boats, but were forced to stay close in to the coast and had to return to shore much more frequently to discharge their catch.

The herring fishing on the Yorkshire coast commenced about August, and was very productive. For herring the drift-net was used, a long net which hung down into the water from a series of cork floats spaced along its upper edge, one end being

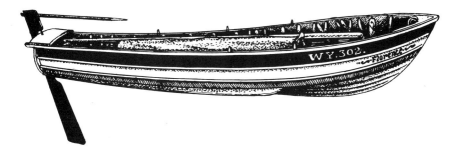

A Whitby coble, showing the deep bow, high shoulders and square stern which made this vessel ideal for launching into the waves and breaching stern first on the sloping shores of the North Yorkshire fishing villages.

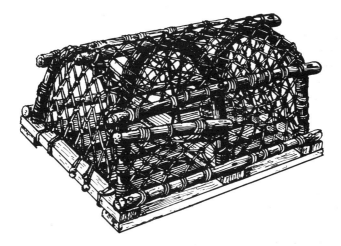

In the early nineteenth century crabs and lobsters were caught using bag-nets or 'trunks' fixed to iron hoops about twenty inches in diameter. From around the 1850s these were replaced by crab and lobster pots (such as the example seen here) which were baited and dropped on to the seabed from cobles, lines and floats enabling them to be drawn up to remove the catch.

made fast to the boat while the other reached out across the current. The main herring season lasted from mid-September to early November, when some forty boats left their local harbours to join the great fishing fleet which assembled down the coast at Yarmouth. Just before their departure the fishermen sent a piece of sea-beef on shore from each boat to their chief friends at the public houses. As a result, a bit of a supper' was held at which those who were going away could enjoy a good evening in the company of those who were staying behind. Similarly the Sunday just before they set sail was called 'boat Sunday', when all their friends from the neighbouring villages came to bid them farewell.[3]

In the course of these few weeks each vessel might easily catch 300,000 herrings which sold for around £200 on the Yarmouth quays. On returning home, the boats

After being drysalted overnight, the herring were kippered by being threaded on to long sticks and hung up in the smoke of smouldering oak chippings as seen here in Mary Ellen Best's painting of a herring curing house at Whitby in October, 1837.

were then laid up for the winter, although cobles carrying three men continued to fish through to the following spring.

Most of the fish landed on the Yorkshire coast was sold fresh to supply the markets at Whitby, Scarborough and Newcastle, from where, particularly from Whitby, great quantities were carried inland. Every year some 750 to 900 tons were distributed in this way, teams of pack ponies equipped with panniers proceeding by the way of Pickering, Malton and York across to the towns of the industrial West Riding.

During the summer months some 150 to 180 tons of cod, ling, skate and coal-fish were preserved at the coast by being cut into pieces and salted by the women. After passing through brine and pickle, it was spread out on the beach to dry, the smell it produced at this time being disagreeable in the extreme.[4] Dried fish was usually purchased by London merchants or their agents who might pay £20-£30 a ton in good years. In the winter months the surplus fish was salted down in barrels, each one containing from 22 to 24 stone of cod or ling selling at around £2.

Up to the 1820s locally caught herrings were sold fresh at the markets, but within

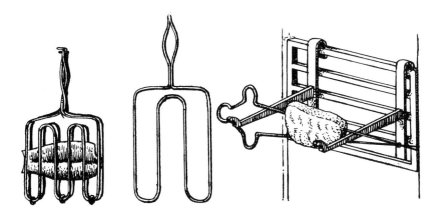

In the home, the fish could be cooked between thin wire grid irons (left), on a grid iron placed over the firebars (centre), or on 'speets' hung on racks in front of the fire (right), the latter two both being used at Staithes.

the next ten years they were being preserved by kippering. Having been cleaned and split, they were packed overnight in coarse-grained salt, the coarser the better, since it prevented the fish from lying too close together.[5] Next morning long sticks were passed through their eyes and, thus arranged in rows, they were hung from beams in specially-built smoke-houses where the fumes from smouldering oak chips slowly changed their colour from silver to burnished copper.

During the 1830s the North Sea began to be fished by trawlers from Brixham in Devon who worked out of Hull and Scarborough.[6] In contrast to the traditional Yorkshire drift nets, their beam trawls had conical nets a hundred feet long with 36ft. mouths kept open by means of a horizontal beam attached to the trawler by a hauser or warp. As the trawl was dragged across the seabed it efficiently scooped up all the fish lying in its path. During a spell of bad weather in 1843 the Brixham fishermen were driven off the Dogger Bank while their nets were still down. When the nets were drawn up they found that they had made the biggest catch of sole that any of them had ever seen. They had discovered a rich new deepwater fishing ground which came to be known as the Silver Pits. Over the next few years more than a thousand Devon men moved to Hull and Scarborough to take advantage of the new grounds, while the French and Dutch also came to poach its rich produce.[7] Soon the use of ice to preserve the fish, and the development of the fleeting system by which the smacks could remain at sea for three months, their catch being transferred to the shore by series of carriers, had revolutionised the local fishing industry. A contributory factor in this great expansion was the development of an efficient distribution system from the ports. As early as 1836 dealers had been able to transport their fish from Whitby as far as Pickering by rail, but in the 1840s Hull, Bridlington, Filey, Scarborough and Whitby were all connected to the major industrial conurbations of the West Riding by efficient railway services. Fish could now arrive at the markets only a few hours after being landed, in contrast to taking half a week or more to traverse the 70 or 80 miles along the dusty roads by pack pony.

Steam power was also adapted to produce more efficient fishing vessels, steam paddle trawlers and screw paddle trawlers both appearing in the 1880s. From this time there was no shortage of fish, even miles inland, a fact which enabled that great institution of the northern industrial towns, the fish and chip shop, to come into existence. Some time before 1880, 'Granny' Duce had established two of three combined greengrocery and fish and chip shops in Bradford, but by the end of the century hundreds of these shops were providing cheap, hot, and satisfying takeaway meals for thousands of working families.[8]

In the home, fish was cooked in a variety of fairly simple ways, being fried, baked, boiled, simmered in milk, or grilled before the fire. This was usually carried out by gripping the fish between a pair of light wire grids and holding them close to the firebars, or putting it on a heavier grid placed over the glowing coals. Along the northern section of the Yorkshire coast, pieces of fish were also speared on sharp-pointed iron tongs called 'speets' hung on a pair of racks which hooked on to the topmost firebar. Ling or 'woof' pie was a speciality of these fishing towns, the following version coming from Scarborough:[9]

Ling Pie

1 lb ling, cut in pieces	½pt. milk
4 oz bacon, cut in small pieces	Salt & pepper
2 hard boiled eggs, sliced	1 oz flour
2 oz chopped onion	12 oz puff pastry

Arrange half the ling in a greased pie dish, season with salt and pepper and sprinkle with a little flour. Add half the bacon, egg, and onion, then the remaining ling, seasoning, flour, and bacon, egg and onion. Pour the milk over all, cover with the pastry, and bake for 10 minutes at 425°F gas mark 7 then at 350°F gas mark 4 for about 20 minutes until cooked through with golden brown pastry.

Of all the fish sold in the industrial areas, the herring was the most useful, especially in one of its preserved forms. In the Scammonden valley in the South Pennines, for example, groups of farmers used to club together to buy barrels of salt herrings for consumption through the winter. These were usually soaked in cold water before being cooked. Kippers meanwhile were known as 'soldiers'; they were described as 'red herrin' – sea beef wi' forty ribs tul t'inch; can be scented hawf a mile off, or a mile wi' a stiff breeze blowing' fro' t'quarter it's in!'[10] For a better quality of preservation, the following recipe might be used:[11]

To Pickle Herrings and Mackerel

Cut off the heads and tails of your fish, gut them, wash them and dry them well: then take two ounces and a half of salt-petre, three quarters of an ounce of Jamaica pepper, pounded small, an ounce of sweet marjoram and thyme, chopped small, mix them together and put some

Cockles and mussels were both popular in Yorkshire. This impressive covered dish was made to serve these hot cooked shellfish in the home of the Routh family of Gayle in Wensleydale for whom it was made by the potters of Burton in Lonsdale in 1815.

within and without the fish, lay them on an earthen pan, the roes at the top, and cover them with white wine vinegar, then set them in an oven, not too hot, for two hours. This is for fifteen, but after this rule do as many as you please.

There are some 3,000 miles of beautiful clean rivers and feeder streams in Yorkshire, but freshwater fish rarely if ever appeared on the tables of most working families. The upper reaches of the rivers of South and West Yorkshire were far too polluted with the effluent of chemical plants, dyeworks, soap factories and tanneries etc. to support any amount of fish life. Weirs and locks built to control and harness the power of the rivers tended to inhibit the movement of fish, while many stretches of water were preserved for private fishing. Even so, quite a number of freshwater fish were taken both legally and illegally within the county.

Every spring the salmon returned from their feeding grounds around Greenland to find their way back up their native rivers, passing up the Esk or the Humber and its tributaries.[12] In the Humber estuary and on entering the Ouse they had to run the gauntlet of the click nets, particularly when they shoaled back towards the sea at the start of the ebb tide after failing to negotiate Naburn Locks just below York. Standing in an eleven-foot boat, the oarsman manoeuvred into the path of a salmon swimming just below the surface, so that the netsman could catch it in his click-net, a large net rather like an outsize landing net. In this way salmon up to fifty pounds

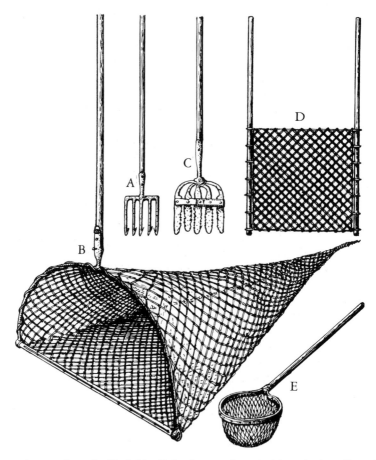

Fishing equipment from the Yorkshire Dales. It comprises a) a leister for impaling salmon, b) a salmon 'cowp' net from Teesdale, c) a glave from Richmond, its tines being barbed to firmly grip the eels, d) a Swaledale prodding net, used to catch eels hiding in hollows in the river banks e) a Wensleydale 'Crabbing' net in which crayfish were scooped up from the river while still clinging to the bait.

or more might be caught. The next obstacle facing the fish was the draft nets operating in the lower reaches of the Ouse below Naburn. These were long nets worked by two men, one holding an end on the bank while his partner towed the other end in a broad sweep three quarters of the way across the river, thus trapping all the fish within that area. From Naburn, the salmon proceeded up the Swale and Ure where they might be caught with rod and line, but frequently more effective but highly illegal methods were used. In click hooking, three large fish hooks bound back to back on to the end of a line were put into the river where the fish were expected to lie. Then, when a fish was within reach, it was suddenly jerked or clicked up, catching the fish in the belly so that it could be hauled out of the water. It is recorded that up to 30 salmon a day have been caught at Wensley using click hooks.

In blazing, which took place at night, a tar light fixed in the cleft of a strong stick was held over an area of shallow water, the strange light attracting all the salmon within sight to this spot. While their attention was taken, a second man entered the water and came up behind the fish so that he could impale them on his leister, an iron fork with a number of sharp barbed prongs mounted at the end of a six- or eight-foot shaft. The leister was also used to spear salmon which were resting beneath the tree roots at the bank after they had been tired out by being chased around the river for hours by men throwing stones from both banks. Nets were also used to take salmon, one from Teesdale being preserved in the collections of the North of England Open Air Museum at Beamish. It has a seven-foot long conical net mounted on to a four-foot diameter semicircular frame which was swept through the shallow waters in the path of the oncoming fish.

To catch trout, some boys in the Dales used a crude but effective version of the leister – a sharpened kitchen knife tied on to the end of a stick, but tickling was by far the most widespread method of poaching.[13] In addition to being caught in the rivers, trout were taken from specially stocked waters ranging from artificial ponds to mill dams, nets being used to clear them from time to time when only the larger fish were removed, the remainder being returned for further growth.

The eels found in Yorkshire's rivers were formerly caught for food, even though they are rarely, if ever, eaten today. Usually they were taken with glaves made by the local blacksmiths, pieces of old cart spring providing the favoured material for forging the broad barb-edged tines between which the eels were caught. In Swaledale a prodding net made of a square of netting mounted between two long poles was thrust about in holes under the banks and other likely places to ensnare the eels, while at Middleham in Wensleydale a system of hooks was used. About a hundred hazel or willow sticks some two yards long were stuck into the banks of the Ure about twelve yards apart, each one having a long line with two hooks baited with dew worms tied on their tips. The larger eels might weigh up to $3\frac{1}{2}$lb, although most were about 2lb or less.[14]

To take crayfish, the small lobster-like crustaceans probably introduced into Wensleydale in the sixteenth century by Sir Christopher Metcalfe, the men of Bainbridge also used lines hung from sticks stuck into the banks. Instead of hooks, however, they used dog's flesh or beast livers, weighing about half a pound, for bait, these being set five or six yards apart in the deep places amongst stones or hollow banks where the fish gathered. Every halfhour or so the fisherman suddenly raised the bait just sufficient to admit his cray-net underneath, then lifting it out completely to enable him to remove anything up to twenty crayfish hanging on to the meat. Having replaced the bait, he then transferred his catch to a wooden store chest bored full of holes and moored to the bank by a strong cord. When he had caught a sufficiently large number of crayfish, he then sold them to the fashionable watering places in the neighbourhood, where they were greatly appreciated stewed, potted, or in the form of soup.

The other freshwater fish were usually fried, grilled or poached, the eels being skinned and boiled, stewed or spitchcocked by being skewered into a circle, dipped in egg, breadcrumbed, and cooked before the fire.[15]

Chapter 11

Puddings

Here's to Yorkshire, my lads,
The land of good cheer;
The home of the pudding
Well known far and near,
Wed a lass who can make one
Is the theme of my song;
But so long as she's Yorkshire
You cannot go wrong.[1]

Of all the regional foods associated with Yorkshire, none can compare with the Yorkshire pudding, justly celebrated in poetry and prose by writers and performers as diverse as Stanley Holloway and Abe Clegg. Great mystique surrounded its preparation, and it was popularly claimed that it could only be made successfully by a native of the county. Light, slightly crisp, and served with real beef gravy, it was one of the county's greatest delicacies:[2] 'There's nowt nicer when it is nice, wi' a sup o' gooid beef gravy – an' when ah sez gravy ah mean gravy, not weshin' up wotter – but ther's plenty 'at can't make a Yorkshire puddin' fit to eyt. They'll gi'e tha a gurt dollop o' clammy soggy stuff at looks an' tastes as mich like putty as owt, an' wi' gurt lumps o' raw flah i't middle; or happen it'll be same as a buffalo hide wi' black blisters all ower it'.

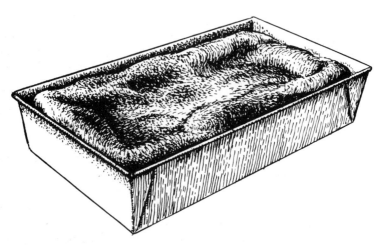

A Yorkshire Pudding.

The Yorkshire pudding was originally baked in a dripping pan placed beneath the meat as it slowly rotated in front of a hot fire. As the juices dripped from the joint they were absorbed into the pudding, giving it a unique flavour. The method is clearly described in Hannah Glasse's *Art of Cookery* of 1796:

A Yorkshire Pudding

Take a quart of milk and five eggs, beat them up well together, and mix them with flour till it is of a good batter, and very smooth; put in a little salt, some grated nutmeg and ginger; butter a dripping or frying pan and put it under a piece of beef, mutton, or a loin of veal that is roasting, and then put in your batter, and when the top side is brown, cut it in square pieces, and turn it, and then let the under side be brown: then put it in a hot dish as clean of fat as you can, and send it to table hot.

John Bramley, a weaver living at Bramley near Leeds, recorded the same scene, in which:

> Ther' t' meyt hung dahn afore t'fire to rooast,
> Ther's t'puddin' on t'brandree afore it ta tooast,
> Potatoes top o't' hob, they'll be don enif sooin,
> But Ah think tha can weive a few more bobbins bi nooin.

When ranges came into use, both the meat and dripping pan tended to be transferred into the oven, the Yorkshire pudding now being baked on one side only, instead of being cooked on both sides by the radiant heat of the fire. The usual recipe was as follows:

Yorkshire Pudding

2 eggs	½ pint milk and water
4 oz flour	Pinch of salt

Mix the flour and salt in a basin, and make a hole in the centre. Break in the eggs and gradually add the milk and water, beating the mixture continually to obtain a smooth batter. Put a little dripping (hot from the roast if possible) into a dripping pan and pre-heat in the oven until smoking hot. Pour in the batter, and bake for 30 minutes at 400° F, gas mark 6, until crisp and brown, then cut into squares and serve immediately.

This basic recipe could be enriched by the addition of a wide variety of savoury or sweet ingredients, including:

1. 4 oz seasoned minced meat sprinkled over the batter when it had just been poured into the pan.
2. A small onion, sliced thinly and separated into rings.
3. A large onion, boiled, chopped finely, and mixed into the batter with a teasponful of dried sage. This was served with mutton or pork.
4. 4 oz Cheshire cheese, finely grated and mixed into the batter.
5. 2 oz currants mixed into the batter. This too was served with roast pork.

6. A large baking apple, peeled, sliced, and spread over the batter when it has just been poured into the dripping pan.
7. A large baking apple, peeled, cored and grated, and mixed into the batter.
8. 1 or 2 sticks of forced rhubarb cut in short pieces and mixed into the batter. This was served with a sweet white sauce at the end of the meal.

The plain Yorkshire pudding could also be spread with any of the following:

9. Treacle or golden syrup.
10. Raspberry jam.
11. Raspberry jam and malt vinegar, to give a fruity 'sweet and sour' taste.
12. Raspberry or blackberry vinegar, made by washing 1lb of the fruit, and soaking it in a pint of malt vinegar in a covered basin for three or four days, stirring occasionally. Strain off the juice, and add a pound of sugar to each pint. Boil for 15 minutes, cool, strain and bottle.
13. Mint sauce.
14. Yorkshire ploughman's salad, described by Eliza Acton in 1845 as a tablespoon of treacle mixed with two tablespoons of malt vinegar and a pinch of black pepper, *or:*
15. Mint sauce salad, made with a handful of mint, finely chopped, together with finely shredded lettuce and spring onions all dressed with sugar and vinegar.
16. Parsley sauce.
17. Butter and sugar.

Although the Yorkshire pudding was cooked with the roast, it was traditionally eaten quite separately as a first course, the effect being to take the edge off the appetite. The motto 'Them as has most pudding can have most meat' was well known in families where meat was a great luxury. Squares of pudding left over from the first course, or specially baked to use up the surplus batter, could be served as a dessert with one of the sweet accompaniments listed above.

In some households, including the farms of the East Riding, the Yorkshire pudding might be replaced by a suet pudding:

Suet Pudding

6 oz plain flour	Pinch of salt
3 oz suet	⅓pt. cold water or milk
2 teaspoons baking powder	

Mix the dry ingredients, and work into a soft dough with the cold water. Having preheated a walnut-sized piece of fat in a hot dripping pan, place the dough on the hot fat, turn it over, and cook for 20-30 minutes at 400°F, gas mark 6. Alternatively, the dough can be divided into a number of balls and put in the fat at the side of a joint of roasting beef 20 minutes before it has finished cooking. When they have risen and gone crisp, turn them over, and leave until the meat is done.

Light and crisp on the outside, moist, spongy and absorbent within, it ideally complemented the roast beef and gravy, as well as adding satisfying bulk to the entire meal.

The other pudding traditionally served as a separate course at the start of the meal was the seasoned or herb pudding. From the seventeenth century herb puddings of this type had been cooked by being tied in a cloth and simmered for an hour and a half, but the introduction of the oven enabled them to be baked as slab-like puddings in dripping pans.[3] In our family, we used this recipe:

Season Pudding

1 lb white bread	Chopped sage & marjoram
6 oz suet	Grated nutmeg
2 eggs, beaten	Salt & pepper
1 lb boiled & chopped onions	Boiling water or milk

Break the bread into a bowl and pour over sufficient boiling water or milk to barely soak it. Mash with a fork, and mix in the remainder of the ingredients. Spread evenly in a greased dripping pan and bake for 30 minutes at 400° F, gas mark 6 until crisp and brown on top. Other versions added two to four tablespoonfuls of coarse oatmeal to the mixture.

Particularly in the East Riding, puddings were eaten either as part of the main course, such as the dumplings served with hot boiled meats, or as substantial main courses in their own right:

Pork Pudding

Pastry:	8 oz belly pork cut in strips
8 oz flour	1 onion, finely chopped
4 oz suet	1 teaspoon sage
1 teaspoon baking powder	large potato, finely sliced
Pinch of salt	
¼ pt. cold water	

Line a greased pudding basin with the pastry, reserving sufficient to make a lid. Fill the basin with alternate layers of pork and the remainder of the ingredients, pour in ⅛ pt. of water, put on the lid, and tie down with a pudding cloth. Steam for three hours.

Bacon Roll Pudding

Pastry:	Filling:
1½ lb flour	1 lb bacon fat
12 oz suet	6 apples, peeled and sliced
1 teaspoon salt	1 large onion, peeled and sliced
½–¾ pt, cold water	

Boil the fat bacon for half an hour, then cut it up into slices. Roll the pastry into a thin sheet, and lay over it the slices of bacon, then the apples and onion. Roll up the pastry, enclosing the bacon etc., then wrap it in a cloth, tie it securely at each end, and boil for two hours.

The old-style boiled puddings intended for eating as a dessert at the end of the meal tended to be extremely plain, being made from wheat flour, barley or oatmeal mixed with suet and cold water. Occasionally currants might be added to make a spotted dog', or the pudding might be served either with custard, with a hot treacle and water sauce, or with Yorkshire dip. According to the dietary of the York Female Friendly Society's school, this consisted of half a pint of vinegar, a quart of water, three tablespoons of flour and half a pound of treacle all boiled together for a few minutes. From the mid-nineteenth century, when richer foodstuffs became more readily available, and steaming tended to replace boiling as the usual method of cooking puddings, they became much lighter, sweeter, and flavoursome. With the addition of sugar, treacle, jam, lemons, fresh soft fruit, dried fruit, figs, ginger or eggs, a whole range of delicious new puddings began to be served in many working households.

The introduction of ranges enabled puddings to be baked, a much simpler and more convenient arrangement, since the ingredients had only to be poured into a greased dish and put into the oven rather than being tied up in a pudding cloth and boiled for hours. This method was particularly suitable for making milk puddings, such as the native bread-and-butter or barley varieties, but baked puddings became much more popular when the expanding empire trade enabled every small village grocery to stock supplies of sago from Sarawak, tapioca from the Straits Settlements, and rice from Burmah and Japan, together with semolina and macaroni from Italy. With these materials at her disposal, the housewife could now make excellent cheap, filling puddings whenever they were required.

West Yorkshire and the upper Calder Valley in particular, was the home of the dock pudding.[5] Unlike the usual varieties of baked and boiled farinaceous puddings, this was made from the Passion dock or sweet dock, *polygonum bistorta*, and closely resembled the Welsh laverbread in its appearance and use. In springtime the fresh young leaves are still gathered by the carrier-bag full, together with nettles, and prepared as follows:

Dock Pudding

1 lb Passion dock leaves	2–4 oz oatmeal
1 lb young nettles	Salt & pepper to taste
2 onions, chopped small	

Wash the dock and nettle leaves thoroughly, and separate them from the stalks. Then either mince them with the onions, or place them directly in a saucepan, before adding the salt and pepper and boiling until soft and tender. Stir in the oatmeal, and continue stirring occasionally as the pudding simmers for a further 15-20 minutes. Serve for breakfast or supper, by frying the mixture in bacon fat, and dishing up with bacon and fried potatoes. It was reputed to have good tonic qualities, 'cleaning the blood' and curing spots and pimples.

Chapter 12

Home-Brewed Beers and Whisky

In the seventeenth and eighteenth centuries home brewing and home baking formed an essential part of the wife's role in virtually every household, but by the opening of the nineteenth century both were entering a period of rapid decline. The main problems facing the home brewer were the availability of fuel and the high cost of the necessary equipment. In the agricultural areas of the County, particularly in the Vale of York and the East Riding, the enclosure of the commons had robbed the labourer of the vast heaths where he had been able to gather sticks, logs and brushwood merely for the trouble of it. Now he had to buy his fuel, or risk pilfering from the hedgerows. This disappearance of free fuel, and the prohibitive cost of the coal brought in from County Durham or south-west Yorkshire, had profound effects on his diet and standard of living generally. From Old Malton in the early 1840s, it was reported that all the labourers had ceased to brew at home, a situation which was typical of many parts of the country.[1] It has been calculated that between 1801 and 1830 a fifth of England's beer was home-brewed. By 1850 this had dropped to one seventh, and by 1870 to one fortieth.[2] The only area of Yorkshire where this rate of decline did not take place was in the industrial belt concentrated around the textile and steel towns of the West Riding. Here there were vast reserves of cheap coal, and the tradition of working-class home brewing was thus allowed to continue through into the 1920s or '30s, while even today one estate brewery continues to produce excellent beer for home consumption.[3] However plentiful the supply of fuel might be, it was still necessary to have access to all the required plant, including a vessel to boil the water in, a mash tub, brewing tub, hop tems and briggs, besides a funnel, barrels or 'drink pots' which, as a group, were beyond the means of many poor families. They therefore worked on a co-operative basis, borrowing and loaning the various items so that they could all brew at regular intervals. In Pudsey in the 1820s, for example, it was hardly possible to walk through the village without seeing some item of brewing equipment being carried from one house to another.[4]

Before brewing could commence, it was necessary to assemble all the various ingredients. Malt was purchased from the local shops, where individual customers might grind it in a small mill kept for the purpose.[5] Hops were usually purchased too, although some cottagers preferred to grow their own, while other herbs for flavouring and enriching the beer were gathered in the dry-bottomed fields at earliest sunrise when still wet with dew:

> She goes and gathers in the fields,
> As wild bees gather honey;
> Her apron full of pleasant things –

125

The joyous and the sunny . . ...
The low of cattle on the hills,
The smell of grouse and heather,
She mixes with her malt and hops
And boils them well together.[6]

Coltsfoot (*Tussilago farfara*) was reputed to improve the medicinal quality of the beer, being 'good for the blood', Alecost (*Tanacetum balsamita*) gave a sharper tang, while ale-hoof or ground ivy (*Nepeta glechoma*) could be used instead of hops.[7] As Culpeper advised, the latter was 'good to tun up with new drink, for it will clarify it in a night, that it will be fitter to be drank the next morning'.

The selection of a yeast of good quality was of the greatest importance, some women being noted for always having nice yeast on their beer. There was always much lending and borrowing of yeast, the brewers arranging with each other to brew at stated times in turn so as to ensure a continuing supply. Public houses also provided yeast for the domestic brewers, but this, like the German dried yeast introduced in the late nineteenth century, was usually considered to be a second-rate alternative to the home-brewed variety.[8]

The water for brewing was first boiled in the set pot, a large cast-iron cauldron built into a brick casing incorporating a small firebox and ashpit. It was situated between the main fireplace and the outside wall in most kitchens in the industrial areas of West and South Yorkshire. Around Sheffield, where it was called the potside, its brickwork was painted red with white mortar to give a colourful chequered design.[9] Having cooled to around 165°F, the water was poured on to the ground malt lying in the mash tub. The size of this glazed earthenware vessel varied greatly according to the size of the household. Most were of about five gallons capacity, but the largest could receive over thirty-six gallons, sufficient to brew an entire barrel of beer. Near the base of the vessel a round bung-hole was usually provided. Into this a wooden spigot or tap was driven, its inner opening being shielded by the betony, a basket-like framework of twigs which effectively prevented the tap from being blocked by the grains of malt.[10]

The volume of water to malt was normally three to three and a half gallons of water to every two gallons of malt, although for special occasions, such as Christenings, weddings and funerals, two gallons of water would be used to mash an equal volume of malt, resulting in a very strong brew, similar to today's barley wine. Having been thoroughly stirred with a long elm paddle and allowed to stand for an hour or two covered with layers of white flannel, the sweet brown wort was run off through the tap into the brewing tub. A horsehair tempse or sieve supported on a wooden brig or trow strained off the smaller particles of malt grains. A second and a third mashing of the same malt would then be completed, each progressively decreasing in quality. In Sheffield, the beer brewed from the first mashing was called 'Romtom', that from the second 'middle mie', and that from the third 'pinkie', while in Todmorden the same products were known as 'Stingo', 'Tip Lash' and 'grout'.[11]

Whatever its quality, each separate batch of wort was then boiled with hops to impart the characteristic bitter flavour and to improve its keeping qualities. Once it

Home Brewing Equipment. This group of utensils from the Pennine hills of south and west Yorkshire includes (left to right); a) an elm paddle for stirring the mash (A.2.62); b) a lading-pot used to bale hot water from the set pot on to the malt; c) a mash pot (A.1.62); d) a sycamore (?) spigot; e) a horse-hair tempse for straining off the malt and hops (A.2.62); f) a Y-shaped brig to support the tempse (A.5.62), and a rectangular brig; g) a sycamore (?) yeast basin (A.28.62); h) a stoneware yeast-or barm-pot. (a & c-g) were presented to the Tolson Memorial Museum, Huddersfield, by Mrs Whitaker of Cawthorne in 1947.)

had been returned through the tempse into the brewing tub, the wort was allowed to cool to around 75°F before the yeast was 'set on'. Thermometers were never available, and so the accurate assessment of temperature was solely a matter of personal skill, one which largely determined the brewer's ability to make good beer.

As fermentation proceeded, a light foaming head rose above the surface of the wort, some of this being skimmed off with a wooden yeast basin for use in starting a fresh brew. The remainder of the first crop of yeast was then 'ding in' by being stirred into the wort, aerating it and promoting further fermentation. If the

Brewing Jars. These black-glazed redware vessels were sufficiently large to brew a complete barrel of beer. The first example was collected from the brewhouse of Tatefield Hall near Harrogate, while the second comes from the Halifax area. Both are in the collections of Shibden Hall Museum, Halifax.

fermentation did not proceed as well as it should have done, particularly in the cold winter months, the cause was often attributed to witchcraft. The remedy was to throw a piece of red-hot chain into the wort, thus mastering the witch, and allowing a vigorous fermentation to proceed. This charm was always successful, since it effectively brought the wort up to the required working temperature.[12] Joseph Baron recorded the following delightful story of a mouse which tumbled into the brewing tub or 'gilevat' full of fermenting wort: 'T' cat sat watchin on it. When it was like to drown, it says to 't cat 'If tha'll help me out, and' let me shake mysen, tha shall eat me'. So t'cat agreed, an helped it out; but t'mouse ran off into its hole. Says t'cat 'I thowt tha said I mun eat thee'. 'Eah', says mouse wi a grin, 'but folk says owt when they're i' drink!'[13]

Once the wort had completely finished working, it was tunned into either barrels or earthenware drink pots in which it was kept ready for use. Occasionally the cottagers might be given surplus 'unfermented grout but publicans who brewed their own beer. To this they added a little sugar or treacle, and yeast, the liquid then being poured into bottles and allowed to work out at the neck overnight. By morning this 'treacle drink' was ready for use as small beer, either being drunk alone, or mixed with old milk and taken with porridge. Weak grout might also be drunk in a fresh and heady state, especially if strong drink was not available.[14] It was no real substitute, however, and weak, sour beer was never popular. This can be seen in the various dialect names it received, including 'prich', 'blashment', 'belsh' (since it caused eructation), 'swipes', 'tinsey-winsey' or even 'belly-vengeance', of which he who drank the most certainly got the worst share.[15]

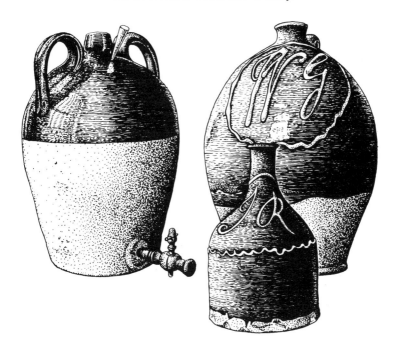

Drink Pots. (left) This drink pot in black-glazed redware, with its spiggot and spile peg, is a typical product of the Halifax potteries.

(right) The drink pot and smaller forenoon drinking bottle seen here come from the Midhope Potteries in South Yorkshire, the former being made for Mr. W. Grayson. (Sheffield City Museums nos. 1921.50 & 1921.49.)

In contrast, the strong beers from the first mashing, the 'Stingo', 'Romtom', 'Ale of the Hunter's Moon', 'Floorum' or 'lying down ale' always enjoyed the fulsome praise of its drinkers. It would keep for long periods and improved its quality when stored in the constant temperature of a cool cellar. As an alternative, sheepwashing ale, once called the strongest ale in Yorkshire, was buried in peat by the shepherds of the Saddleworth moors ready for the washing day. It is remembered that two old farming brothers once buried four gallons of their ale for the haytime, but although they spent several days looking for it when they were about to start mowing, they never could find it, and presumably it still lies beneath the slopes of Woodward Hill.[16] Wherever it matured, the strong home-brewed ale had 'cream an' sparkle, an' made folks feel all of a glow under their waistcoats, an' ivvryboddy aboght 'em lively'.[17] Similarly Ammon Wrigley commemorated the qualities of the home-brewed ale of Friezland near Saddleworth:

> When e'er I drink of Friezland ale,
> Drawn from an old brown bottle;
> I feel as if a summer morn
> Was running down my throttle;

> As white as milk when newly drawn,
> And never milk is richer!
> With creamy puffs, in bunches blown
> Like Roses in a pitcher.[18]

On cold days, or after a long winter journey, the home-brewed ale could be made into a number of rich and comforting hot drinks. For mulled ale, the liquor was heated almost to boiling point with a little brown sugar, cinnamon and cloves. Having been poured into a warm jug, a spoonful of ginger, a little grated nutmeg and half a glass of rum or brandy were added to each pint to produce a drink which would drive out the deepest chill.[19]

Mulled ale was fairly costly to make, and so tended to be a middle-class drink. Its working-class equivalent was the hot ale posset, the ale being heated, spiced, and sweetened with treacle. This formed a major element in the entertainment provided at weddings besides being served on rive-kite Sunday in the East Riding, when farm lads and lasses returned home at Martinmas. As an alternative, they might have drunk 'Whistlejacket' made from gin, hot water and treacle, a similarly satisfying beverage.[20]

In the weaving settlements of the West Yorkshire Pennines, meanwhile, a drink called 'dog's-nose' has maintained its popularity from at least the middle of last century. As cold and healthy as its namesake, it is made by pouring a tot of rum into the bottom of a nearly-finished glass of beer.

In most farmhouses and on the great estates beer was brewed in quantity for use both at table and for refreshment in the field. There might be a variety of 'beer-jobs', ranging from carpet beating to chimney sweeping and tree felling, but the main distribution of beer took place at haytime and harvest. Even the Middleton Colliery pay books record the supply of beer to the haymakers:[21]

31st December, 1814 By cash paid Jaques & Nell for Beer
got during Haymaking in 1813 & 1814

£13. 19. 11d.

or

21st Sept-5th Oct, 1831, Mrs Bedford
Ale to Workmen (Hay Making)

£3. 8. 9d.

On these occasions the ale was carried into the field and distributed among the workers. On the Hickleton estates, for example, 'Owd Arry' used to carry a green two-gallon can into the field, where everyone formed a circle, sitting or standing according to the state of the weather. He then proceeded to 'bole aht' the ale, giving each person a mugful using a single battered tin mug or a horn beaker each holding about half a pint.[22]

In North Yorkshire, the ale might be drunk with the lowance or down-dinner taken in the field in the middle of the afternoon, but in the West Riding, from the Craven dales down to Sheffield it was quite usual for the ploughmen to drink both in the morning, or forenoon, and in the afternoon whatever work was in hand. As Robert Brown commented in 1799, it was 'a ridiculous custom, and ought to be abolished without loss of time. What can be more absurd than to see a ploughman stopping his horses half an hour in a cold winter day, drinking ale? [It is] an encouragement to idleness, and, from wasting much time, a great object to improvements'.[23] His objection carried little weight, however, and the ploughmen continued to carry their 'forenoon drinkings' into the field every working day in one of the purpose-made bottles available from one of the local potteries.

Home-brewed beer also formed an important part of the diet of the country's foundrymen and forgemen. In a single day of intensive labour in the hot, dry furnace shops, with temperatures ranging between 90° and 140°F, a man could lose up to 20lb a day in sweat. To replace this great volume of liquid, from eight to twenty-four pints of home-brewed were consumed throughout each shift. It had to be a comparatively weak drink, for this quantity of strong ale would soon have rendered the man totally unfit for hot work, and thus led to a 75% reduction in his wages.[24] At some factories, particularly during the latter half of the nineteenth century, beer was provided by the management. At the Yorkshire Copper Works in Leeds, for example, a barrel of beer from Bentley's Yorkshire Brewery at Woodlesford was provided each week for the men in the foundry. The foundrymen's drinking habits brought them a great reputation for being able to hold their liquor, drinking competitions occasionally being arranged between individual workers. At one of these, held at the Crooked Billet, a public house in South Leeds. Carter from the Copper Works foundry was challenged by Phillips, who worked in the steel rolling mills at the nearby Coghlan's forge. Two rows of eight quart jugs of beer were laid out along one of the tables in the bar, and the contest began. Carter rapidly despatching his own eight before proceeding to finish a further four of his competitor's to claim an overwhelming victory.[25]

In South and West Yorkshire the medieval practice of celebrating Whitsuntide with a church ale, a communal brew for the benefit of the local congregation, continued through to the mid-nineteenth century. This is clearly illustrated by entries in the accounts of both the established and nonconformist churches of the region:

Greenacres Sabbath-day Schools, 1835: 'Cakes and ale for the children at Whitsuntide £2. 5. 2d.'

Bolsterstone Sunday School 1840–6: 'three pecks of malt & hops for the children's feast. . .

Slaithwaite, 1854: 'that we brew one peck of malt for singers.'

Slaithwaite, 1855: 'That one strike of malt be brewed for singers and players.'[26]

Once the ale had been brewed, probably at a convenient public house, it was kept in readiness for Whitsuntide. Then, having assembled at the Sunday schools, the children set off in procession to sing outside the homes of the leading parishioners, farmers and gentry. From a piece of tape or string slung around their necks they carried their own pottery mugs, having them filled with beer both at the school and

at the houses of friends visited during the walk:[27] 'The teachers served them with
buns and home-brewed ale, two cups each for the big lads and one cup for the little
lads; how the youngsters used to stretch themselves up and stand on their toes for
the second cup'. At this time it was believed that home-brewed beer was a good and
nourishing drink for children, and one which no doubt improved the quality of their
singing. Soon the teetotal movement with its Bands of Hope and Rechabites began
to change the churches' attitude to alcoholic liquors, and they were slowly replaced
by more acceptable alternatives. In 1848 Mr Bell decided to provide tea and sugar for
the Bolsterstone Sunday School feast, for example, while a few years later the
Slaithwaite Sunday School announced that they would not sing before any public
house during their Whitsuntide walks.[28]

The sale of beer had been greatly promoted by the Duke of Wellington's
Beerhouse Act of 1830. In an attempt to curb the nation's addiction to cheap gin, it
gave the public a much greater capacity for purchasing beer. Any householder
assessed for the poor rate was now entitled to obtain an excise licence for two
guineas which thus enabled him to retail beer on or off his premises between 4am
and 10pm. An immediate explosion in the number of sales outlets for beer followed
the passing of the act, the number of public houses in Leeds increasing by 80%
between 1826 and 1836, for example. The working population certainly appear to
have appreciated this expansion of their social facilities, and flocked to the
beerhouses both for the beer and for the enjoyment of good company. Many tried to
obtain their beer on credit, but this could easily ruin the publican. To this end, the
following lines might be painted on the wall above the fireplace in the bar, where it
could be seen by all:

> Customers came and I did trust them,
> Till I lost my money and my custom;
> To lose them both it grieved me sore,
> So I resolved to trust no more,
> Chalk is useful, say what you will,
> But chalk ne'er paid the maltster's bill,
> I'll try to keep a decent tap For ready money,
> but no strap![29]

Much of the ale drunk in these new establishments was purchased from commercial
brewers, but where the householder had a good reputation for the quality of his
home-brewed, he could now obtain a licence and offer it for general sale. If he did
not live in a rateable property, however, or if he could not afford the two guineas
licence fee, he might still try to sell his ale by operating an illegal drinking house or
'hush-shop'. In some ancient market towns the householders were permitted to
exercise their prescriptive right to sell their ale to the public during the annual fairs,
hanging a bush over the doorway by way of a temporary inn-sign.[30] Elsewhere, the
hush shops continued a popular, if precarious, existence. Since the hush seller paid
no licence or excise duty, his ale was stronger, riper and cheaper than that sold by
publicans:

We fellows delight in hush I declare
We spend with our host all the brass we can spare
We deem a man's foolish who spends at an inn
When he knows very well the gauger has been
Derry down, high derry down.[31]

It was difficult to prove that a hush seller was in fact selling ale to his customers, rather than just entertaining a group of friends in his own home, but in the late 1840s and early 1850s the hush shops were virtually all closed down as a result of clashes with two formidable enemies. The first was the increasingly efficient constabulary, whose activities now secured frequent convictions with massive fines of some £10, while the second was the militant Methodist church, vigorously propagating the new gospel of teetotalism. Preachers such as Isaac Marsden of Doncaster swept into Sabbath-breaking hush shops like avenging angels, crashing their sticks down onto the bar-room tables and crying out for the Lord's salvation from the poor misguided drunkard's hell. There was no escape for the men – they were caught red-handed breaking the law by drinking in unlicensed premises during prohibited hours. Their only course of action was to become total abstainers, join the Methodists and be saved – or else face the unabated rigour of law and church alike.[32] Faced with this pressure, it is not surprising that most hush shops were extinct by the 1860s.

Ginger, Herb & Black Beers

As well as producing beers made solely from malt and hops, the home brewer was able to produce an interesting range of fermented drinks using various other ingredients. The oldest of these was 'honey-drink' or 'botchet' which, like its aristocratic counterpart 'bragget', took its name from 'bracem', an old Celtic or Gaulish word for a kind of grain. This honey ale was a speciality of the North York Moors and the South Pennines where numerous stocks of bees gave plentiful supplies of heather honey, renowned for its high colour and strong distinctive taste. Once all the liquid honey had been drained off, the comb was immersed in water to extract all the remaining honey. Then, the comb having been removed, the liquid was allowed to ferment before being bottled and stored ready for use. The resulting liquor had the reputation of being highly intoxicating, and was very liable to give the drinker a headache even if it had not been drunk in any large quantity.[33]

Ginger, nettles, sweet gale or bog myrtle (*Myrica gale*), raspberry and strawberry leaves, and dandelions were also used to make beers.[34] The early nineteenth-century recipes, such as the following example by Miss Monica Tempest of Eshton, rely on yeast alone to work the sweetened, clarified and flavoured liquor:

Ginger Beer

To ten gallons of water put 12 lb. of white sugar and six whites of Eggs well beaten. Stir them well together then set them on the Fire and when near boiling skim very well. Take half a pound of Ginger bruised a little and put it into the liquor whilst boiling and let it boil 20 minutes. Pare 10 lemons and slice them. Pour the liquor boiling upon them. When cool put it into a cask with two spoonfuls of fresh yeast, the pips of the lemons having been previously taken out, and the slices to be put into the cask with one ounce of Isinglass. Bung it well up and let it stand 3 weeks but if the weather be hot only 10 days and then bottle it. March and April are the best months for making it – it will keep a year.[35]

Most of the later recipes include an ounce or two of cream of tartar (calcium phosphate) to improve the flavour. Even though they might vary a little in detail, they all tend to follow the same methods overall:

For ginger beer	1 oz bruised root ginger.
For nettle beer	2 lb young nettles.
For gale beer	1 large bunch of gale

each with:

1 lb sugar	1 gallon boiling water
1 lemon, sliced	½oz fresh yeast, or
1 oz cream of tartar	two level teaspoons dried yeast.

For nettle beer, boil the nettles with half the water for twenty minutes, then strain off the nettle tops and pour the liquid onto the sugar, lemon, cream of tartar, and remaining water. For ginger or gale beer, scald the ginger or gale, the sugar, lemon and cream of tartar with the water.

Allow the liquor to cool to around 75° F, then either spread the fresh yeast on a piece of toast and float it on the surface, or activate the dried yeast and stir it in. Cover with a cloth, and keep in a warm place for two days, skimming off the yeast as it rises. When fermentation has ceased, move the beer into a cool place and allow the sediment to settle before syphoning off the clear liquid into pint bottles primed with half a teaspoonful of white sugar and stopper tightly. Return the bottles to the warm for two days, then store in the cool for ten days, when it will be ready for drinking.

From the middle of the century the trouble of brewing could be greatly alleviated by purchasing one of the various extracts of herbs which were now readily available from chemists and grocers. Local almanacs and magazines carried advertisements for Kemp's 'Compound Essence of Hops & Herbs' and Mason's extracts of dandelion, hops, sarsparilla, ginger or horehound. Of these, a sixpenny bottle would make eight gallons, 'giving herbaceous flavour and a creamy head like bottled ale without the trouble of boiling herbs. Always acceptable at Picnics. In the home it is the pleasantest and most refreshing drink obtainable. Experience has proved that [it is] the best temperance beer for the harvest field . . . .'

Similarly it was possible to buy a bottle of black beer, a sharp-flavoured alcoholic drink made by flavouring a concentrated malt and cane sugar liquor with young shoots of spruce. It was commercially made in Yorkshire from the 1820s at least, when there were four black beer brewers working in the town of Leeds.

By the late nineteenth century the spruce was usually omitted to leave a sweet malty taste, the beer either being drunk on its own, or with rum as a short, or made into a long drink by mixing with lemonade, ginger beer or milk. Its popularity began to wane after the Second World War, and J.E. Mather and Sons of Upper Wortley Road, Leeds, the last company to make black beer in Yorkshire, closed down their works in the late 1970s.[36]

Whisky

In the remote dales of the North and West Ridings there was little respect for the excise regulations introduced by a distant parliament in Westminster. Whisky was much cheaper when made illegally in a small, isolated cottage, and there was certainly a great local demand for the 'whisky-spinner's' products. The spirit vendors travelled round the neighbourhood, calling from door to door 'with a serious other-worldly cast of countenance and sheeps-bladders full of whisky hidden underneath their coats'.[37] Ammon Wrigley has recorded the short career of Mary Robinson who began to distil in an old house near Saddleworth about 1852. Her whisky was known as 'sparrow bills' because it pecked sharply in the throat and stomach and then ran with a warm glow throughout a man's veins, ideal for celebrations, for use as a medicine, and to fortify one against the chill north-east winds which wuthered over Standedge moors. Unfortunately her house was raided by the police and she had to pay a fine of £30 or face three months' imprisonment, a similar fate coming to virtually all the contemporary distillers in the county.[38]

Chapter 13

Beverages

In most parts of Yorkshire ample supplies of water for drinking, cooking and washing were readily available, the whole pattern of settlement being greatly influenced by the distribution of this most essential of commodities. In the Dales, for example, the majority of the villages lay close to the confluence of the main rivers with their small swift-running tributaries, thus ensuring a constant source of fresh, clean water. In the South Pennine valleys, such as Calderdale, the older settlements ranged along the steep scarps six or seven hundred feet above the valley floors to take advantage of the elevated spring-line. Similarly the villages and hamlets closely-spaced around the perimeter of the North Yorks Moors were able to utilise the springs and streams flowing from the higher land. Throughout the remainder of the county springs, streams, rivers and wells were all widely used, the necessary well-heads, troughs and pumps often being supplied and maintained either by the local township or by private patronage.

Wherever there was a sufficient head of water, it was usually made to flow through a spout elevated a foot or more above a stone trough so that vessels could be readily filled with fresh water from the spout itself, while bucketfuls could be baled from the trough for general domestic use or watering livestock. A number of wells of this type, particularly in the Pennines, were decorated with stone heads, the water actually issuing from the lips of the Slabbering' Baby on Adel Moor or Slavverin' Sal of Witton Fell. These probably represent the vestigial remains of Celtic head-cults dating from prehistoric times. In other areas, where the water had to be raised from some depth, draw-wells fitted with a bucket, rope and winch were used, but where possible, these were replaced by mechanical lift- or force-pumps. Besides being safer, and relatively free from accidental pollution, they were far more convenient, a few strokes on the long pump handle producing just as much water as would otherwise have been raised by laboriously winding up a bucketful at a time. But however efficient the pumps were, they were only as good as the water supply to which they were connected, and so they could easily run dry if subject to over-use:[1]

> Sum at's living' remember t'owd pumps –
> Hah offen they've had a good douse,
> An' t'watter cans, t'buckets, and' hoops
> An' t'watter pots reared up i't haase.
> Hah hundreds were waiting o' turns
> I' different places i' t'taan:
> Hah a extra good thump nah an' then
> 'Ud cause t'poor owd pump ta break daan.

Water for drinking, washing, and all domestic purposes came from a variety of local sources. In many towns, even up to the mid nineteenth century, river water was hawked around the streets in water-carts, such as the examples seen here, which were being filled in the River Calder at Wakefield in 1793 (top left). Until piped water supplies were introduced, many communities relied on wells, such as the Bramley pump of 1821, with its elaborate cast-iron lion-mask spout, and the Great Well at Heptonstall.

The pre-historic Celtic use of stone heads to guard springs survived into the nineteenth century. These examples come from 'the slabberin' Baby' on Adel Moor (left) and a trough at the side of the main road through Hebden Bridge.

The hoops mentioned in these lines measured about three feet in diameter, and were gripped by each hand when carrying two buckets of water. This arrangement allowed the load to be evenly distributed to each side of the body, thus leaving the legs free from any impediment and reducing the risk of spillage.

The only area of Yorkshire not to have a readily available water supply was the high Wold of the East Riding. Here most of the rain immediately sank down into the chalk and was totally lost to the inhabitants unless they collected it from their roofs. A piece of old sacking was usually fastened across the bottom of the down-spout to act as a crude filter before the water entered the wooden butt where it was kept ready for use.[2] On the larger farms up to 100,000 gallons could be gathered in this way, storage in these circumstances being in a number of large tanks or cisterns.[3]

In virtually every farm and village on the Wolds, as well as in many of their outlying fields, the water required for both domestic and agricultural purposes was gathered in ponds. The majority of these were constructed during the late eighteenth and early nineteenth centuries as part of the great agricultural improvement of the region. Measuring anything up to 160ft in diameter and 10–15ft in depth, they were scooped out of the chalk and carefully lined with clay to keep them waterproof. The quality of the water in some of the ponds was execrable. When the pond at Fimber was cleaned out in 1821, a 10ft mound of dead matter was left at its centre. Over the following years it accumulated a further eight hundred cartloads of decomposing vegetation, dead dogs and drowned cats etc., so that by the 1850s it had become a seething mass of disease and animal life.[4] J.R. Mortimer remembered it in this state 'infested with innumerable water toads and frogs of all sizes (making at certain times loud and disagreeable croakings) which the boys often hooked out of the water with long sticks and then killed them. At times I have known the young frogs leave the water and crawl rather than hop about the streets in such numbers as to make it difficult for anyone to avoid stepping upon them. Besides, at certain times, the mere would be literally alive with water-lice, which had to be removed from the water before using it, by what was termed 'sarling it'. This was done by running the water through a muslin or straining cloth, which intercepted the insects. Though objectionable in appearance, they were not considered injurious, and the inhabitants, having become so far familiar with these occurrences, and not being over-nice in fancy, these little flea-like bodies caused little compunction. I can remember old Matthew Wilson, a retired farmer, having mugs of unfiltered water, since he could strain it through his front teeth'.[5]

The other great problem with the ponds was that they tended to dry up in times of drought. During the summer of 1826, for example, all the ponds and cisterns around Wetwang and Fridaythorpe went dry, the livestock gnawing the bark of the trees and hedges to obtain some moisture. To try to keep their stock alive, the local farmers had been allowed to take them to Fimber pond once a day, but since this was not sufficient, they began to come more frequently, thus seriously threatening the village's only source of water. This caused such friction between the communities that an actual battle took place on Sunday towards the end of June, the inhabitants of Fimber trying to defend their pond with sticks, pokers and stones, but being driven back by the rush of their neighbours' cattle, maddened by thirst. In the ensuing melee there were broken heads, scratched faces and torn clothes, while the owners of the stock were soaked in the pond, but fortunately there was no loss of life.[6]

In order to prevent such disturbances, and to improve the whole health and cleanliness of the village, various attempts were made to bore a well down to the water, and make it accessible with a force-pump. This was finally completed in 1867, but instead of welcoming this great improvement, the people of Fimber found the expense of maintaining the pump and the labour of using it far too troublesome, and so they returned to their stagnant pond. By 1900 the new well was out of use, and completely covered up.[7]

While the population remained fairly constant, the traditional sources of water were quite adequate, serious shortages occurring only in years of extreme drought. The situation deteriorated rapidly, however, when the towns and villages began to expand in the opening decades of the nineteenth century. Some towns had already established extensive waterworks to pump river water to the houses of subscribers. The York Waterworks'Company of 1677 and its Leeds equivalent of 1694 were still operating, albeit in an improved form, in the 1830s, but by this time they were totally unable to face the demands now being placed upon them, while the quality of the water they supplied was worse than ever before. In Castleford, for example, the river Aire was used for drinking water by the majority of the inhabitants up to the 1850s, even though it received the greater part of the sewage of some 495,000 people living in the textile towns upstream.[8] In these circumstances it is hardly surprising that the death rate soared as typhus, typhoid, dysentery and the cholera epidemics of 1832 and 1848-9 took their toll. When the medical profession eventually proved the connection between these diseases and polluted water, they were able to persuade the local authorities to take the appropriate action. During the 1820s, '30s and '40s, therefore, numerous local acts for the better supplying of towns with water were passed through Parliament and all the necessary civil engineering works commenced. Fortunately most of the larger towns lay close to the Pennine valleys and dales, where land was cheap, and the combination of a high rainfall with a very low population provided ideal sites for the construction of new dams capable of holding millions of gallons of clean, unpolluted water. By the end of the century virtually every house in the urban areas of the county had been provided with tapped water supplies, although some years were to pass before the same could be said of the outlying rural areas.

In northern England in 1797, 'besides water the general drink of the labouring classes is whey or milk, or rather milk and water, or at best very weak small beer'.[9]

The quantity of milk consumed by each household, and the manner in which it was obtained, varied greatly from one region of the county to another. But in most areas it was possible for the more prosperous workers to buy a cow and provide it with adequate grazing fairly close to their homes. In the East Riding, for example, the agricultural labourers commonly kept a cow or two in paddocks, on cottage pastures or by the roadside. Some places were fairly well off in this respect, villagers at Hummanby, Birdsall and Hayton all having cottage pastures, while at Warter there were a number of three-acre holdings.[10]

Similarly in the North Riding many men kept one or two cows and attended to them before and after work. On the Feversham estate several villagers had cow-gates or grazing rights on a large pasture together with small pieces of land on which to make hay for winter feed. There were also ten or twelve cows owned by various people which grazed by the roadside during the summer, for here there was plenty of grass, particularly since the cattle were driven along a different route each day by someone who was getting too old to do much active work. He received a small wage in return for both tending the animals and bringing them back home for milking twice each day.[11]

A similar system of grazing was to be found in the towns during the early nineteenth century, particularly in those major medieval centres such as Hull, Beverley and York which had retained large acreages of free-men's pastures or strays around their periphery. In Richmond in the 1830s virtually every small tradesman kept a cow and a 'bit o' land' to grow hay for winter feed. The cattle were turned out in the West Field from May 13th through to November on payment of a cow-gate of four pounds a year. During this period they were collected by the pinder and brought back to the gate nearest the town at six in the morning and at six in the evening, scores of people with shining milk cans, stools and cow-ties then coming out to milk their own animals.[12]

If it was not possible to keep a cow for one's own use, milk could usually be fetched from a nearby farm. In some areas this useful facility did not exist, however, for the farmers might find it more economical to feed their milk to the pigs, or sell it in the towns nearby. Thus in the rural areas there might be some parishes in which milk was scarce, while in others only a mile or so distant there was a plentiful supply and an informal arrangement which ensured that those who wanted milk were able to get it. Even so it is unlikely that milk consumption in most East Riding Farm labourers' families exceeded between half and one pint per week, unless they lived-in as farm servants.[13] In the West Riding, particularly in and around the industrial towns, milk formed a much more substantial part of the diet, perhaps half a pint or more being taken each day with bowls of porridge. Here the milk they used was three meals old, being taken from the cow one morning, stood in the dairy until the evening of the next day, when the cream was removed, and the remainder then sold to the 'producing class'.[14] Every morning and evening troops of men and women, boys and girls could be seen walking to the farms to collect their milk. The ensuing scene has been clearly described by Charlotte Bronte: in *Shirley*:[15] as Caroline and Shirley reached Fieldhead, the substantial gritstone house now identified as Oakwell Hall, Birstall, 'they found the back-yard gates open, and the court and kitchen crowded with excited milk-fetchers – men, women and children, whom Mrs Gill, the housekeeper, appeared vainly persuading to take their milk-cans and depart. It is, or was, by-the-by, the custom in the north of England for the cottagers on a country squire's estate to receive their supplies of milk and butter from the dairy of the Manor-House, on whose pastures a herd of milch-kine was usually fed for the convenience of the neighbourhood. Miss Keeldar owned such a herd – all deep-dewlapped Craven cows, reared on the sweet herbage and clear waters of bonnie Airedale'. In order to avoid troublesome cash transactions for each of these numerous sales, 'strap' or credit was commonly used. Since most of the customers were illiterate, written accounts were of little use, and so a very simple, yet foolproof system was employed. When the milk was fetched, each customer took a long three-sided piece of stick on one ridge of which a fresh notch was cut for each purchase. When the account was paid off, nothing could be simpler than to slice off the notches at one sweep and begin again.[16]

In addition to being collected, milk from these farms was also carried into the industrial towns where it was either sold from shops or hawked around the streets by milk sellers. The transport of this milk was undertaken by boys called milk-joggers, who rode astride donkeys already weighed down by large cans or casks of milk strapped on to each side. Great pride was taken in the speed of the respective animals, the streets often being enlivened with colourful donkey races on which various sums were bet.[17] George Walker illustrated and interviewed one of these milk boys in 1814, and found him to be extremely proud of his animal: 'Eye, ittle pay onny mule a toppot rooad: we gets 'em all ov a eeup and then they rawm and kick while they scrammel owt ageean'. In plain English: 'Yes, it will beat any ass upon the road: we get them all together in a heap, and then they rear and kick till they scramble out again'.[18] In the Dales, tinplate back-cans or budgets hung from shoulder-straps similar to those of a rucksack were used to carry up to five gallons of milk down from the scattered hill-barns and pastures where milking traditionally took place. If the milk was to be transported for any greater distance a pair of these cans was strapped on to the sides of a donkey, a system which continued up to the 1950s. The last milk donkey to be used in this way died at Castle Bolton in Wensleydale in 1967.[19]

Much of the milk consumed within the larger towns in the early nineteenth century was provided by cow-keepers who maintained a number of animals in sheds

Milk was delivered into the towns by milk boys, such as this one illustrated in George Walker's *Costume of Yorkshire* of 1814. Note the donkey, with its cropped ears and jagged tail.

located in odd corners and yards in the most populous inner-city areas. Here the conditions were far from ideal, the cow-houses frequently being without supplied of water, without any convenience for storing manure, and without adequate ventilation or drainage. The cows might be kept in these unhealthy conditions throughout the entire year, with no opportunity for summer grazing or exercise. From the 1850s the situation began to improve due to a variety of factors; the increasing urbanisation of the towns with its higher rents and rates tended to drive the cow-keepers further out into the more rural suburbs, for example, while the local authorities now began to impose higher standards of hygiene. By the 1880s further advances were being made, as educational courses in dairywork were introduced, and the first generation of commercial creameries came into existence. Even so, perhaps half the milk sold in the towns in the late nineteenth century was still coming out of urban cow-houses.[20] The actual delivery around the streets was undertaken by carrying either a pair of milk-cans suspended from a yoke, or a churn or further milk-cans in a horsedrawn milk-float. Those householders who had ordered regular daily supplies of milk would usually leave a quart jug on their windowsill or doorstep which would then be filled with the required quantity tipped out of one of the measures hanging within the milk can. Using these methods, which continued up to the 1960s in some areas, it was always necessary to place a saucer or bead-weighted cloth over the top of the jug to keep out smuts falling from the soot-laden atmosphere. Even so, little could be done to ward off the attentions of marauding cats and dogs who were always on the lookout for a free drink.

Up to the eighteenth century most people drank only water, milk or beer to satisfy their thirst, but these were now to be replaced by new drinks introduced as a direct result of Britain's growing international trade. In the wealthiest households of late seventeenth-century England the drinking of tea imported from China, coffee from Turkey and chocolate from the West Indies was already an established fashion. It was to take more than a century, however, before these beverages came within the reach of the working class. Griffith Wright has left the following description of a tea-party held by a Leeds clothier's wife while her husband was buying his wool on the Wolds in the 1730s:

And while the good man is away
The neighbour-wives all set a day
To meet, and drink a dish of tea!
With Dame, while she is left a widow,
As neighbours should, without being bid, you know,
'We ne'er stand knocking – Mistress, how do ye?'
Thank you and you, I am glad to see ye!
Pray walk in, put off your things –
Bess, yet aforehand with the bobbins –
Pray ye, walk into the other room,
What stand ye for? come, set ye doon!'
When they have sat and chat a while,
The kettle is brought in to boil,
The Tea-Table in order spread,
Rolls buttered, cold, some toasted!
'Bohea or Green – mixed or clear?
Which you please – do pray draw near!'
So we will leave them at their ease,
And to discourse in what they please . . .

The mention of a dish of tea is quite interesting. Even within living memory the older people in the Huddersfield area used to pour their tea into deep saucers where it quickly cooled and could be slurped with obvious satisfaction.[21]

When tea first began to be introduced into the rural parts of the county around the late eighteenth and early nineteenth centuries the correct methods of making and drinking it were still quite unknown. At Bainbridge in Wensleydale, for example, it is recorded that 'a bagman called on an old farmer and fascinated him by praising the virtues of the new leaf from China, so that with his wife's approval he ordered a stone to begin with. The trader ventured to suggest that a stone of tea would be a costly experiment, and sent them only a pound. Some months afterwards he called again for 'money and orders', and asked how the couple liked their tea. 'Them was the nastiest greens we ever tasted' was the answer, 'The parcel came one morning afore dinner, so the missus tied 'em up in a cloth and put 'em into t'pot wi't bacon. But we couldn't abear 'em when they was done; and as for t'broth we couldn't sup a drop on't!'[22]

Tea, coffee and cocoa were promoted as beverages for working men by the teetotal movement. The Thornton Road Branch of the Bradford Coffee Tavern Company was opened in 1879 by Mr. W.E. Forster, the Bradford M.P.

In spite of these initial problems tea soon became one of the most popular drinks to be enjoyed by all levels of society. By the 1840s it was being drunk by weavers, lead miners and colliers alike, even though it might easily cost sevenpence halfpenny (3p) or tenpence (4p) out of a weekly income of around fifteen to twenty shillings (75–100p). One of the major reasons for its success was that large volumes of this hot liquid tended to reduce the intake of other more nutritious foods. The poor found that they could enjoy a quite deceptive feeling of warmth and satisfaction after drinking a pot of tea, even though it had minimal food value. It was also extremely economical to make, requiring little more than a kettle full of boiling water. Between the 1840s and the 1890s the national average annual consumption of tea rose from 1.6 lb to 5.7 lb per head, as it was freed from tax and new cheap supplies were imported from India and Ceylon.[23] Tea now became the most widely used drink of all, being drunk at breakfast, at work, with dinner, with supper, and at social gatherings ranging from family parties to church and chapel functions. Usually it was taken with milk and sugar, but lacing with alcohol was a very common practice, even though it was only polite to voice some objection to this most welcome addition. When Miss Maffin poured the festive cream and hospitable rum into the Wharfedale blacksmith's wife's cup in the 1860s, she was not at all offended by the gentle remonstration 'There! There! that'll do! not a drop more thank ye. Well, I reckon I shall have to sup it nah ye've put it in; but its worse than poison when ye don't want it!'

For those who could not afford tea, or who preferred a different taste, a variety of herb teas were made from plants either grown in the cottage garden, or bought from street traders who obtained their supplies from specialist herb gardens. Hyssop and tansy were used in this way, but the most popular were the various mints, including pennyroyal, which tasted remarkably similar to strong tea when sweetened with treacle.[24] Mint tea was also a favourite drink of the men working in the devil rooms at the shoddy mills, for it was particularly effective for slaking the thirst and refreshing those who had to spend hours in the dusty and dirty atmosphere of the rag-grinding shops.[25]

Coffee and cocoa were also drunk to a limited extent from around the 1840s. Their use tended to be largely restricted to the urban areas, however, where they never offered any serious competition to tea as the major drink of the working population.

Chapter 14

Feasts, Fairs and Celebrations

Although the everyday food consumed by the majority of the population could be dull and monotonous in the extreme, every attempt was made to provide good and substantial meals for special occasions. Weddings, funerals and Christmastime were all celebrated with their own particular delicacies, but the fairs and feasts held in each village and town gave an equally important opportunity for dispensing hospitality to relations, friends and neighbours.

Most of the fairs held in the market centres had been founded by Royal charters obtained by the Lords of the Manor in the early medieval period, their primary functions being to promote the sale of livestock and other goods, and the exchange of labour. The most significant fairs were held in October and November, particularly around Martinmas week (November 11th), when the shaggy long-horned black cattle driven down from the Highlands of Scotland were sold for conversion into salt-beef for the coming winter. In 1799 John Russell recorded his impressions of a typical fair in Leeds: 'Nov. 8th, . . . the shops were shut up, as the fair was for cattle. The whole of Briggate was filled. It was dangerous to pass, and droves passing other streets filled the whole town with bustle. Nov. 9th was the Toy Fair. A few irregular stalls with cakes etc. were all I saw, with clowns who I could not understand. Young women and men offering themselves for service stood about, to be hired for the year'.[1] Other fairs had monastic origins, Lee Fair, still held at Woodkirk, being granted to the canons of Nostell Priory by Henry I, while the Bird Fair intended to supply Kirkham Abbey with poultry continued to take place in front of the abbey gates for centuries after the Dissolution.[2]

In addition to these legally-established fairs, almost every town and village held its own annual feast, the title of this event varying greatly from one place to another. Saddleworth had its 'Wakes'. Almondbury its 'Rushbearing', Longroyd its 'Thump', Kirkheaton its 'Rant', and Muker its 'Awd Roy', for example.[3] Other titles preserved the medieval ecclesiastic origins of the feasts, as in Slaithwaite's 'Sanjimis', Kirkburton's 'Trinity Burton', or Reeth's 'Bartle', held on the Feasts of St James, Holy Trinity and St Bartholomew respectively.[4]

As *the* great communal festival of the year, the feast was the scene of many lively and colourful events, including the trading activities of itinerant dealers offering Sheffield and Birmingham metalwork, Staffordshire pottery, or locally made furniture and domestic utensils. There might also be horse races, dances, and a variety of games, competitions and side-shows. Some of these, such as bull, badger and bear baiting, cockfighting, wrestling, fighting and even races and athletic exercises, were all vigorously suppressed by the parish constables in the opening decades of the nineteenth century, since they now caused offence to an increasingly

146

Hunslet Feast, 1850. Note the swing-boats, roundabouts and Punch and Judy. Around the sides of the showground are the stalls selling fruit and sweets.

sensitive and refined middle class. Writing in 1858, Walter White states that the annual feasts and fairs of Wensleydale 'would attract visitors for twenty miles around. Here, at Aysgarth, not the least part of the amusements were the races, run by men stark naked, as people not more than forty years old can well remember. But times are changed; and throughout the dale drunknness and revelry are giving way to teetotalism, lectures, tea gatherings, and other moral recreations'.[5]

The latter half of the century certainly did see the abolition of the more brutal aspects of the feasts, but their place tended to be taken by travelling fairgrounds rather than by the morally improving activities suggested by Mr White. At Honley, as elsewhere, there came 'Pablo's Circus, Wombwell's Menagerie, Wild's Theatre, and other celebrated travelling shows. In addition, there were Taylor's Bazaar, Waxworks, Swings, Roundabouts, Flying-boxes, Shooting-tents, Pea Saloons, and numerous other alluring attractions in the fields, whilst stores containing brandy-snap, nuts, fruit and other tempting contents lined the streets from end to end'.[6] Other contemporary writers noted the various foods offered for sale at the feasts, these ranging from gobstoppers, toffee apples and parkin pigs with currant eyes, to nuts, and 'a stick and a glass for a a'penny'. This was a stick of toffee the size of a pencil wrapped in white paper twirled at the ends, dispensed from a tin candlebox hung from the hawker's neck, and accompanied by a glass of treacle-drink.[7] The most popular sweetmeats by far were the brandy-snaps and parkin pigs, which were made as follows:

Brandy Snap

4 oz butter	1 teaspoon ground ginger
4 oz treacle	4 oz sugar
4 oz flour	

Melt the butter and treacle, and then mix in the sugar, flour and ginger. Place teaspoonsful of the mixture on greased baking trays, spacing them about six inches apart, and bake for 8 to 10 minutes at 350° F, gas Mark 4. Allow to cool for 1 to 2 minutes, then loosen with a knife and roll around the lightly greased handles of wooden spoons until they have hardened, when they can be slipped off and stored ready for use.

Parkin Biscuits

8 oz flour	1 teaspoon bicarbonate of soda
8 oz medium oatmeal	Pinch of salt
8 oz treacle	2 oz brown sugar
2 oz butter	1 teaspoonful ground ginger

Melt the butter, treacle and sugar together, and stir into the remainder of the ingredients to form a stiff dough. Turn out on to a floured board, roll out and cut into rounds or pigs, and bake at 350°F, for 10-15 minutes.[8]

One of the best-known makers of parkin pigs was Chatterton, a spice-merchant of Ivegate, Bradford, who proudly displayed an exhibition of his spicy handiwork in a room over his shop. It included all the illustrious characters of the day, occasionally varied by a most dazzling representation of Daniel in the Lion's Den, all in spice.

Other foods found at the feasts attracted considerable attention from the crowds. On entering the fairground at Leeds, the 100,000 visitors would pass the 'Original Pea Shop' or 'Uncle Tom's Cabin Pea Shop' selling boiled peas. Opening a huge tin pan, a man would thrust in a spoon and draw it out filled with black hard-looking pellets about the size of marbles. These he deposited on a small plate with a minimal flavouring of vinegar, salt and pepper before selling them at a halfpenny a portion.

At Grassington Feast a tea-cake race was held for the boys. Five or six boys would climb on to a wall, where they were each given a dry teacake which had to be eaten as quickly as possible. At a given signal, the race was on, and all went well until one or two who had bitten off more than they could chew showed signs of distress, with bulging cheeks and eyes agog. The first to finish then gave a whistle, to prove that his mouth was empty, before jumping down ready to be proclaimed as the winner.

Further amusement, but of a much more revolting nature, could be found in the rat-eating booths, where the climax of the performance was provided by a young man, 'one of the savage tribes of North Americkay', naked to the waist and coloured up with soot and oil. Having been presented with a cage of six or eight half-dead

Clifton Feast. Mary Ellen Best, the York artist, recorded the sweet stall which was erected close to her sister's house on Clifton Green for the May-day feast in 1833. It displays piles of fruit, jars of striped rock, gingerbread and cakes.

rats, he proceeded to shake his head and smack his lips in preparation for his disgusting meal. Taking up one of the rats, he placed its head in his mouth as the showman announced 'He's now sucking the blood'. Cries of 'Bite off his head' from the crowd were not heeded, however, and the show ended with the 'savage' walking off the stage still sucking his rat.[9]

In the home, the preparations for the feast commenced with a week of 'liver and whitewash', the liver, fried with onions, providing a cheap and quickly-prepared meal at a time when the housewife was fully occupied in cleaning and redecorating her home ready for the reception of numerous guests.[10] The arrival of the beef for the feast was a rousing event in the villages, everyone running to their doors as the butchers drove their fat beasts to the slaughterhouses. The grocers, meanwhile, got in extra supplies of malt, hops, and cheese, while the greengrocers stocked more red cabbage than they would otherwise sell throughout the entire year.[10]

Some of the best accounts of the domestic preparations for the feasts are provided by local poets, as may be seen from the following verses extracted from Richard Spencer's 'Holbeck Feast':[11]

The kitchen table looks quite smart
O'erspread with many a tempting tart
And one enormous custard,
And other real, essential things
Such as befit the board of kings,
As pepper, salt and mustard.

There is a host of goodly pies,
Besieged by swarms of busy flies
Some over them are creeping;
Some, as if wondering what is hid
Beneath the surface of the lid,
Are down the vent-hole peeping ...

The snow-white cloth is neatly spread
And graced with celery and bread,
With dishes, plates and glasses.
All is so very bright and clean,
The table's fit for any queen,
And credit to the lasses! ...

But see how changed the joint of beef!
The bones stand out in bold relief,
The meat sinks in the shade;
Yet still how great are the supplies!
In fact the joint's so large in size,
It braves the knife's keen blade.

Usually the feast started on a Sunday, when many friends and relatives who would otherwise be at work were free to attend. Early in the century everyone kept open house, and all visitors to the village were welcome to call in and enjoy the hearty, open-handed hospitality, but later there was a tendency to entertain only those guests who were well-known to the family. For the dinner, taken at midday, it was usual to serve a currant pudding as the first course, bringing it to the table smoking hot and, if possible, flamed with brandy. This was followed by pies of various kinds, including veal, gooseberry, damson and custard, after which the guests were reminded to 'leave a bit of room' for the final course of roast beef and vegetables. The quality and quantity of the beef was of the greatest importance, men earning only 24s (£1.20p) a week buying joints weighing as much as 18lb.[14] It used to be said that on a Wakes Sunday morning, if the wind was in the south-west, they could smell the roasting of Standedge beef down in Marsden beyond the moors. A man coming from the deep cutting towards the Floating Light inn would walk into a warm greasy mist which had gathered from the many pitchers of hot gravy. On a Sunday morning at feast time Ammon Wrigley went to a house in the Deanhead Valley. Every house was tenanted, full of busy looms and lusty weavers singing at their work: 'How well do I remember seeing the big table set in the middle of the floor, seated round by men and women, and the head of the house without a coat and waistcoat carving from a great joint of beef. How he sweat, and every now and then drew his white shirt sleeve across his forehead and said 'By th'Mass this is warm wark'.[15]

The beef was eaten with pickled cucumber, the rich gravy being soaked up with oatcake.[16] All was washed down with strong home-brewed beer. Afterwards the men continued to enjoy the home-brewed, together with snuff and tobacco, for the rest of the afternoon.

On the Monday, the family gathered in the homes of their married sons for a similar feast, while on the Tuesday they proceeded to their married daughters, each secretly vying with the other as to which could provide the best entertainment. It was also the practice for publicans and other tradesmen to present their regular customers with a plate of cold beef and pickles on the Monday, but by the 1880s such gifts were fast becoming obsolete.[17]

The beef dinners described above were largely characteristic of the West Riding, but in the North Riding dales and in parts of East Yorkshire a communal meal of cheesecakes formed the highlight of the feast. About the size of a saucer, or a little smaller, they were made to recipes such as this:

Cheese Cakes

8 oz curds, either purchased, or made by

(a) stirring 1 teaspoon rennet into 2pts. warm milk, leave to form a curd, strain off through a fine cloth and allow to drain overnight.

(b) heating 2pts. of new milk almost to boiling point, then mix in 4pts. fresh cold buttermilk, or

(c) beating 3 eggs and a pinch of salt into a pint of milk, heating almost to boiling point while stirring gently, then allowing to stand until a curd has formed, draining this in a fine cloth for half an hour.

2 eggs	2 tablespoons double cream
4 oz melted butter	Grated peel of one lemon
4 oz sugar	Nutmeg to taste
2 oz currants	8 oz shortcrust pastry

Roll out the pastry and use it to line four saucer-size tart tins. Mix the remainder of the ingredients together and fill the tarts before baking for 30 minutes at 350° F until the top begins to brown.

In Swaledale these cheesecakes were made on the Fridays before the Whitsuntide and Midsummer festivities, their pastry being moistened with dripping from the joint of beef roasting before the fire.[18] Later they were eaten with the beef, replacing the more usual bread. On the eve of Muker 'Awd Roy', held on the Wednesday before January 6th, Old Christmas Day, it was the custom for eight or ten strong lads to go about the village asking for food. They wore large aprons held out at the corners, and into these the housewives threw the cheesecakes, together with Christmas loaves, secret cakes, and even meat and poultry to be used for communal feasts for all-comers held at the local inns.[19] The Redmire Cheesecake gatherers followed a similar procedure, but blackened their faces and wore fancy dress up to about 1910, while those at Fulford used butter-baskets to hold their cheesecakes, gooseberry tarts, and money.[20] Cheesecakes and jam tarts, known as 'Wilfra tarts', were also eaten at Ripon in early August, when a mounted procession re-enacted the return of St. Wilfred to the town.[21]

The Cheesecake Gatherers, Redmire Feast, Wensleydale 1907. Here they blackened their faces and wore fancy dress while collecting cheesecakes for a communal feast.

Gooseberries were grown in most parts of the country, the juicy and sharp-flavoured pies made from them being simply known as 'berry pies', as opposed to those made with 'blackberries' (black currants), 'blaeberries' (bilberries) or currant-berries (redcurrants).[22] Competition for growing the heaviest gooseberries developed to such an extent that competitive shows began to be organised, one formed in 1843 at the Ship Inn, Egton, still taking place on the first Tuesday in August each year.[23] It is not surprising that berry pies were one of the most popular of all the delicacies made for the feast.

At Stamford Bridge, however, the residents baked small pear pies for their village feast, held every year on September 25th. On this day in 1066, the attack of the English army, led by King Harold, upon the Norwegian army, under Harold Hardrada and Tostig, was brought to a standstill by a single soldier who fiercely defended the wooden bridge across the Derwent. He was only removed by the exploit of an Englishmen who sailed under the bridge in a swine-tub or small boat, to spear his adversary from below. To celebrate this crucial event in the English victory, each pie was made in the form of a boat, having a skewer sticking out of it to represent the spear.[24]

The village feast often proved to be a convenient occasion on which to hold the Club Day of the local friendly society, although Whit Monday, May Day and Royal Oak Day might well be chosen in preference. The friendly societies, many of which were founded in the eighteenth century, collected subscriptions of a few pence each week from their members, thus establishing a substantial fund from which grants of sick pay, medical fees, old age benefit or burial money could be made to those in need. On the club day each member dressed in his best clothes, and, carrying his ceremonial staff, joined a procession to the village church for a service, afterwards retiring to a local inn where a substantial midday dinner was provided from club funds. A course of beef and mutton might be followed by one of veal and lamb, with a couple of chickens for the top table. Plum pudding and sweets concluded the banquet, after which there were speeches from local dignitaries, or society officers, with tobacco and ale to finish off the afternoon.[25]

If the dining room was too small to take all the members at one sitting, the landlord might place a manservant at a large table in a lower room, whose duty it was to break up several stones of oatcake into pieces and put them into broth. The table was covered with dark lead-glazed pint pots called meeas-pots, all steaming with broth, ready to be served out to those from afar as a 'biting on' while waiting their turn for dinner proper. In later years the broth and oatcake was distributed to poor neighbours who thronged around the kitchen door at the close of the feast with the request 'Pray, dame! will you' gie' me a meeas o' broth?'[26]

The village feast was certainly the pleasantest time of year for all working families, giving a brief spell of relaxation and sport in a period when holidays away from home were quite unknown. The only section of society to abhor the feasts were the employers, colliery owners finding their pits without men for a week at a time, while millowners just could not induce their men to return to work. 'I wish the devil had him who first invented feasts,' complained Joseph Rogerson after Pudsey Feast, 'Our slubbers have not given over feasting yet; they have done nothing these three days past; they are a set of clever fellows. I doubt I shall see some of them be glad to work when they cannot get any!'[27]

During the course of the year there were many other occasions when the community could come together to enjoy educational, sporting or religious activities for a few hours or perhaps even for a whole day:

> Our minds wander back, past joys we recall,
> Bazaars, and 'At Homes', so happy for all;
> The Christian Endeavour, Prayer Meetings, Talks,
> Band of Hope meetings, Whitsuntide Walks.
> The boys that have gone, o'er land, and o'er sea
> Are loud in their praise, O Zion, of thee ... [28]

The church and especially the nonconformist church, took a leading part in the lives of the majority of the inhabitants of both the rural and urban areas of the county. In church halls, and in the school-rooms at the Bethels, Rehoboths, Salems and Zions, a social or religious event was probably taking place virtually every day of the week. Of these, the most important was the annual Chapel Anniversary, when the congregation was joined by members from other chapels in the vicinity to enjoy a day of praise and good fellowship. The variety and order of the events varied from place to place, but the following account of the Levisham Primitive Methodist Chapel Anniversary is typical: 'There were special preachers on the Sunday, and on the next day the tea-feast was held in the Chapel, and lemon-cheese cakes and curd-cheese cakes and good tea and rich cream were enjoyed by everyone. Then a public meeting was held in Mr Dixon's big barn and recitations, speeches, and hymn-

The love-feast was a nonconformist religious meeting which started with a symbolic meal of bread biscuits and cake. At the same time a large communal love-feast drinking cup made of white earthenware neatly inscribed in hand-painted black lettering, was filled with water and passed around the congregation.

singing ended the day'.[29] The quality and quantity of the hospitality provided was always carefully noted, for the ladies of each chapel took great care to uphold the reputation of *their* anniversary against all others.

Another important event was the love feast. This was a form of religious assembly adopted from the Moravians by John Wesley in 1774, and subsequently held both by the Methodists and by their various offshoots, the Wesleyans, Independents, Primitives, New Connexion, Bible Christians, etc. In no sense was the love feast a form of Eucharist, it was simply an opportunity for the congregation to eat joyfully together, to sing, to give testimony, hear exhortations, and 'start for heaven'. The symbolic meal started with the serving of bread, biscuits or fruit loaf to each person. At the same time, a large communal cup of water was passed around. From around 1830 to 1880 the more prosperous chapels acquired large two-handled tankards for this purpose, each being made in white earthenware with hand-painted inscriptions in black recording the name of the chapel, probably the date, and the word 'Lovefeast'. After these refreshments, individual members stood up and related their religious experiences for two or three minutes.[30] The minister might then address the congregation, and lead them in prayer. At this time the whole atmosphere could become charged with a dynamic emotional force, the affecting cries of the penitents being lost amid the bursting joy of triumphant faith.[31] As in most parts of England, great national and local events were celebrated by a large communal feast provided either by public subscription or, more usually, by the generosity of a benevolent patron. A coronation jubilee, wedding, coming-of-age, declaration of peace, or the passing of a popular piece of legislation, would often provide a suitable opportunity for roasting whole oxen or sheep. For this purpose a large fireplace, perhaps three yards long, was built in a wide, open space, and specially-made giant spits, ladles and carving sets were used to turn, baste and serve the meat for the assembled crowds. Great pride was taken in every aspect of the operation, even to the extent of using a traction engine to turn the spit, commissioning elaborate commemorative knives and forks from the leading Sheffield cutlers, and recording the event for posterity by means of photographs and postcards.

In the first half of the nineteenth century celebratory feasts were often of roast beef and plum pudding, as described in John Yewdall's account of the coronation festival held by James Hargreaves, the Leeds clothier, in 1827:[27]

> His servants to treat, with plenty of meat,
> And cheer up their hearts for a while,
> The scene was the yard, where duly prepar'd
> The following sight made 'em smile.
>
> The table was made, upon which were laid,
> Twenty four plum puddings compact;
> Roast beef and good beer, that old English cheer,
> Were plac'd in their order exact.
>
> The master and dame, and misses too came,
> To sit and partake with the rest;
> And many good folks, who cracked their jokes,
> And heighten'd the charms of the feast.
>
> Two hundred or more, of rich and of poor,
> Were all seated down in one ring;
> When silence profound, was kept all around,
> While the band play'd 'God save the King'.

Even more sumptuous fare was provided for the two thousand people who gathered in a field near Bagdale in Whitby, in 1832, to celebrate the enfranchisement of the town.[33] Here 'the plum-puddings were brought to the field in a waggon drawn by three horses richly decorated with pink ribbons and rosettes [pink then being the conservatives' colour]. These puddings, 176 in number, weighing 10 lbs each, with 40 gallons of sauce, in which were 5 gallons of best French brandy, were all prepared by the Misses Yeoman of the Angel Inn, and they reflected great credit on those ladies. There were, in all, 5,000 lbs of meat, 4,050 three-halfpenny loaves, 5 cwt. of biscuits and 1,700 gallons of ale provided'. The boiling of such a great number of puddings would have to be undertaken by an almost equal number of households, no-one being able to boil more than one or at most two puddings on their domestic fireplaces. There were no such problems in the textile towns of West Yorkshire, however, for here the enormous dye-house boilers could be employed to cook single puddings of truly gigantic proportions. To celebrate the repeal of the corn laws of 1846 villages such as Clayton West, Holmfirth and Pudsey all made huge puddings, the 'tremendous big Plum Pudding boiled in a large Dye Pan at one of the mills' at Pudsey being hoisted on a strong flat cart and drawn through the streets by four horses, followed by large crowds of people and bands of music before being cut up and served.

There were similar celebrations for the opening of the Haworth Railway, now better known as the Worth Valley line, in 1876, when:

> Twelve stone o' flour (3 lbs to a man)
> Wur boiled i' oud Bingleechin's kah lickin pan,
> Wi' gert lumps o' suet 'at the cook had put in't
> 'At shane like a ginney just new aht o't mint;
> Wi' knives made o' purpose to cut it i' rowls,
> And the sauce wur i' buckets and mighty big bowls ...
> Yo' sud a seen Locker-taaners brandishing their knives,
> An' choppin' an cutting their wallopin' shives;
> An' all on 'em shaatin they like'd the puddin' th' best,
> For nowt were like 'the puddin for standin th' test.

Unfortunately the Clayton West pudding was somewhat eclipsed by the product of the neighbouring village of Denby Dale, for:[34]

> At Clayton West they did their best;
> A pudding they had made.
> But Denby Dale made them turn pale
> When rejoicing at Free Trade.

Ever since it had baked a great pie to celebrate George III's recovery from mental illness in 1788, the village had taken enormous pride in its pie-making. A 'Victory Pie' of 1815 contained two whole sheep and twenty fowl, but the 'Corn Laws Pie' was on an unprecented scale. Baked in a circular dish almost two feet deep and seven feet in diameter, it held seven hares, fourteen rabbits, four pheasant, four partridge, four grouse, two ducks, two geese, two turkeys, two guinea fowl, four hens, six pigeons, sixty-three small birds, five whole sheep, a calf and a hundred pounds of beef. Although this pie was quite eatable, it came to a sudden end when its supporting platform collapsed and a crowd of 15,000 scrambled for pieces, demolishing it utterly and throwing it to the winds.

The next Denby Dale pie was made to commemorate Queen Victoria's Golden Jubilee of 1887. Eight foot three inches in diameter and twenty inches deep, it was made by a firm of professional bakers from Halifax. Day after day they cooked almost a ton and a half of meat, game and potatoes in batches, poured them into the great wrought iron dish, and then proceeded to bake it in a specially-built oven. As Mr Brierley cut the first slice, a powerful stench of decomposing food filled the air. Its method of cooking had caused it to go bad, impossible to eat, and dangerous to the crowd as they hurriedly backed away from the open pie. Only the prompt action of the mounted police prevented a major disaster. The next day the pie was buried in quicklime in Toby Wood with all due ceremony, specially-printed funeral cards being sold to try and recoup some of the considerable expenses. The village's pride in its pies had been severely dented, and so a group of local ladies produced their own 'Resurrection Pie' within the same week, this time with complete success.

In 1896 to celebrate the Jubilee of the repeal of the corn laws, the people of

In Affectionate Remembrance of the

Denby Dale Pie,

WHICH DIED AUGUST 27th, 1887,

AGED THREE DAYS,

And was interred in Quick Lime, with much rejoicing,
in Toby Wood, Sunday, August 28th, 1887.

With the Committee's Regrets.

Strong, strong was the smell that compelled us to part,
From a treat to our stomach and a salve to our heart;
Like the last Denby Pie which the crowd did assail,
Its contents a rank mixture, it quickly turned stale,
Though we could not eat, yet we still lingered near,
Till the stench proved too much for our nasals to bear;
So like sensible men the committee did say:
" 'Twas best to inter it without further delay."
This mystic pie, so large and rare,
Smell'd awful as a tomb,
But came to show how long a pie,
In Denby Dale could bloom.

THE RESURRECTION PIE.

Undeterred by previous efforts the people of Denby Dale have attempted
another pie, which is to be consumed to-day, Saturday. This has been made
by the ladies of the village, and is expected to be a success. It consists of
48 stones flour, 96 stones potatoes, a heifer, two calves, and two sheep.

The Denby Dale Pie of 1887, over eight feet in diameter and twenty inches deep. When it was cut, a foul stench showed that it had already started to decompose, almost causing a riot in the surrounding crowds. This black bordered funeral card was issued to commemorate the interment of the Pie in quicklime in Toby Wood on August 28th, 1887.

Denby Dale decided to make an even bigger pie, ten feet long, six feet six inches wide, and a foot deep. Having no faith in professional bakers, two local men and three women supervised the baking of the one and three-quarter ton beef, veal, mutton and lamb pie in an oven near the corn mill. Fourteen horses then drew it in procession to the local park, where it was served to the public to the accompaniment of brass bands, variety acts, and a firework display. Since that time progressively larger pies have been made in Denby Dale, the 1928 'Infirmary Pie' weighing about four tons and the 1964 pie some six tons as this small South Yorkshire village proudly fought to retain its unique status as the home of the world's biggest pies.

Chapter 15

Calendar Customs

The foods traditionally served on major religious festivals and on significant days in the working year tend to be very conservative, changing at a much slower rate than those eaten every day. In this way, they preserve many features from earlier peiods. A good example is provided by frumenty, a dish of stewed grain which was eaten from prehistoric times through to the early seventeenth century, but which survived only as a Christmas eve speciality almost up to the present day. Similarly, the dietary practices of the medieval church, ranging from using up foodstuffs before Lent, giving up meat during Lent, and eating fish on Fridays, continued in many households for centuries after they had been enforced by either church or state.

This is not to say that festive foods have all remained unchanged, for they have been extensively modified by social and economic circumstances. Relatively plain mince pies, Christmas puddings and Christmas cakes became incredibly rich and sweet when dried fruits, sugar and spices became more plentiful in the mid-nineteenth century, while Easter eggs started to be made from chocolate and sugar once hard-boiled eggs had ceased to be a delicacy. Many of the traditional festive foods were only available to the poorer members of the community by means of begging. The calendar therefore included a number of days, such as Plough Monday, Collop Monday, Pace-egg day, or St. Thomas' day, when begging was formalised, perhaps by being integrated with a play or ceremony. As poverty declined, so did the need for begging, and the Plough Stotts. Pace-eggers and 'mumpers' all disappeared, except where they were preserved as a colourful feature of local life, the funds collected now going to suitable charities.

A further source of change came from the middle class and the clergy, partly from their passive influence as leaders of society, and partly from their deliberate policies of 'improvement'. Thus the harvest homes and mell feasts, with their good food, ale, music and dancing were replaced by the sober ceremonial of the harvest festival, while the police were actively employed to subdue mumming and begging in the streets.

In the following pages, the foods specially associated with the various calendar customs are described in detail. In many cases, they are the Yorkshire versions of practices which were widespread throughout these islands. Even so, they demonstrate the richness and strength of local traditions, which have only been eroded by the great changes in economic conditions and population movement which have taken place over the past century.

The first Monday after 12th night was Plough Monday, when the plough-lads begged through the villages. As George Walker commented 'The principal characters in this farce are the conductors of the ploughs, the plough driver with a blown bladder at the end of a stick by way of whip, the fiddler, a huge clown in female attire, and the commander in chief, Captain Cauf Tail, dressed out with a cockade and a genuine calf's tail, fantastically crossed with various coloured ribbons.'

New Year's Day, January 1st

The first day of the year was the occasion for one of the most remarkable of all traditional meals. It took place at the annual meeting of the manorial court of Hutton Conyers near Ripon, where the shepherds representing the local townships came before the Lord of the Manor's steward and bailiff to obtain their grazing rights for the coming year. Each shepherd brought to court a large apple pie, about 16–18 inches in diameter, a twopenny sweetcake (except for one shepherd who provided ale instead) and a wooden spoon. Having measured and divided the pies and cakes with the aid of ruler and compasses, the bailiff proceeded to cut them in two, (one half being shared between the steward, bailiff and tenant of the coney-warren, and the other divided among the six shepherds). The bailiff then gave each shepherd a slice of cheese and a penny roll, and prepared the frumenty. This was done by mixing it with mustard and placing it in an earthenware pot buried up to its rim in a hole dug in a field near the bailiff's house. The party then ate the frumenty, dipping in their wooden spoons in strict order of precedence, the steward being followed by the bailiff, the tenant, and then the shepherds. Refusing to take the frumenty was considered to be an act of disloyalty to the lord, so that any shepherd who forgot his spoon was forced to lie down and eat directly from the pot, some of his fellows always ensuring that his face was plunged into the glutinous yellow mass. Finally the ale was served out, and the business of the court concluded in the bailiff's house.[1]

Plough Monday, First Monday after Twelfth Night

In eastern Yorkshire the plough-lads or plough stotts, gangs of fantastically-dressed farm lads dragging a plough along with them, danced their way through the towns and villages. Usually they begged for money which they could either divide amongst themselves or use for a communal feast. In Holderness, however, cheesecakes were collected by one of the group who wore a clean white apron and carried a basket.[2]

Collop Monday

On the Monday before Shrove Tuesday collops, slices of bacon or ham, were eaten with fried eggs, this being a survival from the medieval practice of eating the last of the preserved meats before Lent. The poor might ask their wealthier neighbours 'Please will you give me a collop?', which, having been cheerfully given, they would take home and cook, thus enjoying a really good meal, and obtaining a little fat for frying the pancakes on the following day.[3]

Shrove Tuesday

Throughout the county, the church bells started ringing at eleven in the morning, these 'pancake bells' being the signal for housewives to start making the pancakes, and for apprentices and schoolchildren to leave their work for the remainder of the day.[4] In Leeds, for example, the youths went round to all the schools beating old tin cans to bring out the scholars, who then reinforced the troop and proceeded to other establishments. In Cleveland, meanwhile, the lads in the school usually tried to send their master outside and then barred the door, shouting:

> A holiday! a holiday! a holiday! we crave,
> A holiday! a holiday! a holiday! we'll have.
> If you won't give us a holiday, there you must stay,
> For this is our legal barring-out day.[5]

The holiday was supposed to give the children time to 'gather sticks to fry pankeeaks with', but in practice it gave them the opportunity of going home for their pancakes before spending the rest of the day in various sporting activities.[6] Usually the pancakes were eaten with treacle or lemon juice and sugar.[7]

In the evening, the young people might hold a join-night, celebrations of this type being held from time to time throughout the year.[8] Mrs Jagger remembered these toffee-boiling nights, 'when the dwellers in some yard or fold joined their finances for the purpose of purchasing treacle and butter. How we pulled, turned, twisted, thumped and kneaded that toffee until it almost begged to be eaten!' Having been worked into sticks or lumps to harden, the toffee was shared amongst the contributors and their friends:

Treacle Toffee

1 lb demarara sugar	1 tablespoon vinegar
4 oz butter	1 tablespoon water
4 oz treacle	1 tablespoon milk

Gently boil in all the ingredients (except the vinegar) together for 15–20 minutes, stirring continuously, until it becomes brittle when dropped into cold water. Stir in the vinegar, and pour into greased shallow tins to set. Alternatively the mixture can be pulled and twisted when partly cooled and thus formed into sticks.

Ash Wednesday

Due to the mistaken association of 'ash' with 'hash', mutton hash was the main dish of the day in some households.[9] I can certainly remember a few families who still made hash on 'Hash Wednesday' in the Wakefield area in the 1950s.

In the North and East Ridings, and in the Craven region of the West Riding, 'fruttasses' or fritters were made for dinner, these being of fruit, eggs and spices, bound with flour and raised with yeast.[10]

To make Drop Fritters (1773)[11]

Take a quart of milk, six eggs, some salt, and nutmeg, four spoonfuls of ale yeast, and as much flour as will make a stiff batter. Then take six apples pared and sliced thin, a pound of currants washed, dried, and picked, half a pound of sugar, a glass of brandy, mix all well together, and set them before the fire two or three hours to rise; then have ready a brass pan with clarified butter, drop them in with a spoon, and turn them out, lay them on your dish, and strew sugar over them; for sauce, use wine, butter and sugar.

Fritters

2 eggs	2 medium-sized apples, grated
8 oz plain flour	1/2 oz candied peel
1 oz yeast	Pinch nutmeg
2 1/2 oz currants	1 cupful tepid milk
2 1/2 oz caster sugar	Grated rind of a lemon, and the
	juice of half

Dissolve the yeast in the milk, and pour into the remainder of the dry ingredients, and add the eggs, then cover and leave to rise in a warm place for 2–3 hours. Drop large spoonfuls into boiling lard in a frying pan, brown on both sides, drain and serve immediately, sprinkled with sugar.

Any remaining batter was used up on the following Friday.

Bloody Thursday, first in Lent

In Cleveland, black puddings were traditionally eaten on this day.[12]

Carling Sunday, fourth in Lent

Carlin' Sunday we kep up
Wi' grey pez cooked fer t'supper:
They're steeped i' watter ower neet,
Then fried wi' saim or butter.[13]

Carlings were grey or brown dried peas, which, having been soaked in water overnight, were drained, placed in a pan of boiling water with a pinch of salt and simmered for about twenty minutes. Having been drained once more, they were then fried in butter or lard for two to three minutes before being served with either salt and pepper or sugar and vinegar. Along the coast from the Humber to the Tyne there are various legends of carlings first arriving as the cargo of a ship driven ashore by storms, the peas, soaked and swollen by the sea water, then being gathered by the famine-stricken population living along the coast.[14] All these stories appear to be apocryphal, for carlings were cooked and eaten in central Yorkshire too, many miles inland. The Rev. Shaw has recorded how the carlings were eaten with ham by the women and children at home in Filey, while their menfolk assembled in the ale houses, where supplies were provided free of charge.[15] Children might also carry quantities in paper bags or even in their pockets, where they were readily available both for eating and to make suitable missiles for pea-shooters and catapults.[16] Those who tasted the carlings fully appreciated their crisp texture, nutty flavour, and high flatus factor, the latter being succinctly expressed in the East Riding saying 'Carling Sunday, farting Monday'. Even in the 1860s, two or three hundredweight of carlings were being sold each year in some of the smaller North Riding towns, but now the custom survives only to a limited extent in the north-eastern corner of the county.

Good Friday

In addition to providing an appropriate symbol of rebirth and resurrection on this great Christian springtime festival, eggs were also collected as a tythe levied at Lent and Easter in a number of Western European countries. In York, the 1587 registers of St. Michael le Belfrey record the collection of 'certayne egges at East'r, due to the clarke by anncyent customs', while at Burton Fleming in the East Riding, tythes of eggs were collected on Good Friday as late as 1726.[17] Good Friday was the usual day for children to go around the neighbourhood, either individually or in groups, to beg for 'pace eggs', the name being derived from paschal, relating to Easter. The Pace

On Good Friday at Midgley in Calderdale, the Pace Eggers still perform their play in which St George of England triumphs over Bold Slasher and the Black Prince of Paradine. Their elaborate head-dresses are made from rosettes of paper mounted on arched supports. Here too is the Doctor who could cure 'The itch, the stitch, the palsy and the gout. If a man gets nineteen devils in his soul, I cast twenty of them out!'

Egg Play, performed by groups of boys when begging for eggs, varied in content from one locality to another, but usually commenced with their captain entering and singing;

> Here's two or three jolly boys, all o'one mind,
> We've come a pace-egging, and I hope you'll prove kind.
> I hope you'll prove kind, with your eggs and your beer,
> For we'll come no more pace-egging until the next year.

Various characters then entered in turn, each being colourfully decked out in appropriate costume. In addition to Old Tosspot, or a miser, there might be St George, Bold Slasher and the Black Prince of Paradine if the West Riding version was being given.[18] Once the dramatic action had taken place, the request for eggs was made in the following manner:

> Come, search up your money,
> Be jubilant and free,
> And give us your Pace egg
> For Easter Monday.
>
> Go down in your cellars,
> And see what you'll find.
> If your barrels be empty
> I hope you'll provide.

I hope you'll provide
Sweet eggs and strong beer,
And we'll come no more to you
Until the next year.

These times they are hard
And money is scant,
One Pace egg of yours
Is all that we want.

And if you will grant us
This little small thing,
We'll all charm our voices.
And merry we'll sing.[19]

The eating of fish on Good Friday continued to take place in many homes, both Roman Catholic and Protestant, although the herb or Passover pudding died out in the mid-nineteenth century. This pudding was made from eggs, cream, sugar and bread crumbs flavoured with the juice of tansey, *Tanacetum vulgare*, which gave it a green colour and a very bitter taste. As one writer commented, 'it was a most objectionable dish'.[20]

Then, as now, hot cross buns were eaten on this day, both in the morning and through the day. Good Friday Cakes were also made, for it was believed 'That if we do eat of a Cake made purposely on Good Friday we shall never want Money or Victuals all the Year round which for many years . . . has always fallen out true'.[21] Even in the 1870s, best flour biscuits were made on Good Friday in Whitby, holes pierced through their centres allowing them to be strung from the ceiling throughout the coming year. They were used to cure diarrhoea, being grated into milk or brandy and water as required.

Easter Sunday

On Heeaster Sunda' we've Peeast Eggs,
An' lots o' Kustods teea;
An' if you've nowt to put on new
There is a fine to dea.[22]

In Whitby baked custards were the traditional fare for Easter Sunday, the cold easterly winds common at this time being known as custard-winds:

Baked Custard

2 eggs
½pint milk
1 tablespoon sugar

½lb shortcrust pastry
A little grated nutmeg

Roll out the pastry and line an 8″ flan tin. Beat the eggs well, add the sugar, and pour the milk over them, beating all the time. Pour the mixture into the flan case, sprinkle with the nutmeg and bake for 15 min. at 400° F Gas Mark 6, then reduce the temperature to 350° F, Gas Mark 4 for a further 30 minutes.

Easter Monday and Tuesday

By this time, the eggs collected by pace-egging or by way of gifts between friends and relations had been hàrd boiled and decorated. The basic staining of the eggs was carried out by boiling them in a pan of water stained with cochineal for red, with the brown outer skins of onions for yellows to dark red-browns, or with coloured rags of various colours. I can still remember the beautifully mottled pale blue and mauve egg which my grandmother made for me in this way in the 1940s. One of the most effective ways of staining the eggs was to wet them, wrap them in brown onion skins bound in place with knitting wool or a piece of muslin, and boil them for half an hour. On being removed from the pan, their variegated marbling would then be much enhanced by polishing with a little butter.

The decoration of the eggs could be undertaken by a resist technique, immersing the eggs in hot water for a few moments, drying them, and writing a name or initials across their surfaces with candle wax before dipping them in dye.[23] Inscriptions could also be added in pen and ink, in gilded dots, or by scratching through the dyed layer with a sharp point to reveal the white shell beneath.[24]

The finished eggs were initially used as playthings by the children, but then came the trolling, when they were rolled down a nearby hill, perhaps one of the bluffs on the Wolds or Castle Hill or Peaseholme Hill at Scarborough.[25] Maggie Newbery could remember rolling her eggs down Bransby Hill around 1905.[26] If they managed to reach the bottom intact, it was believed to be a sign of good luck for the coming year, but most hit stones and cracked, then being speedily peeled and eaten on the spot. It was quite a social occasion, with the mothers sitting and talking at the top of the hill while their children chased the eggs. The lads, meanwhile, used a much

Pace Eggs were hen's eggs dyed by being boiled either with rags, or with onion skins, as in this example presented to Florence E. Wilson on Easter Monday, 1891.

speedier way of either adding to their store of food or losing their egg by 'jauping', one egg being struck against another until one was broken and forfeited to the victor.[27]

May 14th

On this day the maypole was erected at Slingsby, cheesecakes and spice bread being collected from the houses to furnish a communal 'rearing tea', which was followed by dancing to the music of the local brass band.[28]

Whitsuntide

> Early on this joyous morn,
> What beautious articles are borne
> Through the streets with utmost care,
> Teapots, urns, and chinaware,
> Jugs of sweet delicious cream
> Glitter in the sun's bright beam;
> Great tin boilers you may see,
> To boil the water for the tea.[29]

Whit Monday was the great day for Sunday School Anniversaries when the scholars of both Nonconformist and Anglican congregations walked in procession around their village, singing outside the homes of leading members of the community. Sometimes they were accompanied by their own musicians, perhaps with a harmonium on a horse-drawn cart, or even a military band. Further flat carts might be employed to carry the younger scholars, but the Rev. Baring Gould preferred to rely on the stirring strains of 'Onward, Christian Soldiers' which he wrote to march his scholars up the steep Quarry Hill to reach Horbury Parish Church. Early in the century the scholars might have been fortified with ale and rum and hot tea, but from the 1850s the teetotal movement brought an abrupt end to all alcoholic stimulants.[30]

While the walk was in progress, the ladies were busily employed in the schoolroom preparing the food for the patrons and teachers of the schools, and for the children, the tables being set up out of doors if there was a field near at hand and the weather was fine. The wealthier churches might have sufficient crockery to serve the entire gathering, but it was far more common to ask each child to bring a mug of its own, strands of coloured thread being wound around the handle to clearly establish its ownership. An excellent description of the whitsuntide school feast is given in Charlotte Brontë's *Shirley*.[31]

At four, 'long lines of benches were arranged in the close-shorn fields round the school: there the children were seated, and huge baskets, covered up with white cloths, and great smoking tin vessels were brought out. Ere the distribution of good

At the Whit Walks held on Whit Monday, the members of the church and chapel Sunday schools processed around their village, singing outside the houses of members of their congregation and local dignitaries. Often the younger children and a harmonium to lead the singing were mounted on a horse and cart lent for the occasion.

things commenced, a brief grace was pronounced by Mr Hall, and sung by the children, their young voices sounded melodious, even touching, in the open air. Large currant buns, and hot, well-sweetened tea, were then administered in the proper air of liberality: the rule for each child's allowance being that it was to have about twice as much as it could possibly eat, thus leaving a reserve to be carried home for such as age, sickness, or other impediment, prevented from coming to the feast. Buns and beer circulated, meanwhile, amongst the musicians and church-singers: afterwards the benches were removed, and they were left to unbend their spirits in licensed play'. A century later, the same events were taking place in exactly the same manner (except for the beer), individual paper bags containing a range of potted beef sandwiches and buns being distributed at our chapel at Thorpe near Wakefield.[32]

Trinitytide

At the pea-scaldings or peascod feasts held around Whitby, peas were boiled or steamed in their pods before being served in a large bowl set in the centre of the table. Everyone then took a pod and dipped it into a cup of melted butter and salt resting in the middle of the heap before extracting the peas between the teeth.[33]

Midsummer Eve

Writing in 1814, George Walker observed that in some parts of Craven and other districts of Yorkshire it was customary for new settlers in any town or village to set out a plentiful repast before their doors on the first midsummer eve after their arrival. Those neighbours who wished to make their acquaintance would then come

On Midsummer Eve new settlers in Craven set a table of beef, bread and cheese and ale outside their doors so that all those who wished to make their acquaintance could come and eat and drink themselves into friendship.

and sit down to enjoy the meal of cold beef, bread, cheese and ale, thus eating and drinking themselves into friendship.[34]

Churn Supper

The churn or kern supper was provided by the farmer for his workers once all the crops had been shorn, its name being derived from the churn of cream which was circulated around the company. At the churn suppers held in seventeenth-century East Yorkshire, the farmer provided 'puddings, bacon or boyled beefe, flesh or apple pyes, and then creame brought in platters and every one a spoone; then after all they have hot cakes and ale; for they bake cakes and send for ale against that time. Some will cut their cake and put it into the creame, and this feast is called the creame-potte or creame-kitte'. The cakes were made rather thick, and sweet with carroway seeds and currants. They were crossed on top by small squares cut into their dough just before baking.[35]

By the mid-eighteenth century ale had largely replaced the cream, but the custom continued in the agricultural regions from Craven in the west to the coastal region around Whitby and Scarborough.[36] The churn supper songs varied in the different dales, but the following verse is typical in its praise of ale:[37]

> This ale it is a gallant thing,
> It cheers the spirits of a king,
> It makes a dumb man strive to sing,
>   Aye, and a beggar play!
> A cripple that is lame and halt,
> And scarce a mile a day can walk,
> When he feels the juice of malt,
>   Will throw his crutch away.

From the mid-nineteenth century harvest celebrations of this type gradually passed out of use, as the farmers and clergy preferred the new fashion of holding harvest festivals in the parish church.

Burning the Witch

Up to the 1870s, the evening of the churn supper saw the 'burning of the old witch'. Eight or ten small heaps of peas, still on their dry straw, were gathered together and set on fire in the field. The labourers then ran and danced about, eating the 'brusted peas' and blacking each other's faces with the burnt straw, the lads generally aiming for the lasses, and vice versa.[38]

Mell Supper

The mell supper took place at the end of harvest, when all was gathered in. It was the harvest home. When William Metcalf wrote in his diary for September 3rd, 1798, 'Our folk got Mell', he was recording that the last sheaf, the 'mell' or 'widow', had been cut, and was either to be raced for by the older women, or plaited and decorated with ribbons to take pride of place in the centre of the barn floor at the mell supper.[39] In this form the 'mell doll' might even be dressed in the costume of a harvester, and be further enriched with flowers.[40]

The entertainment provided at mell suppers could be extremely plentiful, as is recorded in the Penistone harvest home song:[41]

> Well, on brave boys, to your lord's hearth,
> Glitt'ring with fire, where for your mirth
> You shall see first the large and the chief
> Foundation of your feast-fat beef;
> With upper stories mutton, veal,
> And bacon, which makes full the meal;
> With sev'ral dishes standing by
> As here a custard, there a pie,
> And here all-tempting frumenty.

or the Cleveland song:[42]

> An' what Mell-suppers there was then!
> All t'warkfooaks went seea smart;
> They'd tea, an' beef, an' ham, an' then
> They'd lots o' keeak an' tart.
>
> An' efter meeat was clear'd away,
> They set out t'yall an' gin;
> An' when t'awd fiddler play'd a tune,
> Now t'lads meead t'lasses spin!

> Then keeak an' yall was handed round
> A gud few tahms through t' neet;
> They nivver thowt o'gahin' off yam
> Till it was breead dayleet.

After a night of singing, dancing, and a visit from the guisers or sword dancers, the harvest supper was over for another year.

Not every farm provided such substantial refreshments, however, but beer would always be served in the field at the end of harvest, the farmer perhaps being prompted by the following song:[43]

> We've gotten all in
> We've left nowt out,
> But we've left our neighbour
> In and out.
> We've worn out shirts,
> And torn our skin
> To get our maister's harvest in.
> And now we'll give him a cheer
> And perhaps he'll give us some beer!

Nutty-crack-night, October 31st

A feast of nuts and apples took place in many homes in north-eastern Yorkshire on Halloween. Young couples would try to divine their future happiness by throwing pairs of nuts into the fire; if they burnt quietly it was a sure sign of a successful marriage, but if they bounced and flew apart, their marriage would fail.[44]

All Souls Day, November 2nd

According to the Rev. Baring-Gould, the Saumas loaves eaten on this day were a survival of the food prepared and offered to the dead at All Souls, the great day of commemoration of the departed.[45] They were small and round, being sold by the bakers at a farthing each around 1820, and given to children as presents.[46] In the 1860s, Mrs Sarah Grayson of Smithy Hill, Stocksbridge, was still baking batches of soul cakes which she gave away, along with a New Testament, but from this time the custom rapidly declined and passed out of use.[47]

Gunpowder Plot, November 5th

'I'th' country they all sit raand th'fire wi' their parkin an' milk or else rooasted puttaties, an' they tell tales, an' they laugh an' talk till they've varry near burned their shoe toas off.'[48] Parkins, a variety of oatmeal gingerbreads, were certainly the most important food eaten around the bonfire. The earlier parkins were baked directly on the bakstone or hot hearthstone, their alternative name of 'tharve cake' probably being derived from 'th' hearth cake'. They were originally made in the form of a flat, round cake of oatmeal, treacle, and either butter or suet,[49] but from the mid-nineteenth century the use of ovens and bicarbonate of soda transformed them into thick, moist loaves. The following recipes are for each variety:[50]

Thar Cakes

1 lb fine oatmeal	$\frac{1}{2}$ teaspoon baking powder
$1\frac{1}{2}$ tablespoons sugar	$\frac{1}{2}$ teaspoon ground ginger
4 oz lard	1–2 tablespoons treacle

Mix together the dry ingredients, rub in the lard, and work in just enough treacle to form a very stiff dough. Roll out to about $\frac{1}{4}$ thick on a floured board, cut into rounds, and bake on a greased baking sheet for 25–30 minutes at 350°F, Gas Mark 4. Allow to cool a little on the baking sheet before removing with a spatula.

Parkin

2 oz butter	2 oz dripping or lard
8 oz oatmeal	2 oz sugar
8 oz flour	$\frac{1}{4}$ oz ginger
14 oz treacle	$\frac{1}{4}$ teacup milk

Rub the butter and dripping into the oatmeal and flour, add the sugar and ginger, and mix with the treacle and milk. Bake in a greased tin at 350°F, Gas Mark 4 for $1\frac{1}{2}$ hours.

Parkin also featured in the barring-out custom held in many schools on November 5th. The schoolmaster having been tricked into leaving the building, it was barricaded against him, re-entry only being granted in return for a half-holiday. A collection was then made amongst the scholars for the materials for making parkins, which, when baked, formed the basis of a parkin party. At Lofthouse in Nidderdale the scholars might receive up to twenty parkins in this way, while at Midhope the schoolmaster was given such a large supply that he could still be seen munching them behind the lid of his open desk in the following April and May.[51]

Back End

After the fields had been ploughed, harrowed and sown, the farms of the East Riding looked as clean and neat as gardens. To celebrate the end of this period of particuarly hard work, the labourers and farm servants enjoyed a back end supper. This might include 'seed cake', so called from the occasion rather than its content, for it was just an ordinary plum or currant cake eaten with ale. On other farms there could be a far more substantial supper, with beef pies, ham, cheesecakes, fruit tarts and cheese.[52]

St Thomas' Day, December 21st

Throughout Yorkshire on this day the old women and children begged at the homes of the farmers and more prosperous members of the community, hoping to obtain supplies of wheat for making frumenty on Christmas eve. In large houses, such as Woodsome Hall, near Huddersfield, a sack of wheat stood at the door with a pint measure ready to serve everyone who came 'a-Thomasin'.[53] In Cleveland, meanwhile, parents sent their children 'mumping', presenting a pillow slip to the farmers, who usually gave them a handful or two of corn.[54] Wheat was still being collected in this way as late as 1909, but from the mid-nineteenth century it tended to be replaced by money and seasonal refreshments. Widows calling at Barnes Hall always received a glass of milk or ale, a slice of plumb cake, a sixpence, and a gossip in the kitchen, while at Darrington children collecting money were entertained at the farmhouses with hot ale, spice cake and cheese, so that they were usually comfortably drunk by the end of the afternoon.[55]

On this day too, the corn millers gave to their customers, the retail flour-dealers, a portion of pearled wheat, which they in turn gave away to their customers. Most millers used a pearling mill in which a large rough gritstone wheel revolved on a horizontal axis within a drum made of thin sheet iron punched out to produce a grater-like surface. The grain was first tipped into the drum through a small sliding shutter and the mill started, the stone revolving in the opposite direction to the drum to remove all the coarse outer husk from the smooth, hard grain.[56] The commercial bakers bought the pearled wheat in this form, soaked and boiled it until it creed into a soft, swollen mass, and thickened it with flour before ladling it into basins. When cool, it solidified into a stiff jelly which could be turned out and arranged in pyramidal mountains in the shop windows ready for sale.[57]

The wheat which had been collected by Thomasing or gleaning, or which had come into the house at harvest time and hung from the rafters at the end of the kitchen nearest the fire, had to be de-husked before it could be used. In some households this was carried out by pouring the grain into a clean sack and beating it with sticks upon the floor.[58] A white sheet was then spread on the floor near the open door and the grain poured onto it from a plate, thus allowing the chaff to be blown away by the draught. In other houses the grain was first soaked in water before it was beaten in the sack, the chaff rising to the surface when the grain was washed in water. The cleaned grain was then placed in a pan or stoneware jar, covered with three times its own column of water, and left in the hot oven for a day and half until it was creed ready for Christmas eve.[59]

Christmas Eve, December 24th

'T'day befoar Crismas mi mother wor as fierce as a buck-ferrit, fettlin' up, an bakin', an' gettin' all reddy for t' next day so as not to be done down.'[60] Christmas Eve was certainly one of the busiest days of the year for the housewife, with the house to be thoroughly cleaned, the shopping done, and the baking completed ready for the

The pearling mill was used to prepare wheat for making frumenty. This example, used by Aaron Robinson at Caydale Mill up to 1875, has a large rough stone wheel revolving within a large wire-mesh drum with punched grater-like sides. Once the wheat had been inserted in the drum, the drum and the stone were rapidly rotated in opposite directions, thus stripping off all the coarse outer husk to leave only the smooth, hard grain.

family's Christmas festivities. The traditional ceremonial of Christmas Eve started, in eastern Yorkshire at least, with the ringing of the frumenty bell from the church towers at six or seven in the evening.[61] This was the signal to start cooking the frumity, the main dish of the day.

The composition of the Christmas Eve supper varied from one part of the county to another, but generally followed the same general pattern. Once the frumenty was ready, the family gathered in the living room, where the yule log saved from the previous year was placed on the fire. From this, the yule candle was lit by the master or youngest daughter of the house, and set in the middle of the table, all other lights being snuffed out. Next, a cross was scraped across the top of an uncut cheese, and, once everyone had been wished 'a merry Christmas', the frumenty was served in individual basins, and the cheese eaten with yule cake, pepper cake, or apple pie, no-one leaving the table until supper was finished.[62]

The frumenty varied in richness and flavour from one household to another, but usually it was made as follows:[63]

Frumenty

1 pint of creed wheat	½ teaspoon allspice, nutmeg, or
1 pint milk	cinnamon
1½ oz flour	2 oz treacle

Mix the flour into the milk and bring to the boil, stirring continuously, add the remainder of the ingredients, and reheat almost to boiling point before pouring out into basins and serving immediately. For a richer mixture, currants may be added (about 4 oz to the above quantities).

Modern recipes which include butter, cream, sugar, rum or brandy to produce something like a liquid Christmas pudding have little in common with the form of frumenty traditionally made in Yorkshire.

Yule cakes were rich fruit cakes, their shape varying from area to area. In East Yorkshire they were about a foot in diameter and three inches thick, their tops being criss-crossed by a mesh of pastry strips.[64] Around Whitby they were made in rectangular cakes marked into squares so that they could be broken into individual portions. In Arkengarthdale they took the form of loaves, while in Nidderdale they were about the size of small teacakes, one being given to each member of the household:[65]

Whitby Yule Cake[66]

1½ lb plain flour	8 oz currants
12 oz butter	4 oz candied lemon peel
8 oz soft brown sugar	4 oz blanched almonds
½ oz cinnamon	3 eggs
½ oz nutmeg, grated	1 glass brandy
	cream

Rub the butter into the flour, mix in the remainder of the dry ingredients, and then stir in the eggs beaten with the brandy, and the cream, to form into a dough. Press into a square cake tin, and cut it halfway through into small squares, then bake for three hours at 350° F, Gas Mark 4. Turn out of the tin on to a wire tray, and, when cold, break it into rough pieces along the knife-cuts.

Nidderdale Yule Cake[67]

3½ lb plain flour	2 eggs
8 oz currants	2 pints lukewarm milk
1 lb raisins	8 oz butter
2 oz candied lemon peel, chopped finely	1 lb sugar
½ teaspoon cinnamon	½ teacupful of yeast (or ½ oz or 1 large teaspoon dried yeast, prepared as directed on the packet)

Activate the yeast with a teaspoonful of sugar in half the milk, and beat the eggs into the remaining milk. Rub the butter into the flour, mix in the remaining dry ingredients, and work in the milk to form a dough. Drop large spoonsful of the mixture on to a greased baking sheet, allowing room for expansion, and place in a warm place to rise for 20–30 minutes. Bake for 15 minutes at 450° F, Gas Mark 8, then reduce the heat to 375° F, Gas Mark 5, for a further 15–20 minutes. When just removed from the oven, glaze the cakes by brushing them with 2 tablespoons demarara sugar dissolved in ¼ pt. of milk.

Carved into a block of wood, this mould impressed a crude version of the royal coat of arms on to the gingerbread dough before it was baked. Dating from the reign of George IV, 1820-30, it was used by the Sonley family of bakers at Kirkbymoorside.

Apple pie followed the frumenty in the eastern half of the North Riding, where it might appear flavoured with the juice and zest of lemons.[68] In the same area, the pie was followed by a ginger bread or pepper cake. If they could afford it, every family acquired a gingerbread weighing anything from four to eight pounds, around twelve tons of it being baked in Whitby each year.[69] The York Castle Museum, and those at Pannett Park, Whitby, and Hutton-le-Hole, preserve examples of the moulds used for stamping the designs of figures or coast of arms on the local gingerbreads. The following recipe is based on one originating from Kirkbymoorside:[70]

Moulded Gingerbread

1 lb flour
8 oz treacle
2 oz brown sugar
2 oz lard

1 teaspoon each of ground coriander, carraway, cinnamon and
allspice
3 teaspoons ground ginger

Melt the treacle, sugar and lard in a pan and pour into the remaining ingredients. Knead it to a firm dough and keep in a warm bowl covered by a cloth. Pull off small pieces of the dough and press into the moulds after dusting with ground ginger. Turn out and bake on a greased baking sheet for 3 hours at 250°F, Gas Mark 1.

The pepper cakes, which acquired their name from the inclusion of allspice, or Jamaica pepper, in their ingredients, had a similar composition but were raised with yeast; as may be seen in Mrs Elizabeth Forth's recipe of 1792:[71]

To make a pepper cake

Four pd of Treacle, ½ oz of Jamaica pepper, as much ginger, an oz of Coriander seed, the Ginger must be beaten & sifted, the rest bruised, ½ oz of Carroway Seeds, beat them & put them all into the Treacle, and let them stand 2 or 3 days, then take 3 pd. of Flour & rub into it a ½ pd. of Butter, then mix these and the other ingredients and a pint of new Yeast, & a little Brandy and Candid Orange. Bake it in a Quick Oven.

The later nineteenth-century recipes use bicarbonate of soda instead of yeast as a raising agent, the following example coming from the York Board School's book of plain cookery recipes of around 1900:

Ginger Bread

1½ lbs flour	1 lb treacle
4 oz butter	4 oz sugar
1½ oz ginger	1 teaspoon bicarbonate of soda
½ pt warm milk	3 eggs

Mix the flour, sugar, and ginger well together, warm the butter and add it with the treacle to the other ingredients, stir well, make the milk just warm, dissolve the soda in it, and mix the whole to a smooth dough with the eggs well beaten. Put the mixture into a buttered tin and bake in a moderate oven [for 50–60 minutes at 350°F, Gas Mark 4].

Although not associated with the traditional Christmas Eve festivities, ginger-breads of this type were also made in the West Riding, Wakefield gingerbread enjoying a widespread reputation for excellent quality from the late eighteenth century. Here bakers such as Whitley's, Gosney's, and Simpson's, the latter established in 1823, made their gingerbreads in shallow tins to emerge an inch thick in a series of two-inch squares, each having a raised dome like a well-stuffed cushion.[72]

Mince pies might also be served from Christmas Eve to Twelfth Night. By the opening of the nineteenth century the substantial minced beef or mutton basis of the pies was already disappearing rapidly as they adopted the entirely sweet filling still popular today. In the following recipes of the 1830s, the first includes a calf's tongue, marking the residual use of meat in minced pies, while the second contains no meat at all:[73]

A Minced Pie

1 lb shredded parboiled tongue	1 oz mixed spice
2 lb suet	Pinch salt
5 pippins, chopped	1 lb sugar
1 green lemon peel, chopped	½ pt dry sherry
4 oz candied peel, chopped	A little brandy
2 lb currants	

Mix these together and fill the pies.

The mince pies of the early nineteenth century were larger than those of today, being, baked in wide patty-pans. Their pastry was different too, still being made with the puff-paste which had been used in earlier centuries when the high meat content of the pies required a comparatively long period of baking.

Minced Pies

1 lb beef suet	$\frac{1}{2}$ nutmeg, grated
8 oz chopped apples	1 teaspoon mace
8 oz currants	$\frac{1}{4}$ oz cinnamon
8 oz raisins	1 teaspoon salt
3 oz chopped blanched almonds	1 glass brandy
3 tablespoons sugar	1 teacup white wine
A little candied peel	

These mixtures were baked in patty-pans with puff-paste, as may be seen from contemporary illustrations.

In some parts of the county the wassail bowl passed round the table as part of the Christmas eve fare (see p 181), but in Penistone a large apple pie with a posset-pot full of hot ale and milk was the last thing to be eaten before going to bed. Once the whole household was seated at the kitchen table, a large spoon was put into the full posset pot. It was then passed from one to another round the table, everyone taking their fill before passing it on to the next, the apple pie then being served in the same manner. A similar custom took place in the East Riding, where everybody took about a wineglass full from a loving cup before standing on their chairs to drink at the same time.[74]

Christmas Day, December 25th

'Many keep Christmas day conscientiously as a day of divine worship,' wrote the Rev. George Young of Whitby in 1817, 'but more are disposed to sanctify it by the worship of the belly, in feasting on roast beef, plum pudding, and goose pie.' Certainly most people believed that Christmas day should be celebrated with

> . . . rooast beef an' mutton a gooise full o' stuffin',
> Boil'd turnips an' taties, an mooar o' sich kind;
> An fooamin hooam brewed, why, – aw think we'd enuff in
> To sail a big ship in if we'd been soa inclined.[75]

Up to the close of the nineteenth century the traditional fare for Christmas dinner remained virtually unchanged, although the quality of the individual dishes varied according to the circumstances of each family. If possible, goose formed the major dish of the day, either roast, or contained within that unique dish, the Yorkshire Christmas pie.[76]

'Rise wives and make your pies, and let your maids lie still, for they have rose all winter long and sore against their will!'. Thus the waits cried around the streets of York in the early hours of Christmas morning.[77] The contents of the Christmas pies were usually very rich indeed, as may be seen in the following recipes:

Yorkshire Christmas Pie from Hannah Glasse, 1796

First make a good standing crust, let the wall and bottom be very thick: bone a turkey, a goose, a fowl, a partridge, and a pigeon; season them all very well, take half an ounce of mace, half an ounce of nutmegs, a quarter of an ounce of cloves, and half an ounce of black pepper, all beat fine together, two large spoonsful of salt, and then mix them together, open the fowls all down the back, and bone them; first the pigeon, then the partridge; cover them; then the fowl, then the goose, and then the turkey, which must be large; season them all well first, and lay them in the crust, so as it will look only like a whole turkey; then have a hare ready cased and wiped with a clean cloth; cut it to pieces, that is, joint it; season it, and lay it as close as you can on one side; on the other side woodcocks, moor game, and what sort of wild fowl you can get; season them well and lay them close; put at least four pounds of butter into the pie, then lay on your lid, which must be a very thick one, and let it be well baked; it must have a very hot oven, and will take at least four hours.

This crust will take a bushel of flour. These pies are often sent to London in a box, as presents; therefore the walls must be well built.

To Make a Goose Pye – Ann Pickham of Leeds, 1773

Take two geese at Christmas, cut them down the backs, and take out all the bones, season them well with mace, pepper, salt and nutmeg; wrap one within the other, and raise a crust that will just hold them, lay them in, run the knife point into the skin in several places to prevent them rising; put butter over and lid it, and when baked, pour in clarified butter. This is a real goose pye.

In the North Riding these goose pies were made on December 26th, St. Stephen's day, and distributed among needy neighbours, except one which was carefully stored ready for eating at Candlemas on February 2nd.[78] Elsewhere the pies could include a greater variety of game, although they usually retained their great size. The 'standing pies' provided for the customers of the hotels and inns in East Yorkshire, for example, were nearly a foot high and were filled with[79] the choicest morsels of

The Yorkshire Christmas pie, a huge pie which might contain a turkey, a goose, a fowl, a partridge and a pigeon wrapped one within another, was made only in the most prosperous households. The pies had ornately decorated hot-water crusts, as may be seen in these examples illustrated by Mary Best of York in 1839, (left) and by Charles Fracatelli in 1855 (right).

hare, rabbit and pheasant. In Sheffield, meanwhile, a noted centre for the making of huge pies, Mr Roberts prepared a noble example for a Christmas party held at his house in Fargate in 1824. Weighing almost fourteen stone, it included 56 lb flour, 30 rabbits, 43 lb pork, 12 lb veal, and 20 lb of butter, pepper and spices.[80] A similarly large pie was sent from Sheffield to Lord Brougham in 1832, but unfortunately it failed to arrive safely, breaking down under its own weight. Even in the 1880s Yorkshire Christmas pies were still being made, albeit on a rather more modest scale, but by 1900 they appear to have passed completely out of use.[81]

Obviously goose, either roast or in a pie, was quite expensive. In most homes its place was taken by a joint of roast beef, mutton, or pork, served with potatoes, vegetables and sage and onion stuffing, all followed by a rich plum pudding:[82]

> Ha well aw remember that big Christmas puddin.
> That puddin mooast famous of all in a year;
> When each lad at th' table mud stuff all he could in,
> And ne'er have a word of refusal to fear.
> Ha its raand speckled face, craand wi' sprigs o' green holly
> Seem'd sweeatin wi' juices of currans an' plums,
> An its fat cheeks made ivvery one laugh an feel jolly,
> For it seem'd like a meetin' of long parted chums,
> That big Christmas puddin, – That rich steeamin' puddin –
> That scrumptious plum puddin, mi mother had made.[83]

The earlier receipts show that the pudding was quite plain, as may be seen in the following version noted down at Guisborough on December 25th, 1807:[84]

A Plum Pudding

12 oz flour	4 oz sugar
4 oz butter	4 beaten eggs
4 oz currants	1 teacup milk

Rub the butter into the flour mix in the remainder of the ingredients, tie into a pudding cloth, and boil for five hours.

As the century progressed, the puddings became much richer, the proportion of fruit, fats, eggs and spices increasing enormously:[85]

A Rich Plum Pudding, Leeds 1883

1½ lb raisins	8 oz flour
1 lb currants	1 lb suet
8 oz citron	9 eggs
8 oz candied orange	Half a nutmeg, grated
12 oz fresh breadcrumbs	Pinch of ground cinnamon

Mix the ingredients, tie into a pudding cloth, and boil for three hours.

Well within living memory, the puddings were usually cooked in the set-pot or copper if one was available in the kitchen or wash-house. The prolonged boiling took place on Christmas morning, or perhaps even throughout the previous evening if it was a particularly large pudding.[86] It was then lifted from the pot and quickly plunged into a pan of cold water so that it could be turned out on to a plate without sticking to the cloth. Finally, it came to the table either flaming in brandy or with a topping of white sauce flavoured with rum or brandy, and a sprig of festive holly.

After dinner, there were a few hours for conversation, reading, and play before high tea, with its cold meats, pork pie, and spice cake.[87] The latter, which eventually took the place of the traditional yule cakes and became the Christmas cake of today, was a rich fruit cake, covered with almond paste and ornamental icing. Its quality was a matter of keen concern to the housewife, for her relations and neighbours would all be extremely critical of its texture, flavour, and richness. As with apple pie, it was always eaten with the white, moist cheese made in the county.[88] Recipes for Christmas cakes varied greatly, each family carefully following its own version, but the following is fairly typical:[89]

Rich Christmas Cake

11 oz butter	4 oz blanched almonds
11 oz flour	8 oz candied peel
10 oz caster sugar	1 wineglass brandy
1 lb raisins	6 eggs, beaten
1 lb currants, chopped	½ oz mixed spice

The Christmas pudding, boiled for hours in the set pot finally emerged as the climax of the Christmas dinner. Hopefully it was flaming with brandy, as seen in this late Victorian Bradford household.

Beat the butter to a cream, add the sugar, then the eggs alternatively with the flour, beat well, then add the remainder of the ingredients in small quantities. When well mixed turn into a tin lined with greased paper, and bake in a moderate oven for $3\frac{1}{2}$ to 4 hours.

Twelfth Night

'In that part of Yorkshire, near Leedes, where I was born and spent my youth,' wrote Josiah Beckwith, 'I remember when I was a boy [about 1700] that it was customary for many families on the eve of the twelfth day of Christmas to invite their relations, friends and neighbours to their houses to play at cards, and partake of a supper, of which mince pies were an indispensible ingredient; and after supper was brought the Wassail Cup or Wassail Bowl, being a large bowl. A plate of spiced cake was first handed around to the company, and then the Wassail bowl, of which everyone partook by taking with a spoon out of the ale a roasted apple, and eating it, and then drinking the health of the company out of the Bowl, wishing them a merry Christmas and a happy New Year. The ingredients put into the bowl; viz. ale, sugar, nutmeg and roasted apples, were usually called Lambs-wool, and the night on which it used to be drunk was called Wassail Eve.'[90] By the early nineteenth century the wassail bowl was rapidly falling out of use, but the Twelfth-Night spice cake continued to be made up to around the 1850s.[91] These richly-decorated cakes were sold by confectioners, who also supplied coloured sheets of comic figures, alternately male and female, under each of which was a comic couplet. These were folded up, numbered, and placed in two containers, the men drawing from one and the women from another, then reading out their respective verses in turn before the cake was cut.

From these descriptions of the rich foods traditionally served at Christmas, it would be easy to gain the impression that everyone enjoyed a happy and plentiful festive season, but unfortunately this was often far from the truth. Particularly in the homes of the urban poor and those of the depressed handloom weavers, Christmas might bring a few small luxuries, but there would be little real change from their spartan subsistence diet.

Chapter 16

Headwashings, Weddings, and Funerals

Today, when virtually all births take place in hospital, with skilled medical aid readily available, it is difficult to imagine the plight of women bringing children into the world in the poor workers' cottages of last century. Robert Howard has described how the labour proceeded at Heptonstall Slack, with the expectant mother standing with her arms round the neck of two of her neighbours, or kneeling on a cushion with her arms and chest supported on a pillow placed on a chair.[1] In prosperous homes the whole experience would take place in more comfortable surroundings, with a doctor usually in attendance, but even so any confinement could pose great risks for mother and child alike.

Since the child was particularly at risk, it might be baptised as soon as possible, with the christening taking place about a month later. These ceremonies need not be carried out in church, however, and up to the 1840s the vicar might be expected to travel out to the house as required, the font remaining out of use for years at a time.[2]

The most notable custom associated with births in Yorkshire was the 'Shout' or 'Crying out' of Dentdale, as soon as the baby had made its first wail, the nearest neighbour immediately ran from house to spread the good news, all the womenfolk then picking up their warming pans and rushing to the house to celebrate with a feast of a particular kind of bread, rum butter, and home-made wines. While the women were thus employed, the father and his male friends proceeded to wash the baby's head with brandy before enjoying numerous glasses of strong drink.[3]

In the north-eastern part of the county, meanwhile, the expectant mother made a rich fruit cake called the baby-cake in preparation for the birth of her child, or alternatively laid in a supply of pepper cake. As soon as the happy event had taken place, the doctor was invited to cut the cake into exactly the same number of pieces as there were friends and relations present, since to cut more pieces would bring great troubles to the child, while to cut too few would lead to material shortages later in life. The cake was then eaten together with a cheese cut in the same manner accompanied by good home-made wines or botchet.[4]

About two weeks after the birth the mother invited her female relations and neighbours to a tea party. In Dent this was usually on the second Sunday following the birth and was known as the Wife-day, each guest contributing a shilling towards the cost of the refreshments. In Saddleworth it was a 'yed-weshin' (head-washing) tea, where they 'sat down to rum and tea, beef and bread, oven bottom muffins, crumpets, seed bread, thodden cake, threddle cake, shouting Roger currant bread, about ten currants in a loaf, and home-made blackberry jam. As soon as the tea was over and the old fashioned china sided away into the corner cupboard, [they] set on the table a bottle of elderberry wine for the spinsters and a bottle of rhubarb wine for the wed women. The guests then gathered round the evening fire, and some lit their pipes ... '[5]

When the baby was christened, a celebratory meal or drink might have been organised either at the parents' home or at a convenient public house, but no particular dishes were connected with this event, except at Gomersal, where oval cakes or buns called 'Dumb Boys' were served at the Old Black Bull, Garfitt Hill.[6] Today's ornately decorated Christening cake only became popular in the latter half of the nineteenth century, when most of the customs described above were passing out of use in favour of established middle-class fashions.

Birthdays

Birthdays were rarely celebrated with any special ceremony or meal, but in Holderness no birthday was considered complete without a specially made cake formed of ten or twelve alternate layers of pastry and currants measuring about an inch in total thickness. By the 1890s this form of cake was fast becoming obsolete, being replaced by the rich oven-baked fruit cake which enjoyed increasing popularity throughout late nineteenth-century England.[7]

Weddings

Yorkshire weddings of the early nineteenth century started with breakfast taken in the morning. At Pudsey, for example, all the men breakfasted at the groom's father's house, where rum posset was served, before collecting their lovers or wives from the bride's father's, but at Denholme[8] 'the whole of the wedding party met at the residence of the bridegroom. Before breakfast proper commenced, or rather it ought to be called the first course of the breakfast, a large pot that would hold two or three quarts, with two, three, and sometimes four handles on, called a posset pot, filled with hot ale and rum posset, would be handed round the party from one to another. Into this posset pot the bride would drop a wedding ring, and it was the object of each one of the party by taking three or four tablespoonsful of the posset at a time to fish up the wedding ring, for it was firmly believed that the one who fished it up, whether male or female, would be the next of that party to be married. Then followed tea with a liberal proportion of rum in it. By the time the breakfast was over the company got quite lively, and their faces, normally quite rosy from living in the bracing atmosphere of the hills, 1,200 feet above the level of the sea, became glowing red, the perspiration standing in drops. Breakfast over, the party would prepare for a journey of six or seven miles to the parish church, headed by the indispensable fiddler'.[9] A number of the posset pots used for this part of the entertainment still survive in local museum collections. Usually dating from before

Made in one of the Halifax potteries, this posset pot is a typical example of the vessels from which the guests spooned hot ale and rum posset at the start of the wedding breakfast.

1850, they bear the initials of the couple and the date of the wedding in bold white slip trailing on a rich dark brown background.

If it was a walking wedding, each couple would go arm in arm in procession to the church, but it it was a riding wedding, usually a sign of prosperity, the guests proceeded on horseback, the women being carried pillion behind their menfolk. After the ceremony, the younger men raced to the bride's new home, running barefoot at a walking wedding, or galloping in a cross-country steeplechase for a riding wedding. In addition to gaining a yard-long ribbon as a prize, the winner was awarded the privilege of either removing the bride's garter, gaining a kiss, or being admitted into the bridal chamber to turn down the bedclothes.[10] In Craven and the South Pennines he then retraced his steps carrying a pitcher or tankard of warm ale and rum, the 'Bride-Ale', which he presented to the bride before receiving his prize and accompanying the bridal party back to their new home.[11] In Cleveland, meanwhile, it was customary to give them 'Hot-pots', bowls of hot ale, sweetened and spiced. These pots were then carried from door to door together with a plate covered with a saucer, money being slipped under the saucer to enable the hot-pot to be replenished and thus continue on its way. So popular was this custom, that as many as twelve hot-pots have been presented and drunk on the mile-long route between the church and village at Robin Hood's Bay, where all 1,800 inhabitants participated.[12]

The bride cake featured prominently in the wedding celebrations of Craven and eastern Yorkshire. Here the bride was presented with a small cake on a plate when she arrived at her home. Having eaten a little, she threw the remainder over her head to symbolise the hope that they would always have plenty and something to

Taken from Gordon Home's *Evolution of an English Town*, this illustration shows a bridal garter from north-east Yorkshire. The blank squares were intended to receive the initials of the lovers.

spare. The husband would then throw the plate over his head, the couple's luck depending on its breaking into pieces.[13] Alternatively the groom might throw a plate of bridecake over the bride's head, a friend seizing it and stamping it into fragments to ensure their continuing good fortune.[14] From Craven, meanwhile, it is recorded that the bridal party went directly from the church to a neighbouring inn, where a thin currant cake, marked in squares, though not entirely cut through, was ready for their arrival, having spread a fine linen napkin over the bride's head, the groom proceeded to break the cake over her, the squares being scrambled for by the attendants.[15] This description of the cake bears a close resemblance to a contemporary account of the East Riding matrimony cake: 'a large round cake having a layer of currants between two layers of pastry, is covered with sugar, then cut into as many pieces as there are persons at the feast. Into one piece would be placed a silver coin; into another a wedding ring; . . . in a third, a button. Those to whom the money fell would be rich; the receiver of the ring was to be married soon; while the luckless wight whose piece contained the button was to die in single blessedness . . . '[16] Cakes of this type, variously known as Dewsbury cakes or perhaps Halifax cakes, were popular in the county from the early eighteenth century, one of their great advantages being that they could be baked on a bakstone at a period when ovens were not readily available for large sections of the community.[17]

If they could afford it, the bridal party and their guests enjoyed a good dinner in the evening, with plum pudding served as a first course followed by roast beef and mutton with vegetables, finished off with fruit pies and tarts.[18] In the Craven area, the main element of the dinner was the bride's pie. This was always made round, with a very strong crust ornamented with various devices. In the middle of it was a fat laying hen, full of eggs, probably intended as an emblem of fecundity. It was also garnished with minced and sweet meats. Every guest was expected to eat a little, for it was considered an act of great neglect or rudeness not to partake of this special dish:[19]

to make a BRIDE PYE by Ann Peckham of Leeds, 1773

> parboil cocks-combs, lamb-stones, and veal sweet breads, blanch ox-palates, and cut them in slices; add to them a pint of oysters, slices of interlarded bacon, some blanched chestnuts, a handful of pine kernels, and some dates sliced; season them with salt, nutmeg and mace, and fill your pie with them; lay slices of butter over them, and close it up; when baked, take veal gravy, a handful of white wine, a little butter rolled in flour, made hot, and pour it in; so serve it up.

Since a wedding was seen as a significant event for the whole community, and not just for the family and friends of the bride and groom, it was important that entertainment should be provided for all comers. Anyone who joined the wedding party at the public house after the ceremony could expect a good supply of free ale.[20] At these events a series of catch-songs might be sung, anyone failing to sing them correctly being fined by having to pay for glasses of drink all round. The following verse was common in Cleveland up to the 1880s. Each time it was sung the glasses were drained, someone else being called upon to repeat the song at once, toasting the bride if the last singer had toasted the groom, and vice versa:

> The brahdgroom's health we all will sing,
> In spite of Turk or Spanish king,
> The brahd's good health we will not pass,
> Put them both into one glass.
> See, see, see that he drink it all,
> See, see, see that he none let fall,
> For if he do, he shall drink two,
> And so shall the rest of the company do.

Another catch must have resulted in innumerable glasses having to be paid for each time the song was sung. The bride's garter, or a substitute for it, was placed in the centre of the table and surrounded with a circle of glasses. Each person then sang a line in turn, the glasses being raised on the word 'DRINK', tapped against that of its right and left-hand neighbours at 'CHINK', then set on the table once more without spilling – otherwise someone would have to pay for glasses round. The verse ran:

Wa lift each glass to t'brahdgroom's health,

DRINK, DRINK, DRINK,

T'yan 'at slaps pays for t'next roond

CHINK, CHINK, CHINK.

An' here's to t'brahd, good luck to t'lass

Drink, Drink, Drink.

Wa thruff her band noo pass each glass,
[each in turn slipping the garter over his glass on to his wrist]   Wink, Wink, Wink.
Wer liquor will all 't better seem,

Chink, Chink, Chink.

When wa call to mahnd wheer it hez been,

Drink, Drink, Drink.

But him 'at trimm'ls, smiles, or slaps [spills],

Chink, Chink, Chink.

Pays for wer glasses gahin to 't taps,

Drink, Drink, Drink.[21]

Later, the candle in the cup might be introduced. In this dangerous game a tot was filled with beer in which a candle was placed and lighted. The company then sang 'T' candle's i't cup, an' aboot she goes', then each in turn removed his cap and tried to drain the glass without blowing out the candle. It was not so bad when the candle was first lit and of reasonable length, but if the drinker failed to hold it against the side of the glass with his nose, it set his hair on fire. When the candle had burnt to two thirds of its length it became even more dangerous, quickly singeing off the eyebrows if not skilfully performed.[22]

In parts of the West Riding a rather different form of entertainment took place. On the morning after the wedding a friend called on the newly married couple to receive the 'embrass' or 'embrace', a sum of money which was used to provide a tea for the women and for the men at a public house. Having subscribed say a shilling each to add to the embrass, an evening of dancing, singing and fun was then enjoyed by everyone, the event frequently ending in considerable drunkenness.[23]

From the mid-nineteenth century these traditional celebrations started to decline as society began to expect rather different standards of behaviour. The teetotal movement brought a great decrease in the amount of drinking tolerated by many households, particularly in those which had joined the various nonconformist churches. The clergy were no longer the hunting squarsons of earlier years, but were now a new breed of sincere and energetic men who propounded a very proper and orthodox approach to life, the greatly improved communication systems, ranging from railways to newspapers and magazines, also tended to make fashionable middle-class practices popular throughout the whole country. Thus, by the last quarter of the century, weddings had lost much of their regional character, being replaced by the fairly standard form of celebration which is still in use today. This change is clearly illustrated by the bride cake. From being a thin current pasty, it rapidly became the rich, elaborately decorated iced fruit cake now to be found in most parts of the western world.

When Ellen Bulmer of St Mark's Villa, Leeds, noted down the following recipe in 1878, it was clearly this type of cake which she intended to make:

Brides Cake

1 lb butter	½ lb Candied Lemon
1 lb sugar	1 lb Valencia raisins, stoned
8 eggs	1½ lb Currants
1 lb dried flour	¼ lb Almonds blanched and chopped
½ lb Citron	a nutmeg grated.

Make & bake in the usual way – a glass of Brandy can be added or not at pleasure.
Almond Iceing (improved)
1 lb Almonds pounded in the usual way. 1½ lb of very fine sifted sugar. Mix with eggs unbeaten, put on the cake & let dry of itself.
Sugar Iceing
Iceing sugar mixed with whites of eggs until stiff enough, add a few drops of brandy.

Although the custom of placing a wedding ring in the cake was discontinued, the cake was now cut up into tiny slices, wrapped in napkins, neatly boxed and presented to friends and neighbours who were not invited to the wedding. This was certainly a poor and relatively anti-social substitute for the embrass of earlier years, even if it did reflect a more stylish and fashionable approach to the wedding.

Funerals

Of all the ceremonies which marked the progress of life from the cradle to the grave, the funeral was considered to be of the greatest importance. The entertainment provided for the mourners was always the most lavish and plentiful which could be afforded, since it indicated the family's status and prosperity, besides serving as a mark of respect for the deceased. The outlay of large sums of money at funerals was not confined to any one class of society, for the poor would spend just as much if not more in proportion as the rich. When wages might only amount to ten shillings (50p) to a pound a week, the cost of even a simple funeral could prove extremely expensive, as may be seen from the following undertaker's account of 1869:[24]

Laying out	1s 0d
Coffin	£1 11s 0d
Grave clothes	4s 6d
Grave making	14s 0d
Drinkings	£1 13s 0d
Bidding to funeral	2s 6d
Standing at door	6d
Biscuits	4s 6d
	£4 11s 0d

Some of these expenses were probably paid with 'burying brass', the benefit received from the burial club or friendly society to which weekly subscriptions had been made in former years. Alternatively, in the poorer homes where the funeral and its accompanying refreshments were acknowledged to be a financial burden, each of the mourners was expected to make a small contribution to help cover the costs. In most parts of Yorkshire a near relative sat by the open coffin and received a donation from each visitor who came to take a last look at the body before it was committed to the grave. Everyone was expected to give according to their means and personal circumstances.[25] In other households a collecting basin was placed in a conspicuous position on a table inside the house, wary mourners hovering outside the door to whisper 'Are the' tackin'?' before venturing indoors.[26]

At most funerals guests were invited by a bidder, often the undertaker or his representative in funeral dress, who visited each household in turn and recited a set formula, which varied from one area to another. In Leeds he announced 'You are expected to attend John Smith's burying tomorrow at three o'clock. We bury at . . .', while in Luddenden he informed the residents that 'You are respectfully bidden to the funeral of So-and-So, to be at the house of So-and-So.[27]

Funeral Cakes

'Before leaving the house for the grave-yard, the mourners have refreshment served to them – cheese, spice bread and beer for the men; biscuits and wine, both home-made, for the women. On returning to the house, a funeral feast is prepared, the like of which is only seen at these times ... the expense was so great that families were impoverished for years.'[28] This quotation presents an account of the usual practice throughout northern England, but is particularly interesting in that it distinguishes between spice bread (or cake) and biscuits. The same distinction is made in a Leeds advertisement of c. 1822 for 'Biscuits and Cakes for Funerals'.[29] As a correspondent to the Gentleman's Magazine in 1802 noted, 'in Yorkshire light sweetened cakes were given to those who attended funerals. The cake was put into their pocket or their handkerchief to be carried home and shared with the family, while the same sort of cake was served to the guests in hot spiced ale'.[30] At Eyam in Derbyshire a large round willow basket was used to pass triangular spiced currant cakes to each of the mourners. These, with a large tankard of spiced ale, were served at the door of the house when the funeral procession was just about to start for the church.[31] Perhaps their recipe was similar to the following, published by S.W. Stavely, a Chesterfield confectioner, in 1816:[32]

Funeral Bunns

Take two stone of flour, one pound of butter, one pound of sugar rubbed together, three pounds of currants, ginger, seeds, cinnamon, and a little rose water, mixed up with milk. The above will make forty-eight cakes, each weighing one pound before they are baked; make them round at three-pence each, and bake them a fine brown. They will take one pint of barm.

A small rectangular funeral loaf, made for the funeral of John Alcock who was buried at Elvaston near Derby on September 2nd, 1821, still survives in the Derby Museum.

Funeral cakes were also remembered by Dr. R.W.S. Bishop, in his volume on My Moorland Patients, describing his experiences at Kirkby Malzeard in Wensleydale between 1894 and 1906. Here 'the quality' had good old port and sponge cake and 'the many' mulled ale and Yorkshire parkin. He also illustrates the well-known thrift of the local inhabitants in the following story: 'As an old farmer lay dying, the landlord and his lady walked over the moor to enquire about his health and possibly to see him. The old housewife, who was notoriously mean and miserly, made them a cup of tea, explaining that she was too poor to provide more than simple bread and butter for their entertainment. Unfortunately this was overheard by a grandchild, who, childlike, exclaimed 'Oh grandmother, there's such a beautiful cake in the cupboard'. The old woman then shouted angrily, 'Hod thee noise, doant ye know t'cake's for t'burying!' '

Perhaps this 'cakes and ale' tradition was a predecessor of the biscuits and wine more usual in the late eighteenth and early nineteenth centuries. This is certainly suggested by the early name for the cakes – arval-bread, taken from the Scandinavian 'arval' or Celtic 'arwyl' for a funeral entertainment or rite. Halliwell refers to arval suppers, funeral feasts given to the friends of the deceased, at which a peculiar kind of loaf, called arval-bread, was sometimes distributed amongst the poor. It was a coarse cake composed of flour, water, yeast, currants and some kind of spice, about eight inches in diameter, and the kind of upper surface always scored, perhaps exhibiting originally the sign of the cross.[33]

Funeral biscuits

'At the funeral of the richer sort, instead of hot ale they had burnt wine and Savoy biscuits, and a paper with two Naples biscuits sealed up to carry home to their families. The paper in which these biscuits were sealed was printed on one side with a coffin, cross-bones, skulls, hacks, spades, hour-glass etc.; but this custom is now, I think, left off, and they wrap them only in a sheet of clean writing paper sealed with black wax.'[34] This description of Yorkshire funerals in 1802 tends to show that sponge finger biscuits were largely restricted to upper-class funerals in the late eighteenth century, although they were to become general throughout all sections of society by the early Victorian period.

Just like the funeral cakes, the biscuits were served to the mourners. In Whitby in 1817, for example, 'Two, three or four females, called servers, distribute wine and sugar-biscuits before the procession moves, and walk before it to the grave, dressed in white, with knots of white ribbons on their left breasts'.[35] In Slaithwaite in the 1860s 'the invited mourners were met at the door by a person holding a tray containing wine and biscuits, of which they partook before taking their last look at the departed'.[36] In South and West Yorkshire, the biscuits were also distributed after

This biscuit, showing the typical heart design found in the Yorkshire Dales, was stamped with a mould used by Mrs Nelson of Longber Farm, Burton in Lonsdale.

the funeral: 'small white paper tied with ribbon, containing two biscuits each, were placed in a basket lined with a white cloth, and a man . . . went after the funeral to the house of the friends of the deceased and left one of his little parcels'.[37]

One writer has recorded a rather different tradition for funerals in the Dales. Recalling an event which took place about 1920, Ida Spilsbury mentioned that 'One of the farmers had died, and Maffety was bidden to the funeral and the subsequent feast. I came in and found her with a piece of cake tied round with crape in her hand. This was her invitation!' Presumably this was a local variant of the usual custom.[38]

In the hills of the Yorkshire Dales, the funeral biscuits took the form of rounds of shortbread flavoured with caraway seed. They were stamped with a purposely-made wooden print about four inches in diameter, its face being carved with a heart motif surrounded by a series of zig-zag borders.[39] The heart may appear to be an unsuitable design, since it is usually associated with love and romance, but in this area it was quite appropriate. Here the heart was recognised as a symbol of the soul, and often appeared on gravestones, where each heart indicted the presence of a body interred beneath.[40] The following recipe gives good results:

'Funeral Biscuits'

12oz flour	½ teaspoon baking powder
10oz butter	½ teaspoon caraway seed
9 oz sugar	

Sift the flour and the baking powder, add the sugar and caraway, and rub in the butter. Press out the mixture, stamp with a wooden mould, and bake for 30 minutes at 300° F, mark 2.

Elsewhere, each biscuit measured about six inches in length by one and half inches in width, and had a crisp sponge texture.[43] Stavely give the following useful recipe.[42]

Funeral Biscuits

Take twenty-four eggs, three pounds of flour, and three pounds of lump sugar grated; which will make forty-eight finger biscuits for a funeral (whisk the eggs and caster sugar until stiff enough to retain the impression of the whisk for a few seconds. Gently fold in the flour, and pipe the mixture in 5" lengths on to lightly greased baking sheets dusted with flour and sugar. Bake for 19 minutes at 400° F, mark 6).

Fortunately a number of wrappers for these biscuits have survived in museums and libraries, perhaps being kept as mementoes of funerals significant to their original collectors. Most date from the early nineteenth century, and provide a graphically lugubrious reminder of this period of high mortality.

Usually they bear a printed panel measuring some 4½-5 inches in length by 3-5 inches in width, which was designed to appear neatly on top of the package once the wrappers had been folded and sealed around a pair of biscuits. In the Leeds area the following lines might be printed clockwise around the four sides of the panel:

I am the Resurrection and the Life,
He that believeth in me
Though he were dead, yet shall he live;
And whosoever liveth, and believeth in me,
Shall never die. Believest thou this?
O Death, where is they Sting?
O Grave, where is they Victory?
Thanks be to God which giveth us the Victory,
Through our Lord Jesus Christ

while in York;[43]

This truth how certain, when this life is o'er,
Man dies to live, and lives to die no more.

The central area is reserved for a verse or verses which might celebrate the deceased's joyous reception by his maker, as in M. Wilson's Leeds wrapper:[44]

Come to Judgement
Happy soul thy days are ended
All thy mourning days below
Go, by angel guards attended
To the sight of Jesus go

Waiting to receive thy spirit,
Lo, the Saviour stands above,
Shews the purchase of his merit
Reaches out the crown of love

For the joy he sets before thee
Bear a momentary pain,
Die to live a life of glory,
Suffer with thy Lord to reign.

Hughes and Maudsley preferred to dwell on the resurrection:[45]

My flesh shall slumber in the ground;
Till the last trumpet's joyfull sound
Then burst the chains with sweet surprise,
And in my Saviour's image rise.

Most usual of all, however, were stern verses warning the living of their final end, as in the following from Bramley of Halifax (c.1790):[46]

When ghastly Death, with unrelenting hand,
Cuts down a father! brother! or a friend!
The still small voice should make you understand,
How frail you are – how near your final end.

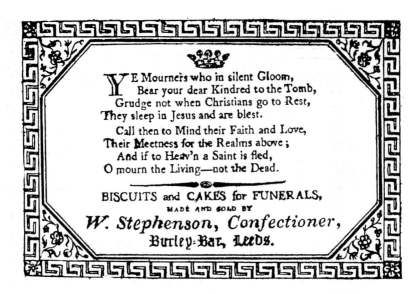

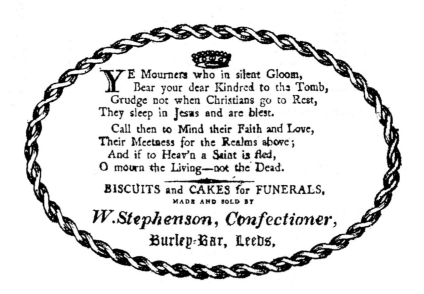

The long finger-shaped funeral biscuits were folded inside printed paper squares and sealed with black sealing wax. The designs usually include appropriate verses and an additional advertisement for the baker. Those made by W. Stephenson and H. Spencer both date from c. 1816-1825.

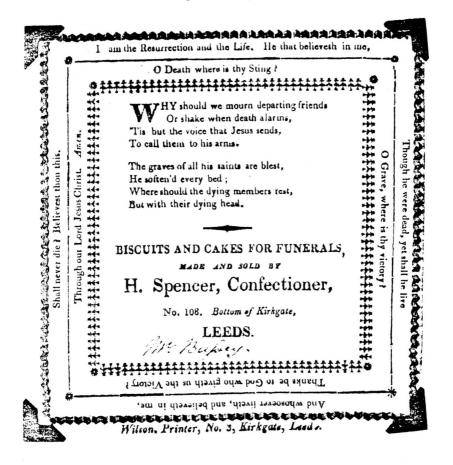

Or from A. & M. Heaps of Leeds, which has a particularly unpleasant twist in its tail:[47]

PREPARE TO DIE

> Death is a friend to all the Saints,
> It calls them to their rest.
> Removes their sorrows and complaints
> And ranks them with the blest.
>
> This awful messenger is come,
> Commissioned from on high
> To call me to my native home
> That world of perfect joy.
>
> Farewell my weeping friends, farewell,
> My dearest friends adieu!
> I hope ere long in heaven to dwell
> And then I'll welcome you.

Finally, the wrappers bear the name and address of their makers, a convenient form of advertising, together with 'Biscuits and cakes for funerals', 'made on the shortest notice', or simply the title 'confectioner'.[48] Sometimes other services were offered by the supplier, such as the provision of funeral wines.[49] One of the most unusual suppliers, however, was 'T. Robinson, Surgeon, Settle', who clearly had an eye for business, profitably selling funeral biscuits to the families of those he failed to cure.[50]

Although the provision of biscuits and cakes formed an important element in most funerals held in northern England from the seventeenth century at least, it began to fall out of fashion from the opening years of the present century. Simpler ceremonies were now preferred, and so mutes, crepe bands, and the practice of holding short services in the home of the deceased before the departure of the coffin to the church, all fell into disuse.[51] Elderly informants alive today can still remember the use of funeral biscuits up to the years around the Second World War, but from that time they appear to have gone out of use completely, and are no longer made either in the home or at commercial bakeries.

After the funeral had taken place, the mourners returned to the family home for the funeral tea, a feast of Yorkshire ham and baked meats with cakes, tea, and a variety of drinks including strong home-brewed beer, the quality and quantity of the provisions being limited only by economic necessity. Then pipes were lit and stories innumerable, long- and short-winded, were recounted of the deceased's skill in bargaining, his sound judgement of a horse, his wondrous sheep dogs, the birth of his first-born, incidents of great snowstorms, of long lost and buried sheep, of good and bad hay harvests, and of all the important things in his life. Then one by one these friends of early youth would yoke up and drive quietly away perhaps thirty or forty miles to a far-off dale'.[52]

Appendix I.

Contents of Weavers' Cottages

a) One-roomed cottage, c. 1810, Allerton near Bradford (Wood)

1 round table standing on three legs
a few turned unpainted chairs
1 old chest
1 cradle
1 half-headed bedstead with chaff mattress
1 or 2 looms
1 bobbin wheel
very few had a clock or a chest of drawers

b) One-roomed cottage of Adam Botheroyd of Almondbury, 7th November, 1820 (Certificate of Distraint, Tolson Memorial Museum, Huddersfield)

1 table	5s
1 pair of looms	–
1 box and 3 chairs	7s
1 delph case and pots	4s
Cans, pots and hustlement	2s
1 cradle	2s
1 fender and fire irons	3s
1 bed and bedding	18s
	£2. 1. 0d.

c) One up and one down cottage, 1832, Ossett, occupied by James Kemp

Kitchen
1 oven, 1 range, facings, 1 grate, 1 fender, 1 set fire irons
1 set pot
1 sink and 1 water kit
1 round table
2 square tables
5 elm chairs
1 corner chair
1 pot case and pots
1 chest of drawers, oak
1 24-hour clock
1 stump bed with flock mattress, 2 blankets, 1 quilt, 1 set of hangings
1 cradle

Utensils
1 jack, 1 spit
2 posnets

1 bakstone
1 tally iron
1 tea tray foot

Cellar
1 stone
2 tubs
1 winter-hedge
1 barrel
Weaving Chamber
1 cotton loom
1 stump bedstead with flock mattress, 2 blankets, 1 quilt 1 box

d) **One up and one down cottage, 1832, Ossett, occupied by Isaac Walby**

Kitchen
1 oven, 1 range facings, 1 grate, 1 fender
1 square table
1 round table
chairs
1 chest of drawers
1 corner cupboard
1 clock
1 tester bedstead, with feather mattress, 2 blankets, 1 quilt, 3 bolsters and hangings

Milkhouse
1 barrel
1 drinkpot, pots etc.

Weaving Chamber
1 broad cloth loom
1 stand bedstead, flock mattress, 2 blankets, 1 quilt, 2 bolsters and 1 hanging

e) **One up and one down cottage, 1832, Ossett, occupied by James Thomas**

Kitchen
1 oven, 1 range, facings, 1 grate, 1 fender, 1 set fire irons
1 square table
1 round table
4 elm chairs
1 corner chair
1 delph case
1 desk
1 corner cupboard
3 boxes, 3 hatboxes
1 stump bedstead with flock mattress, 2 blankets, 4 bolsters
1 cradle
1 picture
1 shoemaker's seat

Utensils
16 plates
1 water kit

1 shovel & brush
knife & forks
1 tea tray
2 posnets
2 candlesticks
1 winter hedge
1 tub
1 iron dish, pots etc.

Chamber
1 jenny

f) Two down and one up cottage, 1832, Ossett, occupied by Job Riley

Kitchen
1 oven, 1 range, facings, 1 grate, 1 fender, 1 set of fire irons
1 round table
1 square table
1 dining table
1 tea table
8 elm chairs   1 nursing chair
1 square cupboard, pots etc.
1 corner cupboard
1 potcase
1 chest of drawers, deal
1 stump bedstead with 1 flock mattress, 3 blankets, 3 bolsters, 1 quilt
1 cradle

Utensils
1 hand wheel
6 plates
3 irons, 1 tally iron
1 salt box
1 spit

Parlour
1 set pot
2 tubs, pots etc.
1 corner chair

Chamber
1 broad cloth loom
2 cotton looms
1 stove
1 set of shafts, 2 pairs of shuttles and bobbins, 1 tub 2 boxes, 2 baskets
1 stump bedstead with 2 flock mattresses, 2 blankets, 2 quilts, 1 bolster

g) One-roomed cottage, 1844, Heptonstall Slack (Howard)

Furniture
1 3-legged table, rugged in appearance
1 or 2 old chairs
1 or more low stools

1 chest of drawers (occasionally)
1 half headed bed, four legs, two side-boards, the head panelled with boards rising about
  two feet above the cording with a small shelf to place a lamp or candlestick upon
1 or 2 cotton blankets
1 rough cotton coverlet
1 pillow of coarse sacking or canvas filled with chopped straw or chaff commonly
  unchanged for 6 to 8 years

Utensils
1 frying pan and/or
1 porridge pot
1 kettle in about one house in twelve
1 or 2 old kitchen knives, frequently none
1 old tea pot
2 or 3 tea cups, saucers and plates
1 or 2 tea spoons
a few mess-pots
1 jug or milk can

h) **Kitchen of one up and one down cottage, 1840s, near Bradford (Scruton)**

1 three-legged table
1 stone shelf built into wall at side of fireplace
1 delph case with cups, saucers, smaller plates
2 looms, with tin oil-lamps at side
1 shut-up bed
1 chest of drawers for clothes
1 pitcher
1 iron pot

i) **Kitchen, early-mid 19th century, Batley (Anon. (1872), 72-7)**

Floor
Stone flags with edge of pottery mould around it, sometimes covered with ruddle or
  scouring stone, with sand where one had to walk

Carpets
Potato sacks, botany bagging for hearthrug with a bit of grey blanket at the bedside

Furniture
|presumably usual table and chairs with:|
1 old long settle
1 arm chair
1 delph case with plates
1 corner cupboard
1 chest of drawers or shut-up bed, with white cover, the bible, hymn books and crockery
1 bread creel
1 copper kettle

On walls
Samplers, silhouette portraits in rosewood frames, framed funeral cards

On mantleshelf
Brass candlesticks and one tally iron

In window
Fuchsias and musk

j) One up and one down cottage, mid-nineteenth century, Saddleworth (Wrigley 1912)

Kitchen
1 round table
3 or more rush seated spindle-back chairs
1 oak couch with print cushion
1 chest with cover and bible on top
1 press, with hunting coat and Paisley shawl
1 corner cupboard with store of spices etc.
1 long case clock
1 spinning wheel
1 mash tub

On ceiling
1 breadflake with oatcakes and onions
1 horn lantern
Mint and sage
1 gun and ramrod hung from straps

On walls
1 sampler
2 small pictures

Weaving Chamber
1 bed
1 handloom
1 50-spindle jenny
1 cuckoo-clock with flowered face and weights of lead
Skeps, slubbing creel, chafing dish, sizing pan and a twelve-stave wheel

k) Three-storey weaver's cottage, 1860s, Slaithwaite (Sykes)

Basement Living Room
1 turn-up bed
1 delf case or sideboard
1 looking glass with lash and small-tooth comb

First Floor Warehouse
1 warping frame, and/or
1 20 or 30-spindle jenny, and/or
1 burling table and/or
1 turn-up bed
Bags of wool, bales of shoddy, mungo, etc.

Second Floor Mill
2 or 4 handlooms
1 turn-up bed (perhaps)
Miscellaneous equipment, including bobbin wheels, healds, reeds, warping frame etc.

N.B: There might also be further parlours, cellars and attics according to circumstances.

l) One up and one down weaver's cottage, Timmy Feather's house, Stanbury, set up c. 1834, as seen in the 1890s (Turner, and photographs at Cliffe Castle Museum, Keighley)

Kitchen
1 long table
3 or 4 old chairs
2 oak chests
1 chest of drawers
1 8-day clock
1 bobbin winder
1 bread flake and oatcake

On walls
1 warming pan
4 cases stuffed animals
4 cages for larks and thrushes
1 cuckoo clock, weights and pendulum
Various framed pictures, funeral cards and miniature silhouettes

On Mantleshelf
4 Staffordshire pottery figures
1 pair pot dogs

In window
Jerusalem lily and two other plants

Weaving Chamber
1 loom
1 swift
1 clock
2 bird cages
Meal tubs and lumber

m) Suggested Furnishings 'for a Model City Cottage', Faxfleet Street, Bradford, 1902–4

Living Room	£	s.	d.
Table with sycamore top, 3ft. × 3ft.6ins.	1	15	0
5ft. dresser with shelf at back	4	0	0
Couch upholstered in leather cloth	3	10	0
4 upholstered chairs at 22/6d	4	10	0
Arm chair		16	0
Rocking chair		15	6
Hearth rug		18	0
Window cornice pole		6	0
Pair lace curtains		6	0
Bright iron fender and set of fire irons		12	6
Coconut rush mat		4	6
Total	£17	13	6

First Bedroom

	£	s	d
4ft. 6in. iron and brass bedstead		18	6
Wire spring mattress		16	0
Felt pad		5	0
Hair & cotton flock mattress and linen tick	2	10	0
Bolster		9	0
2 feather pillows at 5/6d		11	0
3ft. 6in. ash toilet chest with fixed glass	5	0	0
Corner wash stand with marble slab, marble in back, cupboard under and towel bracket	3	10	0
3ft. 6in. wardrobe with mirror in door to match	5	10	0
2 Rushseat chairs at 7/6		15	0
Carpet 9ft. × 7ft. 6 in.	1	3	9
	£21	8	3

Second Bedroom

	£	s	d
4ft. 6in. iron bedstead		16	0
Wire spring mattress		14	0
Felt pad		5	0
Horse hair and cotton flock mattress	2	0	0
Bolster		5	6
2 feather pillows at 5/6d		11	0
2ft. 9in. painted toilet chest	1	5	0
Dressing glass		9	6
Cane seat chair		3	6
Bedside mat		7	6
	£16	17	0

Third Bedroom (Attic)

	£	s	d
4ft. 6in. iron bedstead		15	0
Wire spring mattress		14	0
Felt pad ;		5	0
Horse hair and cotton flock mattress	2	0	0
Bolster		5	6
2 feather pillows at 5/6d		11	0
3ft. 3in. painted tall boy chest, 3 long and 2 short drawers	1	12	0
Toilet glass		6	6
2 cane seat chairs at 3/6d		7	0
2 bedside mats at 7/6d		15	0
	£17	11	0

Total for the whole house £53 9s 9d

Appendix 2

Descriptions of Miners' Cottages at Flockton from the Reports to the Commissioners on the Employment of Children (1842)

Name	Wages	Rent	Rooms	Beds
George Wood Jane Wood 3 children (2 working)	14/8 6/1 at harvest 12/6	1/-	Kitchen 12 × 15ft Back kitchen 9 × 10½ft. 2 chambers	3 very good hung in winter
Simeon Metcalf Nancy Metcalf 7 children (6 working)	14/4¾ 6/- at harvest 43/7	1/-	Kitchen 12 × 21 ft. Back kitchen & pantry 1 Bedroom 12ft × 21ft	3. One is divided by a curtain for the girls
William Child Margaret Child 5 children (1 working)	21/11½ 3/6		Kitchen 10½ × 15ft Bedroom 10½ × 15ft	2 very good and neatly hung
Joseph Charlesworth Anne Charlesworth	15/-	9½d	House 15 × 18ft Bedroom 10½ × 15ft.	2 decent
Richard Bretton Mary Bretton 6 children (3 working)	6/- 17/9	9d	House 12 × 18ft Bedroom 12 × 18ft Pantry	2
Samuel Tailor Martha Tailor 1 infant	14/9	8d	House 15 × 19½ft Recess 9 × 9ft with a window, bed & chairs	1 very handsomely hung

Furniture	Books	Garden
5 tables; clock; armchair; chairs; delf-case with abundance of cookery utensils	4 Bibles; Herbal; 2 Testaments; Barbauld's Hymns; 2 Hymn books; Catechism; Common Prayer; Questions on N. Testament	Beautiful order 18 × 7yds.
4 tables; chairs; clock; delf-case; book-case & drawers	4 Bibles; Catechism; 2 Testaments; Barbauld's Hymns; Common Prayer; Questions on the Testament; 2 Hymn Books	
tables; clock; easy chair; chairs; delf-case; drawers; cradle	1 Bible; 1 Testament; Common Prayer; Hymn Book	
2 or 3 tables clock; chairs; 8 cages of birds drawers; delf-case	Bible; Testament	Small but neat
table; cradle; chairs; chest; delf-case	2 Testaments	
2 tables; mahogany clock; rocking chair; oak easy chair; 6 chairs; cradle; delf-case; looking glass; brass candlesticks; 3 tea trays; steel fire-irons	Bible; Testament	17 × 7yds

Further Reading

The following sources have been used to provide much of the information contained in this book, and will enable the reader to build up a much more comprehensive view of the traditional life of the people of Yorkshire. Unless otherwise stated, all the following books were published in London.

Adamson, J.I.   'A Mey-as i't Porridge', *Yorkshire Dialect Society* X pt. LVIII (1958) 44.

Addy, S.O.   *The Sheffield Glossary* (1888).
                       A Supplement to the Sheffield Glossary (1891).
                       Traditional Tales & Household Remains (1895).

Alderson, J.   *Under Wetherfell*, Hawes (1980).

Anon.   *The Trial, Conviction, Condemnation, Confession and Execution of William Smith* (1753).
                       An Account of the Celebration of the Enfranchisement of Whitby, Whitby (1832).
                       The Dialect of Leeds (1862).
                       From Village to Town, Batley (1882).
                       Plain Cooking Recipes for use in the York Board Schools, York (?) (c. 1900).
                       The Mammoth Pies of Denby Dale, Denby Dale (1964).

Antrim, A.   *The Yorkshire Wold Rangers*, Beverley (1981).

Aram, E.   *The Trial & Life of Eugene Aram*, Richmond (1832).

Atkinson, J.C.   *Glossary of the Cleveland Dialect* (1868).
                       Forty Years in a Moorland Parish (1891).

Atkinson, J.F.   *Recollections from a Yorkshire Dale* (1934).

Baker, R.   *Report on the Conditions of the Residence of the Labouring Classes in the Town of Leeds*, Leeds (1839).

Balderston, A. & M.   *Ingleton Bygone & Present* (1888).

Baring-Gould, S.   *Strange Survivals* (1892).
                       Yorkshire Oddities & Strange Events (1900).

Baron, J.   *T'Yorkshire Lingo* (undated).

Barrett, M.B.   *In Her Clogs & Her Shawl*, Bradford (1978).

Batty, J.   *The History of Rothwell*, Rothwell (1877).

Bedford, H.	Manuscript notes on traditional life in Yorkshire collected by Henry Bedford in the 1930s & '40s. Leeds University Brotherton Library Ms 432/1–4.
Benson, J.	*British Coalminers in the 19th Century*, Dublin (1980).
Bigland, J.	*A Topographical & Historical Description of the County of York* (1818).
Bischoff, J. (collector)	A Poem descriptive of the Manners of the Clothiers, c.1730. MS in Leeds City Libraries. Reprinted in *Thoresby Society* XLI pt.3, no.95 (1947) 275–82.
Bishop, R.W.S.	*My Moorland Patients* (1926).
Blakeborough, R.	*Yorkshire Wit, Character, Folklore & Customs* (1898).
Blashill, T.	*Sutton-in-Holderness* (1896).
Bloom, J.H.	*Robin Hood's Bay* (c. 1935).
Brears, P.C.D.	'Oatcake in the West Riding', *Folklife* XII (1974) 55–9. *Raindale Mill*, York (1975). *Yorkshire Farmhouse Fare*, York (1978). *The Kitchen Catalogue,* York (1979). 'Heart Gravestones in the Calder Valley', *Folklife* XIX (1981) 84. *The Leeds Christmas Book* Leeds (1982). *The Gentlewoman's Kitchen*, Wakefield (1984). 'of Funeral Biscuits', *Petit Propos Culinaires* XVII (1984) 9–17.
Brontë, C.	*Shirley* (1849), Penguin Books edition (1974).
Brontë, E.	*Wuthering Heights* (1847), Penguin Books edition (1965).
Brooke, A.	*Slingsby & Slingsby Castle* (1904).
Bruff, H.L.	*Yorkshire Dialect Society* VI pt.XXXIX (1938) 69–70.
Brown, L.	'Yorkshire Oatcakes Past & Present', *Petit Propos Culinaires* XX 29–43.
Brown, R.	*General View of the Agriculture of the West Riding of Yorkshire*, Edinburgh (1799).
Bullock, J.	*Bowers Row*, Wakefield (1976).
Burnley, J.	*Phases of Bradford Life*, Bradford (1871).
Bywater, A.	*Sheffield Dialect* 3rd ed. (1877).
Cadman, H.A.	*Gomersal Past & Present*, Armley (1930).
Camidge, W.	*Ouse Bridge to Naburn Lock*, York (1890).
Carr, W.	*The Dialect of Craven* (1828).

Carter, F.A.	'Trinity Burton Feast', *Yorkshire Dialect Society* X pt. LIX, Kendal (1959) 25.
Charlesworth, P.	'The Charlesworths of Bank Bottom', *Old West Riding* IV, Huddersfield (1948) 8.
Cole, J.	*The History & Antiquities of Filey* Scarboro' (1828).
Collier, C.V.	'Funeral Biscuits', *Hunter Archaeological Society Transactions* III, Sheffield (1929).
Commission on the Employment of Children (1842)	Irish University Press Series of British Parliamentary Papers: Industrial Revolution, Children's Employment, Shannon (1968).
Cooper, A.N.	*Round the Home of a Yorkshire Parson* (1910).
Cooper, E.	*Muker, the story of a Yorkshire Parish* (1984).
Crump, W.B.	'The Little Hill Farm in the Calder Valley', *Halifax Antiquarian Society*, Halifax (1938) 114–196.
Cudworth, W.	*Round About Bradford* (1876). *Yorksher Speyks*, Bradford (1906).
Cuff, M.	*Recipes ... used in the Preparation of School Dinners served in School Dining Rooms ...* , Bradford (1908).
Dalton, W.	*Guide to Robin Hood's Bay*, Leeds (1893).
David, E.	*English Bread & Yeast Cookery* (1977).
Dibdin, C.	*Observations on a tour almost through the whole of England* (1801–2).
Dickinson, E.W.	*Yorkshire Life & Character*, Hull (1894).
Dowson, F.E.	*Goathland, its History & Folklore* (1947).
Dransfield, J.N.	*History of Penistone*, Penistone (1906).
Easther, A.	*A Glossary of the Dialect of Almondbury and Huddersfield* (1883).
Edmondson, T.	*History of Fimber*, Malton (1857).
Fairfax-Blakeborough, J.	*Life in a Yorkshire Village* Stockton-on-Tees (1912). *Yorkshire Days & Yorkshire Ways* (1935).
Fenton, A.	*The Shape of the Past*, Edinburgh (1985).
Fieldhouse, R. & Jennings, B.	*A History of Richmond & Swaledale*, Chichester (1978).
Fisher, J.	*History & Antiquities of Masham* (1964).
Forshaw, C.F.	*Holroyd's Collection of Yorkshire Ballads* (1892).
Fothergill, C.	*The Diary of Charles Fothergill*, ed. P. Romney, Leeds (1984).

Fream, W.	*Elements of Agriculture* 11th ed. (1920).
Gaskell, E.	*The Life of Charlotte Brontë* (1851), Penguin Books edition (1975).
Gaskell, M.M.	*A Yorkshire Cookery Book*, Wakefield (1916).
Godfrey, A.	*Yorkshire Fishing Fleets*, Clapham (1974).
Goodchild, J.	*Pope & Pearson and Silkstone Buildings*, Wakefield (1977).
Greenwood, O.	*Dalesman* XXI (1959) 406.
Gutch, E.	*County Folklore II: North Riding of Yorkshire, York & the Ainsty* (1901). *County Folklore VI: East Riding of Yorkshire* (1912).
Haggard, H.R.	*Rural England* II (1902).
Haldane, A.G.	*A Practical Cookery Book*, Wakefield (1936).
Harris, A.	'Rabbit Warrens of East Yorkshire in the 18th & 19th centuries', *Yorkshire Archaeological Journal* XLII (1971) 429–43.
Harris, J.	*Harris on the Pig*, New York (1902).
Harrison, S.	*Yorkshire Farming Memories* (cassette tape & booklet), York (1981).
Hartley, D.	*Food in England* (1954).
Hartley, J.	*The Clock Almanac* (1886). *Yorkshire Ditties I*, Wakefield (1868).
Hartley, M. & Ingilby, J.	*The Yorkshire Dales* (1963). *Life & Traditon in the Yorkshire Dales* (1963). *Life in the Moorlands of North-East Yorkshire* (1972). *Life & Tradition in West Yorkshire* (1976).
Harwood, H.W. & Marsden, M.A.	*The Pace Egg Play*, Halifax (1935).
Heaton, H.	*The Yorkshire Woollen & Worsted Industries*, Oxford (1965).
Heavisides, M.	*Rambles in Cleveland*, Stockton-on-Tees (1901).
Hedge, A.	*York Cook Book*, York (1981).
Hellewell, C.E.	The Hickleton Brew (1984). Typescript article by the brewer to Lord Halifax at Hickleton Hall near Doncaster (1926).
Hird, J.H.	*Mirfield, Life in a West Riding Village, 1900–1914*, Huddersfield (1984).
Hird, R.	*Hird's Annals of Bedale*, Northallerton (1975).

Hone, W.	*The Every-day Book* (1826).
Howard, C.	*A General View of the Agriculture of the East Riding of Yorkshire* (1835).
Howard, R.	*History of the Typhus of Heptonstall Slack* Hebden Bridge (1844).
Howitt, W.	*The Rural Life of England* (1840).
Hunter, J.	*Hallamshire Glossary* (1829).
Hutchinson, P.	*Old English Cookery* (1973).
Ingledew, C.J.D.	*History of Northallerton* (1868).
Jagger, M.A.	*History of Honley*, Honley (1914).
Jennings, B. (ed.)	*A History of Nidderdale*, Pateley Bridge (1983).
Johnson, J.	*The Nagars of Runswick Bay*, Youlgreave (Yorks) (1973).
Jones, D.S.	*Mr. Grass the Gamekeeper*, Birmingham (1985).
Kaye, S.	*Yorkshire Cooking*, Halifax (1970s).
Kenworthy, J.	*Early History of Stocksbridge & District*, Sheffield (1916). *The Midhope Potteries*, Sheffield (1928).
Kenyon, W.	*The Bishop of Kexbro', William Challenger*, Barnsley (1907).
Kightly, C.	*Country Voices* (1984).
Laing, S.	*National Distress, its Causes & Remedies* (1844).
Lawson, J.	*Progress in Pudsey*, Stanningley (1887).
Lloyd, G.	Manuscripts in the collection of the Lloyd family, c. 1800.
Long, J.	*The Book of the Pig* (1906).
Long, W.H.	*Survey of the Agriculture of Yorkshire* (1969).
Lovett, S. (ed.)	*The Armley Album*, Armley (1980).
Lucas, J.	*Studies in Nidderdale* (1882?).
Lumb, W.	*Workshop Shavings and other Poems*, Halifax (1938).
Manley, E.R.	*Meet the Miner*, Lofthouse (1947).
Markham, A.M.	*Back of Beyond*, North Ferriby (1979).
Marshall, W.	*Rural Economy of Yorkshire* (1788).
Metcalfe, W.	*William Metcalfe—His Book*, Leeds (1931).
Montagu, F.	*Gleanings in Craven* (1838).
Moody, F.W.	'Oatcake', *Transactions of the Yorkshire Dialect Society* VIII pt. XLIX, Kendal (1949) 21–30.
Moorman, F.W. (ed.)	*Yorkshire Dialect Poems* (1919). *More Tales of the Ridings* (1920).

Morris, M.C.F.	*Yorkshire Folk Talk* (1892).
	The British Workman Past & Present, Oxford (1928).
Mortimer, J.R.	*A Victorian Boyhood on the Wolds*, Beverley (1978).
Moxon, E.	*Supplement to Moxon's Cookery*, Leeds (1758).
Nellist, S.W.	*The Yorkshire Wolds of Yesteryear*, Driffield (1981).
Newall, V.	*An Egg at Easter* (1971).
Newbery, M.	*Reminiscences of a Bradford Mill Girl*, Bradford (1980).
Newton, G.D.	'Single Storey Cottages in West Yorkshire', *Folk Life* XIV (1976) 65–74.
Nicholson, J.	*The Folklore of East Yorkshire* (1890).
Orton, H.	'Yorkshire terms for Earwig and for the mid-morning meal', *Transactions of the Yorkshire Dialect Society* X pt. LVIII (1958) 52.
Pease, Sir A.	*Dictionary of the North Riding Dialect*, Whitby (1928).
Peckham, A.	*The Complete English Cook or Prudent Housekeeper*, Leeds (1773).
Platts, W.C.	*Betwixt the Ling and the Lowland* (1901).
Pollard, S.	*A History of Labour in Sheffield* (1955).
Priestland, G.	*Frying Tonight* (1972).
Pudsey Civic Society Members.	*The Pudsey Album*, Pudsey (1984).
Reach, A.B.	*The Yorkshire Textile Districts in 1849*, reprinted Helmshore (1974).
Reffold, H.	*Pie for Breakfast*, Beverley (1984).
Rimmer, W.G.	'Working Men's Cottages in Leeds', *Thoresby Society* XLVI (1960) 165–99.
Ring, T.J.	*Ox Tripe*, Sheffield (1920).
Roberts, J.	*Titus of Salts*, Bradford, undated.
Robinson, C.C.	*Dialect of Mid Yorkshire* (1876).
Rogerson, J.	'Diary of Joseph Rogerson', *Thoresby Society* XXXII (1929) 59.
Ross, F.	*History of Driffield*, Driffield (1898).
Roth, H. Ling	*Yorkshire Coiners*, Halifax (1906).
Rowntree, S.	*Poverty, a Study in Town Life* (1901).
Salmon, D.J. (ed.)	*Malton in the early 19th century*, Northallerton (1981).
Samuel, R.	*Miners, Quarrymen and Saltworkers* (1977).
Scruton, W.	*Pen & Pencil Pictures of Old Bradford*, Bradford (1889).
	Bradford Fifty Years Ago, Bradford (1897).

Sedgwick, A.   *Adam Sedgwick's Dent*, Sedbergh & Dent (1984).

Sheppard, A.   'East Yorkshire's Agricultural Labour Force in the mid-nineteenth century', *Agricultural History Review* IX (1961) 45–54.

Sheracy, R.H.   'The White Slaves of England', *Pearson's Magazine.* I (1896) 262–8.

Simpson, M.E.   *Ploughing and Sowing* (1861).

Smith, E.   *Sixth Report of the Medical Officer of the Privy Council* (1863), Appendix No. 6, 'Report on the Food of the Poorer Labouring Classes in England'.

Smith, J.R.   *A Glossary of the Words & Phrases collected in Whitby & the Neighbourhood by an Inhabitant* (1855).

Snowden, J. Keighley *The Web of an Old Weaver* (1896).

Spark, F.R.   *Memories of my Life* (1913).

Speight, H.   *Chronicles & Stories of Old Bingley* (1896).

Spencer, R.   *Field Flowers*, Batley (1890).

Spilsbury, I.K.   'An Old Gentlewoman of the Dales', *Dalesman* II no. 5 (1940).

Staveley, S.W.   *The New Whole Art of Confectionery*, Chesterfield (1816).

Stead, J.   *Food & Cooking in 18th century Britain* (1985).

Stead, R.   *A few notes: Holderness & Holdernessians* (1878).

Strickland, H.E.   *General View of the Agriculture of the East Riding of Yorkshire*, York (1812).

Strong, R. (ed.)   *Israel Roberts, 1827–1881*, Leeds (1984).

Sutcliffe, H.   *By Moor & Fell in West Yorkshire* (1899).

Swires, M.   *A Poacher and a Poet in Nidderdale*, Pateley Bridge (1970s).

Sykes, J.   *Slawit in the Sixties*, Huddersfield (1926).

Taylor, J.   *Reminiscences of Isaac Marsden* (1888).

Thomas, J.E.   *The Housewife's Guide*, Leeds (1830).

Thompson, S.   'The Bay I Remember', *Bayfair* II Robin Hood's Bay (1976).

Thompson, W.   *Sedbergh, Garsdale & Dent*, Leeds (1910).

Thompson, W.H.   *Speech of Holderness & East Yorkshire*, Hull (1890).

Tomlinson, J.   *Some Interesting Yorkshire Scenes* (1865).

Travis, J.   *Historical & Biographical Notes Mainly of Todmorden & District*, Rochdale (1896).

Treddlehoyle, T.   *The Bairnsla' Foakes an' Pogmoor Almanack*, Leeds (1868).

Tuke, J.	*General View of the Agriculture of the North Riding of Yorkshire* (1800).
Turner, J.H.	*Yorkshire Folklore Journal*, Bingley (1888).
	Yorkshire County Magazine, Bingley (1892).
Wagers, J.	'Hazlethorpe Papers', *Leeds Mercury* Supplement, Leeds (c.1870) Leeds Ref. Lib. 3.98.3/W.12Y
Walker, G.	*The Costume of Yorkshire* (1814).
Walker, H.J. & B.M.	*Recollections*, Leeds (1934).
Walker, J.W.	*Wakefield, its History & its People*, Wakefield (1939).
Walker, S.	A Book of Household Recipes (1833). Manuscript Leeds City Reference Library SR/641.5/W15W.
Warner, J.W.	*History of Barnoldswick*, Skipton (1934).
Watkins, J.	*Memoir of George Chambers the Marine Artist*, Whitby (1837).
Whitaker, J.	*History and Antiquities of the Deanery of Craven* (1805).
White, W.	*A Month in Yorkshire* (1859).
Whone, H.	*The Essential West Riding*, East Ardsley (1975).
Wilkinson, E.	*Royal Commissioner on Labour—The Agricultural Labourer* I, England, Pt. VI (1893).
Wilkinson, J.H.	*The Dialect of Leeds* (1862).
Willans, R.	'A List of Ancient Words used in the Mountainous District of the West Riding of Yorkshire', *Antiquaries Journal* (1811) 138.
Williams, E.	*Holmfirth from Forest to Township*, Huddersfield (1975).
Williamson, G.C.	*John Russel R.A.* (1894).
Wilson, G. (ed.)	*Voices: Memories of Home Life*, Loftus (1985).
Wilson, R.M.	'Agricultural Terms in the East Riding', *Transactions of the Yorkshire Dialect Society* VI pt. XXXVIII P.20.
Winder, T.	*T'Heft & Blades of Shevvield*, Sheffield (1907).
	An Old Ecclesfield Diary (1921).
Wise, W.	*Richmond, Yorkshire, in the 1830s*, Richmond (1977).
Wood, J.	*Autobiography of John Wood ... written in the 75th Year of his Age*, Bradford (1877).
Woodcock, H.	*Primitive Methodism on the Yorkshire Wolds* (1889).
Wright, E.M.	*The Story of Joseph Wright, Man and Scholar* (1934).

Wright, G.   Matters of interest to the Town of Leeds.
                    Manuscript of a poem written c.1730 now in Leeds City
                    Reference Library. See Bischoff, above.

Wright, W.   (Bill o'th Hoylus End). *Random Rhymes and Ramblings*,
                    Keighley (1876).

Wrigley, A.   *Songs of a Moorland Parish*, Saddleworth (1912).
                    Old Saddleworth Days, Oldham (1920).
                    At the Sign of the Three Bonny Lasses, Saddleworth (1927).

                    Those were the Days, Stalybridge (1937).

Y.A.S.   Archives of the Yorkshire Archaeological Society, Claren-
                    don Road, Leeds.

Yewdall, J.   *The Toll Bar* (1827).

Young, G.   *A History of Whitby*, Whitby (1817).

Notes

Introduction
1. White, W. 52.
2. Lawson, J. 11 & 55–6.

Chapter 1. *The Wool Textile Workers*
1. Newton, G.D., 68 & Appendix I a & b.
2. Appendix I, c, d, e, j.
3. Report of the Select Committee on the State of the Woollen Manufacture in England (1806) 45.
4. Appendix I, K.
5. Heaton, H, 293
6. Wright, G.
7. Strong, R. 12.
8. Lloyd, G.
9. Wood, J. 1877.
10. Scruton, W. (1897) 92–3.
11. Wrigley, A. (1912) 7.
12. Laing, S. 27.
13. Roberts, S. 19.
14. Rimmer, W.G. 193, 194; Strong, R. 15; Burnett, J. 139.
15. Howard, R. 55–7.
16. Burnett, J. 138–9.
17. See the chapter on Porridge, pp. and Snowden, J.K. 65 & 75.
18. Cudworth, W. 108–9.
19. Strong, R.S.
20. Lovett, S. 35, & Pudsey, 66.
21. Speight, H. 231.
22. Newbery, M. 47.
23. Sykes, D. 655.
24. Newbery, M. 36.
25. Reach, A.B. 15.
26. *Ibid.*, 9.
27. Sykes, D. 655.
28. Newbery, M. 37.
29. Newbery, M. 42, & Dibdin, C. 196.
30. Wright, E.M. 14, & Sykes, D. 655.
31. Tomlinson, J. 25–6.
32. Barrett, M.B. 9.
33. Quoted in Roberts, J. 27.

34. Hartley, M. & Ingilby, J. (1976) 33.
35. Hartley, J. (1886) 12, & Greenwood, O. 406 & 35.
36. Barrett, M.B. 9–10.

Chapter 2. *The West Riding Coal Miner*

1. Benson, J. 21–7.
2. Goodchild, J. 6.
3. Cudworth, W. 18 & Commission (1842) 170.
4. Walker, G. pl.III & Commission (1842) 170.
5. Haggard, H.R. 303 & Commission (1842) 181.
6. Haggard, H.R. 303; Strong, R. 52–3 & Cudworth, W. 108.
7. Hird, J.H. 37.
8. Commission (1842) ...
9. Cudworth, W. 93.
10. Kenyon, W. 12.
11. Manley, E.R. 63–71.
12. Benson, J. 140.
13. Bullock, J. 12.
14. Samuel, R. 326 & 337.
15. Benson, J. 58.
16. Whone, H. 62.

Chapter 3. *The East Riding Farm Worker*

1. Marshall, W. 253.
2. Sheppard, J.A. 47.
3. Gutch, E (1912) 11 & Nicholson, J 29.
4. Markham, A 28 & Wilkinson, E 57.
5. Morris, M.C.F. (1928) 60 & information from Miss. M. Moore, York.
6. Blashill, T. 234
7. Information from Miss M. Moore, York.
8. Nellist, G.W. 8
9. *Ibid.* 9 & Reffold, H. 28.
10. Strickland, H.E. 261.
11. Morris, M.C.F. (1928) 17.
12. Haggard, H.R. 367.
13. Reffold, H. 28.
14. Stead, R. 77.
15. Morris, M.C.F. (1928) 43–4.
16. Howard, C. 32.
17. Morris, M.C.F. (1922) 311 & (1928) 56–60.
18. *We Called them Tigalaries* tape cassette, York (1979).
19. Sheppard, J.A. 47 & 53, & Simpson, M.E. 1–4.
20. Reffold, H. 43.
21. Sheppard, J.A. 53.
22. Howard, C. 21.
23. Wilson, R.M. 21. The recipe was provided by a lady born in 1882 who worked as a cook on an East Riding farm.
24. Harrison, S. & Markham, A.M. 41.
25. Leatham, I. 29 & Woodcock, H. 22.

26. Woodcock, H. 22.
27. Marshall, W. 144; White, W. 54; Woodcock, H. 202; and *Gentlemans Magazine Library of English Topography* XIV 369.
28. White, W. 54 & Marshall, W. 145.
29. Woodcock, H. 201–2.
30. Morris, M.C.F. (1928) 3.
31. Stickland, H.E. 261.
32. Haggard, H.R. II 295.
33. Strickland, H. 261.
34. Smith, E. 265.
35. Morris, M.C.F. (1928) 38.

Chapter 4. *The Urban Poor*

1. Baker, R. 14.
2. Reach, A. 17.
3. Pollard, S. 18.
4. Reach, A. 5.
5. *Ibid*. 37.
6. Baker, R. 45–6.
7. Reach, A. 22 & 38.
8. Sheracy, R. 264.
9. Rowntree, S. 265.
10. Whone, H. 92.
11. Sheracy, R. 267.
12. Spencer, R. 285.
13. *Dalesman* 481.
14. Burnley, J. 26.
15. Baron, J. 32.
16. Burnley, J. 29.
17. *Dalesman* XX 818 & XXVII 566.
18. *Dalesman* XXVII 401 & Barrett, M.B. 4.

Chapter 5. *Fuel & Fireplaces*

1. Balderstone, A. & M. 138.
2. Wilson, G. 18.
3. *Yorkshire Evening Post* 31/5/1978.
4. Lucas, J. 119. See also Hartley, M. & Ingilby, J. (1968) 63–7 & (1972) 73–81.
5. Lucas, J. 26.
6. Moorman, F.W. (1920) 28.
7. Russell, J. 66.
8. Young, G. 818; Atkinson, J.C. 121; Alderson, J. 54; Cunliffe-Lister, S. 151; Jennings, B. 313–5 & 327; Tuke, J. 18–19 & *Dalesman* XIV (1952) 436.
9. Wise, W. 83 & Bigland, J. 80–81.
10. Wise, W. 83 & Mortimer, J.R. 5.
11. Lawson, J. 4. See also Winder, T. 26.
12. Original in Shibden Hall Museum, Halifax.
13. Lawson, J. 4.
14. White, W. 98.
15. Thompson, S.

16. Watkins, J.
17. Tuke, J. 293.
18. Jennings, B. 237.
19. Heavisides, M. 118.
20. Lawson, J. 4.
21. Meriton, G. 39, 83, 93.
22. Fenton, A. 103, 111.
23. Mortimer, J.R. 5.
24. Nicholson, J. 18 & Morris, M.C.F. 287.
25. Hird, R. 367.
26. Brears, P.C.D. (1984) 64.
27. Stead, J. 8.
28. Appendix I & private collection.
29. Reach, A.B. 32.
30. Brears, P.C.D. (1979) 12.
31. Hartley, M. & Ingilby, J. (1972) 14–15.

Chapter 6. *Oatcake*

1. Bigland, 83, 605, & Fieldhouse & Jennings, 466.
2. Fieldhouse & Jennings, 150 & 466.
3. Whitaker, & Crump, 188.
4. Bigland, 786.
5. Tuke, 120 & 127.
6. Morris, 88.
7. Marshall, 22–3.
8. *Leeds Mercury* 16th August, 1800 & Tuke, 121.
9. Whitaker.
10. In the South Pennines notched stone joists were apparently used to support the kiln floor. See R. Cross in *Dalesman* XIII (1962) 886.
11. Pontefract, E., in *Dalesman* V (1943) 113.
12. Raistrick, A., in *Dalesman* XXIII (1961) 25 and example in a private collection.
13. Baring Gould, S., 322.
14. Carr, W., 156.
15. Bywater, 32.
16. Lucas, J., 16, Brears, P., (1974) 57 & Wrigley, A., 190–203.
17. Lucas, J., 19.
18. Lawson, J., 8.
19. Brown, L., 29, & Moody, F.W., 25.
20. Bedford 432/3 p.12.
21. *Ibid.* 432/3 p.29.
22. *Ibid.* 432/4 p.96.
23. *Ibid.* 432/4 p.61.
24. Hutchinson, P., 70.
25. Lawson J., 30.
26. Easther, A., 20.
27. Montagu, F., 15.
28. Easther, A., 20.
29. Carr, W., 131 & Hartley, M. & Ingilby, J. (1968) 26.

30. Moxon, L. (1758) no.37 & Y.A.S. DD148.
31. Lucas, J., 15.
32. Bedford 432/4 pp 49-5 & 72-3.
33. Easther, A., 20, & Bedford 432/4 p.91.
34. Dickinson, I.W., 178 & Easther, 20.
35. Carr, W., 141.
36. Hartley, D., 518-9.
37. *Dalesman* XXIX (1967) 562 & Addy.
38. Bedford 432/4 p.2.
39. Remembered by the mother of Mrs K. Mason of Renyard's Ing, Addingham Moorside.
40. Bedford 432/4 p.2.
41. Brears (1984) 64.
42. Warner, J.H., 87.
43. *Leeds Mercury* Supplement no.563.
44. Walker, J.w., 374.
45. Dickinson, I.W., 179.
46. Brown, L., 37, Moody, F.W., 21, & *Dalesman* IV (1942) 73.
47. *Dalesman* XIV (1952) 437.
48. Bedford 432/4 p.83.
49. Thompson, W., 201.
50. Hutchinson, P., 69.
51. *Dalesman* X (1948) 15.
52. *Leeds Mercury* Supplement no.563.
53. E.g. *Dalesman* XIV (1952) 437, XXIX (1967) 561 & Wilkinson, J.H., 416.
54. *Ibid.* 258 & Easther, A.
55. *Leeds Mercury* Supplement no.563 & Addy.
56. Bedford 432/4 p.34; Kenworthy, J., 128, & Lawson, J., 9.
57. Walker, G., 62.
58. *Leeds Mercury* 10th May, 1800.

Chapter 7. *Porridge*

1. Geo. I chap.18 sec.3; (2) Geo. II sec.33 & (1) Geo. IV cap.93.
2. Wrigley, A. (1940) 41.
3. Wrigley, A. (1912) 152.
4. Thomas, W. (1910) 189.
5. Willans, r. 138.
6. Bronte, E. (1847) 178.
7. Wilkinson, J.H. 434, & Carr, W. 117.
8. Easther, A. 81.
9. Bischoff, J. 9.
10. Wood, J. 10.
11. Bedford 432/4 p.118.
12. Adamson, J.I. 44; Bedford 432/4 p.93; & Charlesworth, P. 8.
13. Bronte, E. (1847) 178.
14. Willans, R. 138 & Atkinson, J.C. (1868) 36.
15. Baron, J. 48.
16. Mellor, S. 30.
17. Snowdon, J.K. 3.

Chapter 8. *Bakery*

1. Dyer, S. 95 & Anon (1862) 290.
2. Alderson, J. 145.
3. Bedford, 462/4/115; *Darlington & Stockton Times* 20/10/1961, & Fairfax-Blakeborough (1935) 119.
4. Anon (1862) 445; Winder, T. 11 & Lawson, J. 8.
5. Information from Horsforth Woodside Methodists.
6. Brears, P. (1984) 69.
7. Information from Hornsey Historical Society.
8. Bedford 462/4/39.
9. *Ibid.* 38.
10. *Ibid.*
11. Brears, P. (1984) 65–6.
12. Kendrew's *Cries of York*, early 19th cent.
13. Haldane, H.C. 71.
14. Armstrong, T. *Crowthers of Bankdam* (1940).
15. Brears, P. (1984) 63–4.
16. Dalton, W. 24.
17. Hird, R. I 32–3.
18. Bigland, J. 88, 605 & Marshall, J. 15.
19. Tuke, J. 117.
20. Castle Museum, York, letter to Dr J. Kirk from John S. Gayner of New Earswick 6/11/1928.
21. *Dalesman* XII (1950) 148.
22. Woodcock, H. 22.
23. Bigland, J. 383.
24. Morris, M.C.F. (1928) 30.
25. Bedford 432/3/7 & 16.
26. Winder, T. 11 & Strong, R. 14.
27. Wise, W. 99.
28. Burnett, J. 203.
29. Wise, W. 57–8 & Morris, M.C.F. (1928) 30.
30. Young, G. 628.
31. Reach, A.B. 34.
32. Based on Bunett, J. 7 & 227.
33. Based on *ibid.* 16–17, 119, 156 & Brown, R. 209.
34. Barrett, M.C. 9–10 & Wilson, G. 24.
35. Blashill, T. 234.
36. Lawson, J. 9 & Kenworthy, J. (1928).
37. David, E. 95.
38. Pudsey Civic Society 38.
39. Information from Woodside Methodists, Horsforth.
40. Baron, J. 18.
41. Platts, W.C. 62–5.

Chapter 9. *Meat*

1. Boorde, A. 1542.
2. Tuke, J. 247–59 & Brown, R. 178–9.

3. See Brears, P.C.D. (1984) 26; Brown, R. 179, and Dewhirst, I. 92.

4. Morris, M.C.F. (1928) 37.

5. Walker, J.W. 500.

6. Drummond, J.C. & Wilbraham, A. 317–22 & Burnett, J. 7 & 100–2.

7. Kightley, C. 94.

8. Ring, T.J.

9. Easther, A. 149.

10. Bedford, 432/4/69.

11. Warner, J.H. 87.

12. Horniman Museum, London, no.4-9-52/1.

13. *Dalesman* XXI (1959) 193 & Kay, S.

14. Gaskell, M.M. 16–17.

15. Select Committee on Agriculture (1836) 49 & Wood, W. 77; White, W. 215, 237.

16. Hewitt, J. 247.

17. Yeadon Ladies' Guild.

18. Baron, J.

19. Newbery, M. 25.

20. Harris, J. 57; Long, J. 113; Long, W.H. 102; Tuke, J. 282, & Strickland, H.E. 245.

21. Fream, W. 536.

22. Long, J. 119–24.

23. Reach, A.B. 17 & 35, & Baker, R. 14 & 17.

24. E.g. Bradford M.O.H. Report (1876) 9.

25. Barrett, M.b. 46.

26. Nellist, S.W. 25.

27. Fairfax-Blakeborough, J. (1935) 105–6.

28. Platts, W.C. 277.

29. Markham, A.M. 31 & thomas, J.e. 46.

30. Nellist, G.W. 26 & Fairfax-Blakeborough, J. (1935), 106.

31. Information from Mrs E. Phillips formerly of Penistone and Haldane, H.C. 33.

32. Fairfax-Blakeborough, J. (1935), 107.

33. Bedford, 432/4 pp. 39–40.

34. Reffold, H. 15 & Haldane, H.C. 126.

35. Harris, A. 429.

36. Antrim, A. 89–93 & information from Mrs J. Stead.

37. Morley Friends Adult School.

38. Jones, D.S. 66–7.

39. Kaye, S. 111.

40. Kightley, C. 85–92 & Fothergill, C. 41–2 & 48.

41. Fothergill, C. 134 & Hartley, M. & Ingilby, J. (1968) 54–5.

42. Thomas, J.E. 41.

43. Easther, A. 57; Bedford 462/4/53; Moxon, E. & information from Mrs J. Stead.

Chapter 10. *Fish*

1. Young, G. 820–23.

2. Cooper, G.H.

3. Cole, J. 143.

4. Bigland, J. 315, & Cooper, A.N. 102–3.

5. White, W. 131.

6. The following paragraphs are based on Godfrey, A.

7. White, W. 132.
8. Priestland, G. 67–8.
9. White, F. 204.
10. Baron, J. 70.
11. Thomas, J.E. 32.
12. Information from Mr Peter Price.
13. Information from Mr G. Dent & Bedford 432/4/41.
14. Fothergill, C. 124, 165, 167, & information from Mr G. Dent.
15. Fothergill, C. 103, & notes 107 & 109.

Chapter 11. *Puddings*

1. Fairfax-Blakeborough, J. (1935) 116.
2. Whone, H. 31.
3. Brears, P. (1984) 81.
4. *Leeds Mercury Supplement* 21/10/1882.
5. See *Dalesman* XVI (1954) 41.

Chapter 12. *Home-Brewed Beers and Whisky*

1. Salmon, J.D.
2. Burnett, J. 5.
3. Hellawell, C. 2.
4. Lawson, J. 8.
5. Lawson, J. 8.
6. Wrigley, A. (1920) 269 & (1912) 28.
7. Wrigley, A. (1920) 18; Carr, W. 6, & Addy, S.O. (1891) 1.
8. Lawson, J. 9.
9. Addy, S.O. (1891) 45.
10. Addy, S.O. (1891) 5.
11. Addy, S.O. (1891) 48, 38, 44; & Travis, J. 379, 384.
12. Easther, A. 52.
13. Baron, J. 34.
14. Carr, W. 300.
15. Carr, W. 57, 37, 32; & Addy, S.O. (1888) 261, 249.
16. Wrigley, A. (1920) 268.
17. Treddlehoyle, T.
18. Wrigley, A. (1912) 27.
19. Atkinson, C.J.F. 23.
20. Nicholson, J. 29; Baron, J. 12; & Morris, M.C.F. (1892) 397.
21. Leeds City Archives, Middleton Colliery Paybooks MC 129–151.
22. Hellawell, C. 5.
23. Brown, R. 203.
24. Cudworth, W. (1876) 51–2.
25. Memories of D.J. Brears, who worked at the Yorkshire Copper Works about this time.
26. Wrigley, A. (1937) 90; Kenworthy, J. (1916) 26; & Sykes, J. 117.
27. Wrigley, A. (1920) 52.
28. Kenworthy, J. (1916) 26; & Sykes, J. 117.
29. Dransfield, J.N. 288; & inscription seen over the fireplace of Springfield Farm, Wrenthorpe, Wakefield.
30. Ross, F. 94.

31. Wrigley, A. (1937) 175, quoting Thomas Shaw, 'Tom o'th Top', writing in 1824.
32. Taylor, J. 77 *et seq.*
33. Addy, S.O. (1888) 111; & Morris, M.C.F. (1892) 280.
34. Addy, S.O. (1888) 289.
35. Yorkshire Archaeological Society Archives MD 423/392.
36. Anon. *The Story of a Drink* (undated) Leeds; *Yorkshire Evening Post* 27th Nov. 1975 & *Yorkshire Post* 12th Sept. 1978.

Chapter 13. *Beverages*

1. Spencer, R. 296.
2. Reffold, H. 59.
3. Morris, M.C.F. (1928) 25.
4. Edmondson, T. 3.
5. Mortimer, J.R. 11–12.
6. Edmondson, T. 12.
7. *Ibid.* & Mortimer, J.R. 12.
8. Babbage, H. 25.
9. Wilson, C.A. 371.
10. Harris, A. 12.
11. Cussons, A.C.H. 5.
12. Wise, W. 91.
13. Cussons, A.C.H. 4 & Harris, A. 25–6.
14. Howard, H. 57.
15. Bronte, C. 345.
16. Sykes, J. 99–100; Scruton, W. 91 & Cudworth, W. 146.
17. Winder, T. 26.
18. Walker, G. 51.
19. *Dalesman* XIII 23; XIX 339; XXI 353; XXIX 37 & Hartley, M. & Ingilby, J. (1968) 12.
20. See Harris, A. for a full discussion of this subject.
21. Information from Mrs J. Stead.
22. White, W. 200.
23. Burnett, J. 98.
24. Howard, 57 & Wood, J. 9.
25. Reach, G. 8.

Chapter 14. *Feasts, Fairs and Celebrations*

1. Williamson, G.G. 70.
2. Walker, J.W. 45–6 & Gutch, E. 156.
3. Wrigley, A. (1920), 99; Carter, F.A. 25 & Sykes, J. 63.
4. Carter, F.A. 25; Cooper, E. 86–7 & Moorman, F.W. (1919) 53.
5. White, W. (1859) 238.
6. Jagger, M.A. (1914) 123.
7. Thompson, S. & Sykes, J. 65; Speight, H. 269; Wrigley, A. (1937) 252; & Scruton, W.
8. Based on a recipe of Mrs Harker, Cyprus Street, Wakefield.
9. *Leeds Mercury* Supplement 563.
10. Wrigley, A. (1920) 100.
11. Spencer, R. 52.
12. *Dalesman* X (1948) 229.
13. Spark, F.R. 136.

14. Sykes, J. 63; Carter, F.A. 28; Charlesworth, P. 8 & *Leeds Mercury* Supplement 563.
15. Wrigley, A. (1920) 107–8.
16. Charlesworth, P. 8; Baron, J. 77; Fisher, J. 464 & *Leeds Mercury* Supplement 563.
17. *Leeds Mercury* Supplement 563.
18. Hutchinson, P. 68–9.
19. Cooper, E. 85 & Bedford, 432/4 p. 42.
20. *Dalesman* X (1948) 216 & Camidge 248–9.
21. White, F. 361.
22. Carr, W. 33 & Atkinson, J.C. (1868) 41, 48, 132.
23. Hartley, M. & Ingilby, J. (1972) 130.
24. Gutch, E. 157.
25. Cooper, A.N. (1910) 172. One Beverley society was known as the 'Duck and Green Peas Club' as this was the fare at their dinner, Nicholson, J. 10.
26. Kenworthy, J. (1928) 93.
27. *Colliery Guardian* 6/1/1905 & Rogerson, J. 30/8/1809.
28. Lumb, W. 62.
29. Walker, H.J. & B.M. 17.
30. Wright, E.M. 26–7.
31. Bartlet, 'Cups for the Lovefeast', *Country Life* 13/2/1975.
32. Yewdall, J. 55.
33. Anon. (1832).
34. Strong, R; Williams, E. 134 & Anon. (1964).

Chapter 15. *Calendar Customs*

1. Hone, W. 21.
2. Gutch, E. (1911) 87.
3. Cole, J. 131; Atkinson, C.J.F. 133; Kenworthy, J. 38; Fisher, J. 463; Addy, S.O. (1891) 13; Gutch, E. (1899) 237.
4. Gutch, E. (1899) 237 & (1911) 90.
5. Heavisides, M. 46.
6. Stead, R. 70.
7. Heavisides, M. 46 & Blakeborough, R. 75.
8. Gutch, E. (1899) 240; Turner, J.H. 31 & Wrigley, A. (1920) 112.
9. Gutch, E. (1911) 92 & Woodcock, H. 25.
10. Gutch, E. (1899) 241 & (1911) 93.
11. Peckham, A. 131.
12. Blakeborough, R. 75.
13. Fairfax-Blakeborough, J. (1935) 160.
14. *Dalesman* XXVI (1964) 129.
15. Gutch, E. (1911) 92.
16. *Ibid.* 93; Blakeborough, R. 76 & *Dalesman* XXVI (1964) 129.
17. Newall, V. 184–5.
18. Gutch, E. (1899) 244 & Harwood, H.W. & Marsden, F.H.
19. *Ibid.*
20. Markham, A. 53, & Turner, J.H. (1892) 40.
21. Anon. 1753.
22. Gutch, E. (1899) 245–6.
23. Bloom, J.H. 52.
24. Gutch, E. (1899) 246.

25. Baker, J.B. 467 & Atkinson, C.J.F. (1868) 368.
26. Newbery, M. 7.
27. Blakeborough, R. 77.
28. Brooke, A. 240.
29. Spencer, R. 86.
30. Strong, R. 11.
31. Brontë, C. 290–303.
32. Barrett, M.B. 36 & Hird, J.H. 110.
33. Atkinson, C.J.F. (1868) 376 & Gutch, E. (1899) 253.
34. Walker, G. Plate XXXVI.
35. Gutch, E. (1911) 104–5.
36. Aram, E. 32.
37. Forshaw, C.F. (1892) 60.
38. Gutch, E. (1911) 105–6 & Thompson, W.H. 61.
39. Metcalfe, W. 75; Blakeborough, R. 85–6 & Fairfax-Blakeborough, R. (1935) 322.
40. Morris, M.C.F. (1892) 213–4.
41. Dransfield, J.N. 306.
42. Gutch, E. (1899) 256.
43. Wise, W. 59 & Markham, A. 41.
44. Gutch, E. (1899) 266.
45. Baring-Gould, S. 272–3.
46. Gutch, E. (1899) 267.
47. Kenworthy, J. (1916) 37–8.
48. Hartley, J. 100.
49. Travis, J; Hunter, J. 125 & Carr, J. 196.
50. Bedford, 432/4/56 and Plain Recipes for use in the York Board Schools 28.
51. Bruff, H.J.L. 70 & Kenworthy, J. (1928) 141.
52. Morris, C.J.F. (1892) 214 & (1928) 45.
53. Easther, A. & Fairfax-Blakeborough, R. (1935) 168.
54. Fairfax-Blakeborough, R. (1912) 37.
55. Fletcher, J.S. (1910) 149–50 & *Blackwood's Magazine* CCXXXV no. 1419.
56. Anon. (1862) 307 & Brears (1975) 4.
57. Anon. (1862) 277.
58. Bedford 432/4/109 & 94, & Fairfax-Blakeborough, R. (1935) 168.
59. Carr, W. 167 & Morris, M.C.F. (1892) 216.
60. Cudworth, W. (1906).
61. Hartley, M. & Ingilby, J. (1972) 126 & Addy, S.O. (1895) 110.
62. Fairfax-Blakeborough, R. (1935) 166 & *Gentleman's Magazine* 1811 pt. I 423–4.
63. Bedford, 432/4/95 & 109; Haldane, H.C. 9 & Cole, J. 136.
64. Addy, S.O. (1895) 104.
65. Hartley, M. & Ingilby, J. (1963) 312 & Atkinson, C.J.F. (1868) 22.
66 White, F. 286.
67. Lucas, J. 43.
68. Young, G. 879; Cole, J. 136 & Ingledew, C.J.D. 341–2.
69. Young, G. 879–80.
70. Hartley, M. & Ingilby, J. (1972) 127.
71. Hedge, A.
72. Information from Mrs Baines of Pontefract, a descendant of the Simpsons.
73. Thomas, J.E. 30 & Walker, S. 40.

74. Addy, S.O. (1895) 103 & 104.
75. Hartley, J. (1898) 73.
76. For goose poems see Spencer, R. 44 & Wright, W. (1876) 76.
77. Wise, W. 50.
78. Gutch, E. (1911) 273 & *Gentleman's Magazine* 1824 pt. II 588.
79. Nicholson, J. 19.
80. *Gentleman's Magazine* 1824 pt. II 588.
81. *Leeds Mercury* Supplement 20/12/1883.
82. Barrett, M.B. 39.
83. Hartley, J. (1898) 73.
84. Brears, P.C.D. (1978).
85. *Leeds Mercury* Supplement 20/12/1883.
86. Spencer, R. 359 & Thomas, J.E. 36.
87. Barrett, M.B. 39 & Winder, T. (1921).
88. *Dalesman* XXIII (1951) 394.
89. Brears, P.C.D. (1982). See also Peckham, A. 149.
90. *Gentleman's Magazine* 1784 pt. I 98–9.
91. Addy, S.O. (1895) 110 & Turner, J.H. (1892) 38.

Chapter 16. *Headwashings, Weddings and Funerals*

1. Howard 58.
2. Atkinson (1891) 45.
3. Howitt, 236 & Sedgwick 97.
4. Bishop 200 & Blakeborough 106.
5. Wriley (1927) 203.
6. Cadman 113.
7. Nicholsn 11.
8. Lawson 18.
9. Wood 23.
10. Atkinson (1891) 206–10.
11. Carr 50 & Lawson 19.
12. Blakeborough 96; Atkinson (1891) 208 & White 98.
13. Blakeborough 96 & Gutch 129.
14. Addy (1895) 122; Nicholson 3 & Gutch, 129.
15. Carr 51.
16. Nicholson 11.
17. Brears (1984) 64.
18. Wood 23.
19. Carr 51 & Peckham A. 105.
20. Lawson, 18 & Fairfax-Blakeborough (1935) 139.
21. Blakeborough, 104–5.
22. Fairfax-Blakeborough (1935) 137–8.
23. Lawson 19.
24. Sykes, J. 150.
25. Local Notes & Queries CCCLXVII & CCCLXXIII, *Leeds Mercury* Supplement (1885).
26. Moody, F.W. 33.
27. Anon. (1862) 249; Roth, H.L., 279 Hone, W. 1079.
28. Nicholson, J. 8.
29. Funeral biscuit wrapper of W. Stephenson, Leeds City Library.

30. *Gentleman's Magazine* (1802) pt. I 105.
31. Addy, S.O. (1895) 124.
32. Staveley, S.W. 15.
33. Atkinson, J.C. (1868) 10–12.
34. *Gentleman's Magazine* (1802) pt. I 105.
35. Young, G. 884 & Atkinson, J.C. (1891) 227.
36. Sykes, J.
37. Collier, C.V. 211 & *Sunday Times* December 4th, 1955.
38. Spilsbury, I.K. 19.
39. E.g. Brears. P.C.D. (1979) no. 627.
40. Brears, P.C.D. (1981) 84.
41. Roth, H.L. 279. The recipe is quoted in Hartley M. & Ingilby, J. (1963) 311.
42. Stavely, S.W. 20.
43. Wrapper of Joseph Hick, 47 Coney Street, York.
44. Do. M. Wilson, 20, Commercial Street, Leeds. Leeds City Museum.
45. Do. Hughes & Maudsley, successors to Mrs Harding, 36 Cheapside, Lancaster. Castle Museum, York, 10/45.
46. Do. Bramley, confectioner, tea dealer, and milliner, Halifax, printed by Jacobs of Halifax c. 1790. Shibden Hall Museum, Halifax.
47. Do. M. Heaps, 60 Woodhouse Lane, Leeds.
48. E.g. Leeds Reference Library, L7 CB: H. Spencer, 108 Kirkgate, Leeds, c. 1817; W. Stephenson, Burley Bar, Leeds; H. Stonehouse, Bramley's Yard, Lower Headrow, Leeds; Craven Museum, Skipton: D1569 & D1504; Ann Oldfield, New Market Street, Skipton, 1817–50; & M. Barraclough (daughter & successor to the above) 1850–.
49. As supplied by 'M. Matthews, confectioner & dealer in funeral wines, Hogg's Field, Holbeck, Leeds', Leeds Reference Library L7 CB.
50. Wrapper for funeral of Mrs Oliver, d. November 7th, 1828 aged 52. Pitt-Rivers Museum, Oxford. Presented by T.G. Burnett, 1919.
51. Bishop, R.W.S. 159.
52. *Ibid.* 139–146.

Index